Formatio books from InterVarsity Press follow the rich tradition of the church in the journey of spiritual formation. These books are not merely about being informed, but about being transformed by Christ and conformed to his image. Formatio stands in InterVarsity Press's evangelical publishing tradition by integrating God's Word with spiritual practice and by prompting readers to move from inward change to outward witness. InterVarsity Press uses the chambered nautilus for Formatio, a symbol of spiritual formation because of its continual spiral journey outward as it moves from its center. We believe that each of us is made with a deep desire to be in God's presence. Formatio books help us to fulfill our deepest desires and to become our true selves in light of God's grace.

SPIRITUAL DISCIPLINES *Devotional*

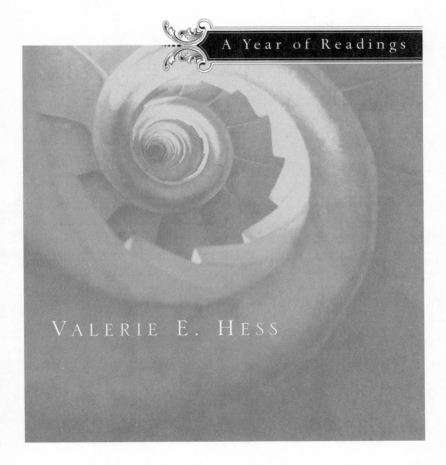

A Year of Readings

VALERIE E. HESS

An imprint of InterVarsity Press
Downers Grove, Illinois

InterVarsity Press
P.O. Box 1400, Downers Grove, IL 60515-1426
World Wide Web: www.ivpress.com
E-mail: email@ivpress.com

InterVarsity Press® is the book-publishing division of InterVarsity Christian Fellowship/USA®, a student movement active on campus at hundreds of universities, colleges and schools of nursing in the United States of America, and a member movement of the International Fellowship of Evangelical Students. For information about local and regional activities, write Public Relations Dept., InterVarsity Christian Fellowship/USA, 6400 Schroeder Rd., P.O. Box 7895, Madison, WI 53707-7895, or visit the IVCF website at <www.intervarsity.org>.

Design: Cindy Kiple
Images: Paul Taylor/Getty Images

ISBN 978-0-8308-3503-4

Printed in the United States of America ∞

Library of Congress Cataloging-in-Publication Data

Hess, Valerie E., 1954-
Spiritual disciplines devotional: a year of readings / Valerie E. Hess.
p. cm.
ISBN 978-0-8308-3503-4 (pbk.: alk. paper)
1. Spiritual life—Christianity. I. Title.
BV4501.3.H48 2007
248.4—dc22

2007011180

P 19 18 17 16 15 14 13 12 11 10 9 8 7 6 5 4 3 2 1
Y 23 22 21 20 19 18 17 16 15 14 13 12 11 10 09 08 07

To Maggie and Lydia,

who always keep me honest

Contents

Acknowledgments

AS ALWAYS, I AM DEEPLY indebted to Richard Foster and his groundbreaking book *Celebration of Discipline*. The timeless truths he presents in that book continue to guide, refresh and challenge people all over the world. I am so grateful for his support, as well as for the loving encouragement I've received from all the great folks at Renovare.

This book attempts to take things I have experienced, read about, or heard told and integrate them into the daily practice of the spiritual disciplines. Where people are identified, I have sought their permission; otherwise, names and details have been changed to protect those who didn't know they were going to end up in this manuscript! But to all who have shared their lives with me, either close up or from afar, I am thankful for all that I have learned from you.

I am very thankful for Cindy Bunch and her coworkers at InterVarsity Press, who continued to pursue this book at some critical junctures. I will always be grateful for her optimism and belief in the project.

And finally, I am grateful to my husband, John, who has so faithfully modeled to me the practice of the spiritual disciplines for over thirty years now, and to Maggie and Lydia who, among other things, taught me that "the cloud of witnesses" referred to in the book of Hebrews sometimes come in the form of little girls who ask piercing questions when they see me say one thing and do another . . . and then love me anyway.

Introduction

WELCOME TO THE WILD AND WONDERFUL world of spiritual formation using the spiritual disciplines!

Spiritual formation simply means developing the holy habits of the Christian faith. These habits are also referred to as the spiritual disciplines. Habits are important because they are the things that carry us through life in all of its seasons. We do certain things every day—like brushing our teeth or combing our hair—regardless of what mood we are in. Often we do them without conscious thought because they are so ingrained in us. We do them because we know they are important and we usually feel better for having done them.

The word *discipline* often sends up red flags for people. They are afraid it can only refer to some joyless routine of drudgery that will add yet another burden to their already full schedule. They don't understand that the spiritual disciplines are meant to lead us to a joyful, rich life like the one Jesus modeled. In fact, if these disciplines don't lead us to joy and goodness, and to show more mercy toward ourselves and others, we need to stop doing them immediately! Legalism is never a reflection of the life Jesus lived and invites us to live.

The word *disciple* comes from the same root word that *discipline* comes from. In learning the spiritual disciplines, we are seeking to become better disciples of Jesus Christ. We are not trying to earn our way into God's favor, but rather we are trying to develop habits that will make us better at living the life Jesus wants for us.

Look at it this way: in any relationship there must be active engagement on both sides. Each person in the relationship needs to respond to the other person appropriately, to anticipate needs and wants and to be sensitive and encouraging to the other person. This analogy breaks down, however, when we are talking about a relationship with the Creator of the universe. God is always the initiator, but at some point we must respond to the goodness and grace God offers us if we consider ourselves believers. We always fail miserably in our part of the relationship, but we are offered forgiveness and a chance to learn a new way whenever we ask God for that opportunity.

This is where the spiritual disciplines come in. These habits, or tools, teach us to respond to God and to the people around us in ways that look more like the ways Jesus responded during his life on earth. But if the spiritual disciplines should ever become sources of pride or legalism, we must discontinue them immediately.

How to Use This Book

In this book we will explore simple ways for Christians of all ages to develop holy habits through the use of the spiritual disciplines. I am deeply indebted to the groundbreaking work of Richard J. Foster in his book *Celebration of Discipline,* where he outlines twelve classical spiritual practices that Christians in all times and places have routinely engaged in. We will focus on one of these twelve disciplines for each month of the year.

Within each discipline, there is an introductory chapter and twenty daily readings that can be used within that month. Each introduction contains a list of suggested activities to help you practice that discipline. Choose only one or two each week—whatever seems appropriate for your schedule. The exercises can be used by small groups or individuals, at home or at camp, in a Christian day school or adult Sunday school class, in confirmation classes or at a youth group meeting. There are only five readings for each week because I want to encourage you to take a reflective pace in studying and acquiring the habit of that particular discipline. The structure of this book is meant to increase the goodness of your daily life, not burden it.

You do not have to go straight through this book. While you can work with the material from beginning to end, you can also turn to a discipline that feels more familiar or interesting to you and start there. Eventually, though, you should engage with all of the spiritual disciplines presented in this book so that you maintain a balanced understanding of these holy habits. And do spend the full month with each discipline once you choose one to focus on. It may take several days to begin to understand what that particular discipline is trying to teach.

A gentle word of caution: sometimes the disciplines we like studying the least are the ones we need the most. The good news is that the Holy Spirit will lead and guide you to the right place to start, and he will gently move you through the disciplines in the order that is best for you.

These disciplines are not meant to be one more thing for us to fail at in our relationship with God. They are meant to help us untie knots of bondage and break old, bad habits that make life more difficult. The disciplines are meant to breathe life into the dead places of our souls.

Your children can learn these disciplines right along with you. You can help them develop spiritual habits just as you do with physical, nutritional and educational habits. Here are some suggestions for getting started:

- Make sure you have a good idea of what the discipline is and how it can help make you a better disciple of Jesus Christ. You do not have to be an expert (no one in this lifetime will ever fully master all of these disciplines!), but you should be reasonably familiar with it before you try to teach it.
- For younger children, teach by doing. Engage in the activities suggested for children, and during the activity talk about what it means to be a follower of Jesus. Much of this can be done as a normal part of your day, for spiritual formation happens in the "everydayness" of our lives.
- For older children, it might be helpful to have a family devotion time once a week (every Sunday evening, for example) to talk about the discipline you are focusing on for the month. Then as a family choose an activity or two to practice that week. Again, try as much as possible to make the activity a part of your everyday life.
- Let adolescents choose their own activity. This will help them take more responsibility for their own spiritual formation, something they will be doing soon enough as they move through high school and into the world of higher education or career.
- Most of all, love your children, encourage them and support them in their growing relationship with God. Remember, your child's relationship with God will not be the same as yours, so try not to get in between your child and her encounters with the living Christ.

Each month you will find a few ideas highlighted that are especially appropriate to do with children.

And so, with a prayer for God's help and blessing, I invite you to a deeper level of discipleship, a level that leads to more joy and goodness. My prayer is that at the end of twelve months, you will have more holy habits at your disposal as you seek to be a more faithful, more joyful disciple of Jesus Christ.

The Discipline of Meditation

IF THE IDEA OF CHRISTIAN MEDITATION seems like an oxymoron to you, then let me assure you that it is not at all the same thing as non-Christian forms of meditation. In those practices, many of which have become popular in the last twenty-five or thirty years, the focus is on emptying the mind. In Christian meditation we seek to clear our minds of the clutter that prevents us from focusing fully on God. We push aside that which keeps us from filling our minds with God's Word and his work in creation, the world and other people.

Meditation could be summed up by this comparison: we seek to soak ourselves in God much like uncooked pasta or rice soaks in hot water, softening so that it becomes useable. We train ourselves for a time to forget about everything we have to do and focus on what God wants us to become. We spend time intentionally listening for the voice of God speaking to us, especially through Scripture.

Its companion disciplines are the discipline of study and the discipline of guidance. We must be careful what we fill our minds with. It is very important that meditating on Scripture be our first priority. Otherwise we may lose our ability to hear the voice of the Good Shepherd, which he promises his followers will recognize (see John 10:3-4). But beyond that meditation on Scripture, we should begin to meditate on how God is working in the various people and situations we encounter, always listening for (meditating on) how God might want us to respond to those encounters. We can also look for (meditate on) God's work in creation.

We must then in all humility take the things we have heard from God in our meditation and process them with other Christians. Since Satan can masquerade as an angel of light (see 2 Corinthians 11:14), we need to have accountability within the Christian community regarding "a word from the Lord." History is littered with the destroyed lives of those who did not heed the warning to seek accountability.

But since "God did not give us a spirit of timidity, but a spirit of power, of love and of self-discipline" (2 Timothy 1:7), let us view the discipline of meditation as an invitation to pull up a comfortable chair, with a hot drink in hand and our shoes off, and relax in the arms of Jesus for a time of restorative conversation.

Each week choose one or two suggested activities from the list below to help you practice this discipline.

For Anyone

- Write seven promises from the Bible on index cards. If you aren't sure where to find them, spend the next several days looking for God's promises as you attend church and read your Bible. Put the cards at your bedside with a small flashlight. Whenever you wake in the night, pick up a card and ask God to show you how this particular promise applies to a situation you are worried about.
- Do a *lectio divina* reading of John 9 (see week one, day five for a full description of this prayerful way to read Scripture).
- Choose a Bible passage to study. Get a Bible commentary from your church's library or a Christian bookstore, and read all you can about the background and meaning of that passage. Then spend ten minutes a day for one week letting words and phrases from that passage soak into your heart. In this way you will end up both with knowledge of God and knowing God.
- Reevaluate the way you do your daily devotions. Focus on a smaller amount of material over the same amount of time so you can meditate on at least one concept and retain it throughout the day.
- Spend some time meditating on a difficult situation in your life. It could involve a family member, a neighbor or your job. Listen for words that God may (or may not) want you to speak in that situation.
- On an index card write the name of a person or a short description of a situation that strikes you as hopeless, and put it in your pocket or wallet.

Look at the card frequently throughout the day, and ask God to give you his perspective on that person or situation.

- Read the book of Jonah. Ask yourself in what areas of your life you may be behaving like him. Ask God to show you the "Ninevehs" you are despising and avoiding. Answer the question God asks in the last verse of the book (Jonah 4:11).
- Begin a Scripture memorization program. Choose short, familiar passages and memorize them. Work up to longer passages.

Especially with Children

- Find something in nature—like a shell, a leaf or a flower—and spend time really looking at it, thinking about what it may tell you of God. Think about the diversity of seashells that God creates to protect even the tiniest and seemingly least significant of creatures, or the intricacy of the veins in a leaf and their importance to the tree. Start a nature journal to record your thoughts every time you have a chance to be out in creation.
- In the fall, buy some hyacinth or narcissus bulbs. Put them in a sack in your refrigerator for at least six weeks, then force them using a special bulb vase (available at many florists and garden centers). Make sure that the flat bottom of the bulb is slightly above the water. In the days ahead, meditate on the length of the roots and the timing of their appearance in relation to the rest of the plant.
- Find a star chart and learn about the constellations and their movements. Spend some time outside at night looking at the stars and marveling at their perfect rotations throughout the seasons. Imagine the sound of the song that the stars sang at creation (see Job 38:4-7). Can you hum that melody?
- Get an age-appropriate art book from the library (such as one from the Sister Wendy series). Spend some time sitting with your child and looking at the artwork. What might a particular piece say about God and his work in the world?

DAY ONE

Deep Roots

Then [Jesus] told them many things in parables, saying: "A farmer went out to sow his seed. . . . Some fell on rocky places, where it did not have much soil. It sprang up quickly, because the soil was shallow. But when the sun came up, the plants were scorched, and they withered because they had no root."

MATTHEW 13:3, 5-6

At the Alpine visitor center in Rocky Mountain National Park, there is a display case featuring the plants of the alpine tundra. One is a flower of minute size and delicate beauty. But this tiny plant also has a three-foot-long root! The disparity between the exquisite, tiny flower and the size of the root needed to support it in that harsh environment still fascinates me.

The discipline of meditation teaches us to read God's Word slowly, phrase by phrase, letting it sink deeply into our minds and hearts. It is like the root that little alpine flower puts down to survive on the tundra. When we meditate on God's Word and his work in the world around us, we lengthen the root of our soul into the life-giving soil of God's transcendent goodness.

On that mountain tundra, the wind blows hard and relentlessly, and the snow is deep and long lasting. But that tiny flower is solidly anchored, allowing it to burst forth in glory each spring. In the same way, may the flower of our soul have such a deep anchor in God and his Word.

DAY TWO

Hard Times

The fruit of the Spirit is love, joy, peace, patience, kindness, goodness, faithfulness, gentleness and self-control. Against such things there is no law.

GALATIANS 5:22-23

Several summers ago, much of the western United States experienced a terrible drought. Here in Colorado, the fire danger was high. Because watering restrictions were in place, everything turned brown at the height of the growing season. The temperatures were hot day after day, with no relief in sight.

Yet in the midst of that hot, dry summer, we were feasting on peaches. Apparently peaches like that kind of weather, so there was a bumper crop. This was a blessing in the midst of the drought, and it was a good reminder that in God, there is always some goodness to look for, even in hard situations.

As Christians, we are called to bear fruit. That means we are to produce the fruit of the Spirit in increasing abundance over the course of our faith walk.

Those of us who have been Christians for a long time know that many of those fruits grow significantly only during times of drought. We learn to love by loving someone unlovable. We learn self-control by saying no to something we want. We understand the meaning of faithfulness when faced with the temptation to be unfaithful.

We are called to focus—to meditate—on developing these characteristics, such that by the end of our lives we have a bumper crop of the fruits of the Spirit.

DAY THREE

New Habits

Within your temple, O God, we meditate on your unfailing love.

PSALM 48:9

For those of us who grew up with an image of God that was less than loving, this verse is important for two reasons. First of all, it implies intentionally thinking about God as a God of love. We won't get rid of wrong ideas unless we consciously seek to counterbalance them with the truth.

Secondly, the verse talks about doing this meditating within the context of corporate worship. This ensures that we don't replace one false notion with another. Within a solid Christian community, we can come to know the fullness of who God is, and we can unlearn any false ideas.

When my husband and I first got a car with the antilock braking system, we had to learn to not pump the brake when that system kicked in on slippery roads. Applying steady pressure instead of pumping the brakes went against the way we had learned to drive in icy conditions, but we had to allow the computer system to control the car. Even now it is a bit unnerving to hold that pedal down while the car is shaking, and to trust that the computer system is handling it.

By training ourselves to say regularly, "God's love is unfailing"—even when we don't feel that love, and life itself seems to be shaking as hard as the ABS trying to regain control of a car on an icy road—we can learn to trust God's care for us.

DAY FOUR

Night Prayers

My eyes stay open through the watches of the night, that I may meditate on your promises.

PSALM 119:148

I generally don't lie awake at night worrying, but sometimes I find myself suddenly awake, almost as if God himself has roused me. I have been training myself during these times to ask God what situation or person needs to be prayed for at that moment. Something or someone usually comes readily to mind. I lift up a short prayer, and then I'm able to fall right back to sleep.

It took time and intentionality to train myself to listen and pray instead of tossing and turning, worrying: *What was that noise I just heard? Who or what is outside? Are the kids OK? Why did I wake up like that?* Now I direct my questions to God and listen for a word from him.

Many of us toss and turn at night. We think about what happened during the day or what will happen tomorrow. We worry about bills, struggles our children are having, work issues, marital problems, things we suddenly realize we forgot to do.

Instead of worrying, we can train ourselves to use those restless nighttime hours to focus on God's promises to us in Jesus. It will take time, but those night hours can be precious times of communication with the God of the universe, who loves us and helps us deal with all of our concerns.

Lectio Divina

As [Jesus] went along, he saw a man blind from birth.

JOHN 9:1

This verse is only the beginning of an incredible story that spans the rest of chapter nine. Among other things, the story begs the question, who is really in need of healing here? It is a good story for learning the art of *lectio divina,* or spiritual reading.

Lectio divina (lex-ee-o dih-vee-na) simply means reading Scripture in such a way that the story becomes part of you: you put yourself into the story through the eyes of different characters; you see the crowds, you feel the tension and ultimately you hear a word of God spoken to you personally. It is best to read the story three times.

The first time you read the story, spend some time thinking about what the scene looked like, how it smelled, what time of day it might have been. The second time you read the story, put yourself into it as one of the characters. For the story in John 9, imagine how you would react if you were the blind man, one of Jesus' disciples or one of the Pharisees. The third time you read, listen for a word or phrase that seems to leap out at you. Spend some time thinking and praying about what that word or phrase may mean for you personally.

If you are a parent, keep in mind that children are "new Christians" who need intentional discipling. These Bible stories need to become part of their own faith history. Read to them slowly, encourage them to use their imaginations and stop to let them ask questions or process a concept. These steps can be critical to the deepening of their own faith. Plus it gives us adults new eyes with which to view stories we think we know so thoroughly. Being open to this kind of reading helps us make these stories our own as well.

Lectio divina can also be done with smaller sections of a story or with other passages that aren't actually stories. However, short sections of biblical stories are the best way to learn *lectio divina,* especially with children.

DAY ONE

Knowledge Versus Knowing

Whatever was to my profit I now consider loss for the sake of Christ. What is more, I consider everything a loss compared to the surpassing greatness of knowing Christ Jesus my Lord, for whose sake I have lost all things. I consider them rubbish, that I may gain Christ.

PHILIPPIANS 3:7-8

I know a woman who is very learned in the Bible but who is also very judgmental. She uses her knowledge of God to put people down or browbeat them to her way of thinking. Often the last stab she takes with her Bible-based knife is "God told me so." It is hard to refute that kind of argument, and most people don't even try. They simply avoid her. Her tactics are manipulative, and it is a terrible witness to non-Christians.

In Philippians 3:4-6, Paul lays out his impeccable background as a faithful Jew. But after outlining his pedigree, Paul writes in verses 7-8 that his qualifications are nothing compared with his knowing Christ. This is why the discipline of meditation must be a significant part of our Bible study time. It doesn't matter how much you know if you don't know the One whom you are studying.

DAY TWO

Speaking Versus Silence

Then the LORD answered Job out of the storm. He said: "Who is this that darkens my counsel with words without knowledge?"

JOB 38:1-2

Because I am an impulsive person, I find the discipline of meditation to be difficult but useful. One of the ways I practice it is by meditating on words I could use in a difficult conversation I'm facing. By slowing down, praying and taking time to think the circumstance through, I often come to a better way of presenting what needs to be said. Sometimes I have even had a strong nudging from the Holy Spirit telling me what not to say.

While we traditionally think of the discipline of meditation as ruminating on a phrase or word from Scripture and letting it sink deeply into our hearts, we must remember that this discipline (as well as all of the spiritual disciplines) is meant to help us go out into the world as better disciples of Jesus Christ. These disciplines, or holy habits, are to have practical applications for real situations in our daily lives.

Throughout the book of Job, Job and his friends engage in much discussion and speculation about what has happened to Job and why. God finally answers, and when he does, he shows them that they have no idea what they are talking about. Sometimes we should simply be quiet and not speak in certain situations, trusting that God's counsel is far above our own common sense.

DAY THREE

Less Is More

Open my eyes that I may see wonderful things in your law.

PSALM 119:18

I love good devotional resources. I tend to have an abundance of them, and then I try to use all of them in one quiet time. I read a bit from here, use a prayer from there, etc. One morning I realized that I couldn't remember a thing I had read just a few minutes earlier! It was as though the time I'd spent reading and praying had no impact on me at all. My mind was saturated with too many readings that were so varied, I wasn't able to absorb much of anything let alone be transformed.

Not long after this I went on vacation, but instead of packing all my resources, I took only one book. I wanted to use my time away for physical refreshment as well as deepening my connection with God. I focused on reading less and retaining more.

The discipline of meditation is more like intricate needlework than painting the side of a barn. In meditation we seek to focus on a Bible passage or a particular aspect of God one small stitch at a time—slowly, carefully—instead of reading large chunks of Scripture that give us an overview in broad strokes (something we do in the discipline of study).

By focusing on less during my time with God each morning, I was able to see more details in Scripture and more ways God was applying them to my life, in a way I hadn't been able to with my overabundance of devotionals.

DAY FOUR

The Big Picture

[Jesus said,] "Do not let your hearts be troubled. Trust in God; trust also in me."

JOHN 14:1

Remember the Y2K scare leading up to the new millennium? Remember how nothing happened? But then three months later a teenager from the Philippines brought the world to a near standstill with the "Love Bug" computer virus. While we were looking for one thing, something else happened and caught us completely off-guard.

War, conflict and strife are certainly not what God wants, but they are the reality of fallen humanity in a fallen world. Jesus calls us to meditate on the truths of his kingdom such that when the kingdoms of the earth are in turmoil, we are not alarmed. Jesus calls us to model the deep peace of knowing that he will bring all of history to a close at the right time. Until then, we are to do what God has called us to do, where he has called us to do it.

A Jew from Israel once told me that he was exploring Buddhism because it was the only religion he had found where the adherents weren't killing someone about something. This man was desperately looking for peace on earth. He wanted to believe that somebody somewhere was doing it right, and if he could just find and join that group, he would find peace for himself. He was crestfallen when I told him that Buddhists were killing Christians in Sri Lanka at that time.

Only in knowing and following Jesus will we find peace here on earth.

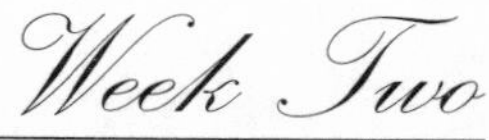

DAY FIVE

God's Hand in Creation

The heavens declare the glory of God; the skies proclaim the work of his hands. Day after day they pour forth speech; night after night they display knowledge.

PSALM 19:1-2

Sixth-century Christian philosopher Anicius Manlius Severinus Boethius wrote a treatise called "The Principles of Music" in which he talked about music as a form of math, "exemplifying in sounds the fundamental principles of order and harmony that prevail throughout the universe."* Boethius and many like him believed there was a perfect harmony that could not be heard with human ears but that kept the orbits of the stars in perfect alignment.

We know that there are additional scientific explanations for the celestial rotations, but as Christians we can also affirm the sense of order and movement that Boethius talks about. We know that the God of the universe created the heavens and all that is in them, and at creation "the morning stars sang together" (Job 38:7).

Sometimes in our mad rush through life we forget to stop and listen for that music still being sung in creation. Let's not forget that we are invited to study and think about God's overarching plan for us and all of creation, and that his plan includes music.

*Donald Jay Grout, *A History of Western Music* (New York: W. W. Norton, 1973), p. 23.

DAY ONE

Fear of Hearing

When the people saw the thunder and lightning and heard the trumpet and saw the mountain in smoke, they trembled with fear. They stayed at a distance and said to Moses, "Speak to us yourself and we will listen. But do not have God speak to us or we will die."

EXODUS 20:18-19

One night at dinnertime I sent my younger daughter to tell the older one to come inside and wash her hands. She did as she was told, but her sister kept playing. Finally I had to go out and get her myself. "Why didn't you come as you were told?" I asked her. "Because I didn't know you had really called!" was her reply.

A command was given and a choice was made. But when my younger daughter went as my messenger, my older child chose to ignore my message on the pretext that it wasn't a valid command. When I came myself, she still had the option to ignore the command, but now the stakes were different. Ignoring me would leave no room for rationalizing her disobedience because she heard my voice directly.

Many of us long to hear a word from God, and yet when that word comes, we sometimes do not like it. We long for intimacy with the God of the universe, but we become frightened when he speaks a word we don't want to hear, like "Forgive that enemy" or "Stop overeating." Like the Israelites at the foot of Mount Sinai, we withdraw and decide that we don't really want to hear what God says except through what someone else tells us. Suddenly we want a Moses to talk to God for us—and then we can decide whether or not we believe the message we receive.

Christian meditation may bring you a word from God that goes contrary to what you want to hear. However, it will also lead you to the promised land. And remember, God loves us, even when correcting us. The voice we are afraid to hear is gentle and loving despite a word that may seem hard at the time.

DAY TWO

A Solid Foundation

Make a table of acacia wood. . . . Overlay it with pure gold and make a gold molding around it. . . . Make the poles of acacia wood, overlay them with gold.

EXODUS 25:23-24, 28

This passage comes from a section of Scripture that I find a bit tedious. God is telling Moses how to build the tabernacle. God describes it in great detail, down to the way the goldsmiths should make the leaves on the lampstand (verses 31-36). As I was going through this section again, I was struck by the fact that God was concerned even about the kind of wood used underneath the gold of these holy objects.

My husband and I have used a lot of wood in remodeling our house. He would meticulously pick out individual boards at the lumberyard, making sure they had a nice grain and color, especially if they were going to be used in very visible ways. If I had been giving the instructions for the tabernacle furnishings, I would have told the people to use plywood since the gold was going to cover it up. But acacia wood is of high quality and is nearly impervious to insects, so God was asking the Israelites to build something on a foundation that would not rot.

As I thought about this detail, I was reminded of how much God cares about what is on the inside as well as how things look on the outside. The fact that God specifically named the wood to be used in the building of the tabernacle, even though it wouldn't be seen, means that God cares about me, inside and out. Instead of skimming through this passage, wondering what a cubit is, I found myself thinking about what's inside of me—my attitudes, my thoughts, my desires. No matter how much gold I use to cover my outside, God is aware of what is being covered up. To God, the inside matters even more than the outside.

Dream Big

Now to him who is able to do immeasurably more than all we ask or imagine, according to his power that is at work within us, to him be glory in the church and in Christ Jesus throughout all generations, for ever and ever! Amen.

EPHESIANS 3:20-21

We had about eight hours before we had to be at the airport to catch our late-night flight home, so we were driving around north of Tel Aviv looking for a place to wait. We had heard about a small area called Dor on the Mediterranean coast, and after much difficulty we found the turnoff that led to it. We came to a tiny, deserted beach community that seemed to offer little interest except for the sea itself. We walked around and went into a small diving shop that was open.

Inside, a man began to talk to us, and soon we were viewing a video of all kinds of treasures from antiquity that have been pulled out of the sea off the west coast of Israel. He even showed us a shell-encrusted sword that is believed to have been from Napoleon's troops. It turns out we had stumbled upon Kurt Raveh, a marine archaeologist who had discovered a shipwreck from the time of King David or Solomon! In that seemingly humble spot, we found so much more than we could have imagined or hoped for.

Sometimes in life we enter a situation expecting to find very little of interest or use. Sometimes we expect very little of interest or use from ourselves. But God does not look at us or our situations that way. God is always able to do more, give more, imagine more and help more than we can even begin to articulate in our minds or our prayers. God invites us through the discipline of meditation to a fresher, higher vision of the people and situations in our lives.

Trading Up

"For I know the plans I have for you," declares the LORD, *"plans to prosper you and not to harm you, plans to give you hope and a future."*

JEREMIAH 29:11

We had finished our marvelous and unexpected time in Hof Dor, Israel. Now we needed to eat and head to the airport to begin the long flight home. We had been told about the Carmel Mizrachi Winery in Zichron Yachov, a town not too far from Hof Dor. We found the restaurant and even managed to change clothes in our rental van without too much embarrassment! We walked up to the door only to discover it was closed for a private party. We were at a loss as to what to do next.

Zichron Yachov is a delightful artist community, but it's not on the beaten path of most Holy Land tours. It was evening, the shops were closed and most people were already home for dinner. We finally found a small restaurant where no one spoke English except a customer who had studied it a bit in school. With the young man's help and the graciousness of the wait staff, we somehow managed to order an incredible meal. It was good, authentic Israeli food, served well in a wonderful environment. The wait staff was genuinely interested in learning about us (and we, them) despite the language barrier. By the time we left for the airport, we were almost glad the winery had been closed because we would have missed that wonderful experience.

So often I have my day, my week, my life all planned out. And plans are good—we can't just drift from moment to moment. But my goal is to learn to thank God in the midst of canceled plans, canceled flights, canceled relationships. I want to have these words from Jeremiah buried in my heart so I can remember this in the midst of the disappointment of changed plans: God wants only good for me, and God's good is far better than what I can imagine for myself.

DAY FIVE

Focusing on Goodness

Finally, brothers, whatever is true, whatever is noble, whatever is right, whatever is pure, whatever is lovely, whatever is admirable—if anything is excellent or praiseworthy—think about such things.

PHILIPPIANS 4:8

When talking about the spiritual disciplines, this verse is often used to explain why celebration is considered a discipline. It also speaks to the discipline of meditation because it implies that when things are not true or noble, or when they are wrong or impure or ugly, we are to focus on the opposite reality as found in God.

This is not a head-in-the-sand solution for dealing with evil in the world. This is acknowledging that many situations are pretty awful, but with the eyes of our soul we can also see another reality. By focusing (meditating) on God's transcendent goodness, we can see through the darkness to the possibilities on the other side.

I recently saw an example of this kind of change of focus in a young woman who was diagnosed with an inoperable brain tumor. While she grieved over the situation, she chose to spend her remaining time on earth in joy. She gathered all of her friends and family at church to celebrate her life. The celebration started with a potluck, followed by a time of singing and sharing stories. There were tears, but there was much joy and laughter, too. That time of focusing on the good in this young woman's life gave everyone a new way of looking at her dying.

DAY ONE

Different Perspectives

A week later [Jesus'] disciples were in the house again, and Thomas was with them. Though the doors were locked, Jesus came and stood among them and said, "Peace be with you!" Then he said to Thomas, "Put your finger here; see my hands. Reach out your hand and put it into my side. Stop doubting and believe."

JOHN 20:26-27

When I travel in countries that are predominantly Roman Catholic, I am fascinated by the images of Christ I see in the churches. Often there is a large cross with a depiction of Jesus in death, blood running down his face and body. As a Protestant, this is not something I see very often. It is an image of the Christian faith that many of us skip over or think about for only an hour on Good Friday.

One of my daily prayer books (*Celtic Daily Prayer* from the Northumbria Community) devotes an entire month to focusing on Jesus' scars. This is not something I had ever spent much time thinking about. It gave me a new perspective as I pictured Jesus in my mind, taking a whole month to focus on Jesus' wounded yet healing hands.

Another way to approach Christian meditation is to go into other churches in your area or when you are traveling and look at the way they portray aspects of God in their architecture, stained-glass windows, crosses, banners, baptismal fonts, altars or tables. Think about (meditate on) what each of these things (or the lack of them) say about God and his loving work of salvation in the world. Consider taking a picture or making a simple drawing of something that really speaks to you so you can use it in your devotional time at home.

DAY TWO

God's Delight

The Lord your God is with you, he is mighty to save. He will take great delight in you, he will quiet you with his love, he will rejoice over you with singing.

ZEPHANIAH 3:17

I love my children dearly. I love them so much it almost hurts sometimes. I have even been known to burst into tears trying to express my love to them. I delight in the things they do (most of the time), and I love spending time with them.

Years ago I made up a little song that I would sing to them when they came to me in tears: "Tell Mama where it hurts. Tell Mama where it doesn't feel good. Tell Mama what's not right so she can make it better." I would sing these words as I held them and comforted them. Even though they are adults now, I still try to find ways to comfort or encourage my children in those moments when they "just need Mom."

It is harder for me to imagine God in that mothering role with me as his child. In recent years I have begun to meditate on this concept of God comforting me and delighting in me as I do my children, and this verse has always given me pause. It is not an image of God that comes naturally to me. I wish it did, because I think obeying and loving God would be much easier if I could embrace this mothering God image that we find here and in other places in Scripture (see, for example, Matthew 23:37, where Jesus likens himself to a mother hen who gathers up her chicks under her wings).

To think that God loves me more than I love my children is a difficult concept for me to grasp, yet I sense it is one God is inviting me to embrace. How wonderful to look forward to interacting with God the same way my children look forward to interacting with me!

DAY THREE

Memorize, Memorize

I have hidden your word in my heart that I might not sin against you.

PSALM 119:11

When my daughter was learning her multiplication tables, she and I would drill them every night to prepare for the next day's quiz. It was hard work, but things were going along well until we came to the fives. She discovered that counting by five in her head was easy to do, so she decided there was no need to memorize that set of numbers. The problem was that the quizzes were timed, and in order for her to move on to the next level she had to have the right answers within the time limit. Needless to say, she failed her first attempt when she tried to count by fives. That night she was frustrated but ready to put in the hard work of memorizing.

Many times after a conversation I find myself thinking about what I should have or could have said to that person. If I had put more time into memorizing God's Word, the Holy Spirit could have more easily pulled a thought or phrase from that treasure chest in my heart and put it in my mouth. But like my daughter, I too often try to take the easy way out. I'm too busy or distracted or tired to focus on memorizing passages of Scripture.

In our relationships with others, over time we begin to learn what the other person might say in a given situation. By memorizing Scripture, we can learn what God might say in a situation where we are called to be Christ's ambassador.

DAY FOUR

God's Command

Look at the birds of the air. . . . See how the lilies of the field grow.

MATTHEW 6:26, 28

These verses come from the part of the Sermon on the Mount where Jesus tells us to "consider the lilies," as some translations put it. Jesus is talking about meditating on birds and flowers to help us understand how God will take care of us. We are to think about how God cares for creation, then apply that to how God will care for us. We are commanded to meditate on these things so that we do not worry.

One of the major differences between non-Christian meditation and Christian meditation is that we are to empty the clutter in our minds so we may fill our minds with the things of God. We are not supposed to empty our minds just for the sake of emptying our minds, but rather that we may clear a space for God to speak to us. We are to chase away distractions for a time so that we might focus on God, God's Word, creation and God's work in the world.

The wonderful thing about Christian meditation is that everything we encounter in a day can lead us to focus our thoughts on how God is at work in us and in the world. We don't need a special technique or a particular place (although deep breathing and sitting in a quiet environment can be helpful).

The goal is to be intentional about looking for God and listening for his voice in all that we do.

Moving Meditation

These commandments that I give you today are to be upon your hearts. Impress them on your children. Talk about them when you sit at home and when you walk along the road, when you lie down and when you get up.

DEUTERONOMY 6:6-7

The idea of getting a child to sit and meditate on God may seem utterly impossible. In fact, some adults may not easily sit and focus on God. But this verse gives us permission to make focusing on God a part of all our activities. Intentionally focusing on God while we are in the car or at the table is certainly one way this can be done.

However, music, art, dance and labyrinths (circular pathways found in many churches) can also be tools to help fidgety people learn to meditate. If you have access to a "walking maze," as some labyrinths are called, you can meditate in motion. Read a passage like John 3:16, where we are told how much God loves us. Then, as you silently walk the circular path, focus on how God's love supports you in all the twists and turns of your life.

Another way to help wiggly ones sit and meditate is to give them art supplies that are age appropriate. Then read a short passage, such as John 3:16, and have them think about God's love for them while coloring or manipulating clay. (Great art talent is not required.) Or put on a CD of hymns, praise songs or classical music like Bach. Use the words to focus on God, or use the instrumental music to encourage bodies to move as they think about the Bible passage. (Great dance talent is not required.)

Or read a passage such as Psalm 19:1-4, and then go on a hike, thinking about (meditating on) what creation tells us about God. Bring along a notebook to record simple drawings and thoughts or a small box to collect treasures found along the path.

Remember, we want to train our minds to focus on God and the good things of God so that we might find nourishment for our hearts and spirits.

The Discipline of Prayer

SOMETIMES IT IS EASY TO FORGET what prayer really is. For a Christian, prayer is nothing more and nothing less than conversation with the God of the universe! Stop and think about that. We are invited to talk to the Creator of all things, at any time and in any place that we want. There isn't a governmental advisor on earth who has more intimate contact with an earthly ruler than we the children of God have with our Father in heaven.

The discipline of prayer teaches us to have regular times of prayer. It teaches us to be so habitual in prayer that when we need quick, on-the-run help and wisdom as we go about our day, we will automatically turn to God. And when we don't know how or what we should pray at that moment, this discipline provides us with prayers from other times and places that we have used or even memorized and that will instantly come to our minds and lips. Such prayers will prime the pump, so to speak.

For some people the idea of a regularly scheduled time of prayer or the thought of using prayers other people throughout Christendom have prayed seems artificial or forced. They think that if prayer isn't spontaneous, it isn't authentic. However, that conclusion isn't realistic when compared to the rest of life.

Most of us can't talk to our spouse, our children, our family members or our friends whenever we want to throughout the day. They have schedules and commitments that don't allow them to drop everything at any given moment and talk with us. So we have a date night with our spouse or we have a girls' (or guys') night out with our friends or we do something special with a child to catch up with them. Or we have a regularly scheduled meeting at work with our boss or coworkers.

Of course, in reality we can come to God anytime, day or night. The problem for many of us is that we don't (or won't) come unless we have an urgent need. Too often we are like those people who write to the newspaper advice columnist, complaining about relatives who only contact them when they need money. If we believe that God is most known to us in the person of Jesus Christ, then don't you think God wants to hear from us more often than when we need something, as any other friend would?

The discipline of prayer can help bring us into a more biblical, accurate understanding of what a relationship with God entails. And what a relationship we are invited to participate in!

Each week choose one or two suggested activities from the list below to help you practice this discipline:

For Anyone

- When you pray "Thy will be done" in a given situation, ask yourself whether it is a petition of confidence in a close Friend whom you are in constant communication with or a petition of fear and resignation, a kind of back door out: "If God says no, then it obviously wasn't God's will." Pray for something specific, coming boldly to God with your request.
- Ask the Holy Spirit to bring to mind three incidents or interactions you remember involving your earthly father or mother. Do those memories affect the way you approach God? Spend some time in prayer asking God to heal any negative feelings you may have developed about your earthly parents or guardians that impact your current relationship with God.
- Experiment with different postures for prayer: kneeling, standing, hands open and low, hands open and raised, prostrate on the floor. How do these postures impact your prayers?
- Commit to praying regularly for persecuted Christians around the world. There are many websites that can help you get started, like Open Doors <www.opendoorsusa.org>, the Voice of the Martyrs <www.persecution.com> or Turkish World Outreach <www.two-fot.org>. You can also find out what missionaries your church supports and how to correspond with them and learn about the conditions in which they are working. Consider doing this with a prayer partner or in a prayer group that meets regularly.

- Take a situation you are anxious about, and thank God for everything you can about that situation. Memorize Philippians 4:6 and say it to yourself every time you are tempted to worry.
- Do you or your children struggle with self-esteem? Are teenagers in your care beginning to date? Are there issues your extended family struggles with, like alcoholism or infidelity? Pray daily against the temptations you and your family may be especially susceptible to.
- After you say your prayers at bedtime, have a time of silent listening. Even if you fall asleep, know that you did so while trying to hear God speak to you. In the morning lie in bed for a few minutes and see if you have a thought or impression that could be God nudging you in a certain direction.
- Develop your own "rule" of prayer—that is, something you do every day no matter how you feel or what your schedule is. Be realistic and start with something simple that you can commit to doing at the same time every day in this season of your life. A simple example is saying the Lord's Prayer before you get out of bed in the morning and when you get back into bed at night.
- Pray for random people you see today, listening for God to give you a word about how to pray for them.
- Pray regularly for your employer, your local governmental officials, the school board, your church leaders—everyone whose authority directly impacts your life.

Especially with Children

- Pray with your child about a difficult homework assignment. Have him lift the book or paper up as if showing it to God while he asks for help and guidance. (You can also do this with a letter or a bill that is troubling you.)
- Make a list of all the members of your family, writing down as many names as you can think of, dead or alive. Think about how those people influenced for good or for ill who you are today. Pray for those still living, that they may make a godly impact on the children in your family. Pray that any evil in the family tree be rendered ineffective. Thank God for his faithfulness to your family throughout the generations.

- Each night read a small portion from the book of Daniel, the book of Esther or the Gospels with your children. (Remember, this is about character formation, not speed reading.) Talk about the characters, and ask your children what gifts they would like to ask God to help them develop in their lives. Record those desires in a notebook. (You could do this for yourself as well.)
- Find a prayer that your family can memorize and use at mealtimes or bedtimes. If possible, find the history behind the prayer, such as who wrote it, the time and place it was written, etc. Talk about why the author may have chosen the particular words of the prayer.

DAY ONE

The Small Wings of Prayer

When Peter saw this, he said to them: "Men of Israel, why does this surprise you? Why do you stare at us as if by our own power or godliness we had made this man walk?"

ACTS 3:12

Chaos theory, something I know very little about, is a hypothesis that says a butterfly flapping its wings in one part of the world will create a hurricane in another part of the world. It's the idea that nothing happens in a vacuum, that everything affects something, somewhere.

Whether or not this is scientifically true, I find it to be an encouraging picture of what prayer is like. I take comfort in knowing that the "tiny wing" prayers I send to God during my devotional time or on the run during the day can, in the hands of God, turn into a hurricane of power for a person or situation somewhere else in the world, or even in the deep recesses of my own heart, soul and mind.

What I find empowering in the above verse is that when Peter and John ordered the lame beggar to rise in the name of Jesus, they assumed he would. "Why does this surprise you?" they asked the astounded crowd. Have we heard this story too many times to be astounded ourselves? Do we really expect things to happen when we pray in Jesus' name? Do we really believe that our butterfly prayers will unleash great power?

I have been experimenting with praying more boldly. When I was on a flight preparing to land in Denver, the plane was bouncing around in significant turbulence. Even the flight attendants had to be seated and buckled in. I lifted up a prayer to the One who stilled storms on the Sea of Galilee, and the bucking plane immediately smoothed out. Coincidence? I don't know, but someone once said that they noticed more "coincidences" when they prayed boldly and in faith.

DAY TWO

Transformed Desires

Pray continually.

1 THESSALONIANS 5:17

This is one of those Bible verses that is pretty clear about what we are supposed to do. The tension comes when we try to figure out how to do it. “Praying without ceasing” can conjure up visions of being on our knees for the rest of our lives, and if we are honest, that picture does not appeal to most of us. So many times we can’t even sustain a conversation with God for five minutes! How can we ever hope to keep it going continually?

One of the ways to approach this is through the ancient idea of purifying our desires. This means struggling to get to the point where we are not distracted by material possessions, worry or trying to get everyone to follow our way of doing things. The goal is to be so in tune with God’s heart that everything God desires, we also desire.

Carefully studying Scripture helps us know what it is that God desires. Then we can pray to have those same desires ourselves. This practice will take a lifetime and will never be perfectly achieved here on earth, but it will bring us closer to praying continually.

Total Honesty

God did not give us a spirit of timidity, but a spirit of power, of love and of self-discipline.

2 TIMOTHY 1:7

My friend was in a very difficult situation. I was very concerned about her, and I encouraged her to see a Christian counselor whom I believed could help her. After she went to the first appointment, she told me the counselor was unwilling to work with her because her issues touched a deep nerve of resentment from his past.

I refused to believe that God wanted this to happen. If God had been physically in front of me, I would have been shaking him by his lapels. I pleaded and yelled and refused to take no for an answer. I told God he needed to change the therapist's heart because my friend wasn't going to make it without that man's help. (I was quite sure of my assessment of the situation.)

That night a miracle occurred! After the therapist went home and talked to his wife, he called my friend, saying he would work with her. It turned out to be a healing experience for both of them.

From this situation I learned not that I would get my way if I had a temper tantrum before God, but that God listens to all of the ways I pray. God simply requests that I come to him honestly.

DAY FOUR

A Gentle God

One day Jesus was praying in a certain place. When he finished, one of his disciples said to him, "Lord, teach us to pray, just as John taught his disciples." He said to them, "When you pray, say: 'Father . . .'"

LUKE 11:1-2

In college I needed a PE credit, so I signed up for an advanced swimming class. I had passed the Red Cross lifesaving course at the public pool back home, so I felt confident I was in the right class. But it soon became apparent that I was not. Besides my poor swimming ability compared to the rest of the class, for some unknown reason the instructor seemed to resent my very presence. He wouldn't talk to me and made it clear that he felt I didn't belong there. He offered no help and was obviously disdainful when it came time to give out grades.

I was only eighteen and didn't have good conflict-management skills. I was afraid to approach the instructor to ask him what I needed to do differently. So all semester I went to class, did what I could and left the pool as quickly as possible afterward.

Many of us have a view of God similar to my view of that instructor. For some it is based on the way our earthly fathers or mothers treated us. Maybe in our relationship with God we feel that we somehow end up in the wrong place doing the wrong thing too many times, so why bother to pray? But Jesus shows us a new way of defining *Father*. We are invited to approach this Father at any time, with all our needs and emotions, trusting that he will give us his love and help.

DAY FIVE

Postures of Prayer

Hear my cry for mercy as I call to you for help, as I lift up my hands toward your Most Holy Place.

PSALM 28:2

Think about your hands and all the different emotions that can be communicated with them: gracious invitation, caring concern, functional help, anger and rage. I once read somewhere that the Assyrians had a word for prayer that meant "to open the fist."

Fists raised in anger or threat, fists closed around things we won't let go of, fists used to inflict hurt on someone else—fists are not usually a posture we think of for prayer. So if we are trying to open ourselves to God, to cry for mercy and help, to worship and praise or to plead for others, we generally don't make fists.

One thing we can think about in the discipline of prayer is our body language when praying. It can be helpful to experiment with different postures since our outer body language often reflects our inner attitude, even in prayer.

For example, try praying with your hands held palms up. This simple gesture can help us open our spirits to what God may want to give us. Or when you are praying about a troubling situation, turn your hands over, palms down, symbolizing giving the concern over to God. When struggling with difficulties, throw yourself face down on the floor as a symbol of your willingness to let God's will be done in your life. Try standing when you are praising God or when you are confessing your faith in him.

These are just some of the postures you could experiment with to infuse new life into your prayers.

DAY ONE

The Bigger Picture

If the world hates you, keep in mind that it hated me first. If you belonged to the world, it would love you as its own. As it is, you do not belong to the world, but I have chosen you out of the world.

JOHN 15:18-19

The church in North America would do well to remember that it lives in an unusual time of peace and relative acceptance. From the beginning Jesus promised that since the world hated him, it would hate us. Today that hatred is still acted out in many places in the world, with the persecution of Christians happening in an increasing number of countries.

This is a sobering subject, but if we believe that when one member of Christ's body suffers, every member suffers (see 1 Corinthians 12:26), we will keep the larger church in mind as we pray, not only for their sake but for ours. When we are aware of persecution, it helps us keep perspective on our own troubles.

My husband is a pastor, and once while he was waiting for a parishioner to arrive for an appointment, he began to dwell on all the frustrations he had dealt with recently. But after the ensuing conversation with his parishioner, my husband came to realize that his irritations were minor compared to the hurts this person was facing. He was filled with a new spirit of gratitude for God's hand in his own life.

If you are struggling with lethargy in your prayers, remember those who are paying a high price for their faith in Christ. Pray for them instead of focusing solely on your own needs and troubles.

DAY TWO

Moving to Action

We prayed to our God and posted a guard day and night to meet this threat.

NEHEMIAH 4:9

I learned this proverb while I was in the Middle East: "Trust in Allah but tether your camel." It means you should trust God to take care of things, but you should also do what you can to ensure a good outcome. This proverb, as well as our verse for today, points to the fact that we are coworkers with God in the situations of our lives. We are invited to pray about all things, but we are also called to do what we can in the situation we are praying about.

For example, when we are sick, certainly we are to ask God in prayer for healing, but we are also to see a doctor, take our medicine, rest, etc. Or when we have financial difficulties, we are to ask God for help, but we should also seek out godly counsel on how we might restructure our finances or find a better job.

The Israelites were trying against great odds to rebuild the destroyed city of Jerusalem. One of their biggest problems was that certain tribal people in the area were dead set against Jerusalem being rebuilt and were doing everything in their power to stop its reconstruction. Nehemiah 4:8 reads, "They all plotted together to come and fight against Jerusalem and stir up trouble against it." Nehemiah and those rebuilding the walls prayed for God to protect them, but they also posted guards day and night. And ultimately they were successful in getting the walls up and defeating their enemies.

In the Dark

Do not be anxious about anything, but in everything, by prayer and petition, with thanksgiving, present your requests to God.

PHILIPPIANS 4:6

When I was preparing to go to graduate school, we moved early in the summer so that we could get settled and find work before school started in the fall. We had already saved the tuition money for the first semester, so we weren't too concerned about finances. But as the summer went by, nothing came together for employment. My husband had trouble finding a job, which caused us to live off the saved tuition money. School was due to start in two weeks, and all the graduate student scholarships were gone by then. With a growing sense of concern and worry, we wondered if we had missed God's call and timing in this venture.

A week later the head of the music department came to see me while I was practicing. He said that a graduate student they had expected to come was not matriculating that fall, freeing up that scholarship money for me. Just a few days later my husband found a good job with the university. In God's timing and provision, I was able to attend school that fall.

That first year, my husband contracted hepatitis A and spent two weeks in the hospital, though we had no health insurance. Our first daughter was born very unexpectedly the next summer, but with God's help, I managed to graduate on time. These were very full years to say the least, but some of our best memories and relationships come from that time period. We prayed many prayers for help during those days, and the temptation to worry was staggering at times. But as we watched God part the waters in each new challenge, we grew in our ability to give thanks and to trust.

DAY FOUR

Resisting Temptation

Jesus went out as usual to the Mount of Olives, and his disciples followed him. On reaching the place, he said to them, "Pray that you will not fall into temptation."

LUKE 22:39-40

The context of this verse is the time before Jesus is arrested in the Garden of Gethsemane. As the scene moves through verse 46, we see that the disciples spend the time sleeping rather than praying against temptation. And despite their brave pronouncements of fidelity, when the soldiers come, they all flee in panic, leaving Jesus alone to face his captors.

The call for us to pray that we will not fall into temptation is still valid because temptation comes in all shapes and sizes and carries with it potentially deadly results. One way to start thinking about the issue of temptation, which is often viewed with derision in our culture, is to use the petition from the Lord's Prayer: "Lead us not into temptation." Repeat it daily, and pray it over and over whenever you are in a situation that brings out the worst in you.

For me, some of those situations involve overeating at food buffets or making unnecessary purchases in stores that carry clothing or kitchen gadgets. I have had good success in resisisting the urge to overeat or buy unneeded items when I keep repeating in my heart, *Lead me not into temptation.* Then I am able to gain the upper hand over the forces that would like to see me fail in living a balanced, healthy lifestyle.

DAY FIVE

Listening and Talking

There is a time for everything, and a season for every activity under heaven: . . . a time to be silent and a time to speak.

ECCLESIASTES 3:1, 7

The Taizé Christian community in France developed a style of worship that is now used in other Christian communities around the world. The community gathers in a room full of candles with a simple visual focus, such as an icon of Christ or a cross. They sing simple choruses over and over, allowing worshipers to practice contemplative prayer while singing. There are also plenty of silent times between readings and songs.

For people who are used to worshiping at a fast clip with never a moment of silence in the service, the slower pace and long silences of Taizé can be uncomfortable. This is something that needs to be practiced because long silences and repetitive choruses in worship are a foreign concept for many of us. Many of us are used to using lots of words with God (and with people), and if we aren't talking, we are used to listening to someone else talk or sing.

It is important that we have a full range of ways to connect with God in prayer. Many of us leave it at "Here is my list of needs, amen." While God wants to hear what is on our hearts, he also wants us to listen for what is on his heart. We need to learn to be silent in our prayers at times.

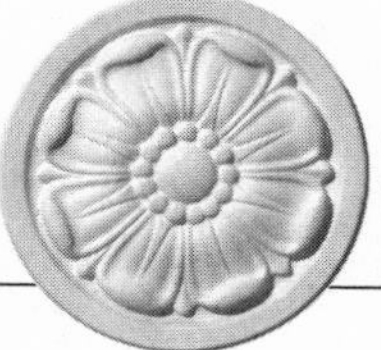

DAY ONE

Developing a Rule

Seven times a day I praise you for your righteous laws.

PSALM 119:164

This is one of the passages that led monastic communities from the sixth century onward to develop the Daily Offices: Matins, Lauds, Prime, Terce, Sext, None, Vespers and Compline. (There are eight offices although this verse only refers to seven prayer times.) In these communities, no matter what a member is doing, when the bell rings, they stop their work and pray, sing and give thanks to God as a community using a prescribed liturgy based on the Psalms.

I'm sure this is a great inconvenience at times. Surely that bell must sometimes ring when they are right in the middle of something important. While several of the offices (especially Prime, Terce, Sext and None) are quite short, the call to prayer is still an interruption.

Yet this "interruption" tells the members of the community that prayer is a work equal to any other kind of work they may be doing. It gives them perspective and helps to set priorities. It also helps them keep balance and rhythm in their day-to-day lives.

We who are not part of a structured faith community like a monastery could also benefit from something that would give our days perspective and balance. For example, the Northumbria Community has a midday prayer service that a person can do in two minutes—the time it takes the tea kettle to come to a boil. Another system I am aware of is to set an alarm to go off at 9 a.m., noon and 3 p.m., alerting you to stop and say the Lord's Prayer.

Prayer, like all of the spiritual disciplines, needs to have structure for it to become effective and more deeply rooted in our lives.

DAY TWO

Learning Trust

Trust in him at all times, O people; pour out your hearts to him, for God is our refuge.

PSALM 62:8

When I was in high school, I played Kim McAfee in our musical production of *Bye Bye Birdie*. In the musical there is a scene where Conrad Birdie, the Elvis-style rock star, comes to town. All of the girls in the cast, me included, were to run around onstage, screaming in mass hysteria. The scene ends with all of us fainting on the floor and my stage boyfriend surveying in disgust the aftermath of Conrad Birdie's appearance.

I had the hardest time learning to "faint" onstage, trusting that my "boyfriend" would catch me. Overcoming the last-minute, knee-jerk reaction to put out a hand to catch myself was difficult but necessary for the dramatic effect needed in that scene.

In prayer, we may find ourselves fighting the same knee-jerk response while learning to trust that God will catch us as we pour out our hearts to him. Even after we pray, we may still feel deeply unsettled or find ourselves worrying. We may need to pray again and again, practicing melting into the arms of our Father, who will restore and heal us in the right way and in the right time.

When I was learning to faint onstage, falling backward onto a bed was good practice. In prayer, "falling" on our face on the bed or on the floor can symbolize our desire to completely trust God in any given situation.

DAY THREE

Praying for Enemies

Also, seek the peace and prosperity of the city to which I have carried you into exile. Pray to the LORD for it, because if it prospers, you too will prosper.

JEREMIAH 29:7

This must have been a bitter pill for the Israelites to swallow. They had been forcibly taken from their home in Jerusalem and resettled in Babylon (modern-day Iraq). Now the Lord told Jeremiah to tell them to settle down, build houses, plant gardens, find spouses for their children and pray for the prosperity of Nebuchadnezzar and his empire. The Lord told these captives that only through the prosperity of their captors would they themselves find prosperity.

I don't know about you, but praying for the prosperity of people who came to my house, dragged me out of it and then burned it down would be tough. I would probably pray that God would send fire from heaven and consume them, not prosper them.

For a modern-day application of this principle, think about the person who got the promotion you were so sure you deserved. Or the relative who managed to get the family heirloom you so coveted. Or the company who moved your family far away from friends and loved ones to a part of the country you don't even like.

While these situations aren't the same as being forcibly relocated to a foreign country, they are still times when we might feel that praying for the prosperity of that person is too painful. Yet that is what God is saying through Jeremiah: in the prosperity of the community in which we find ourselves is our own prosperity.

DAY FOUR

Covering the Uncovered

For this reason, since the day we heard about you, we have not stopped praying for you.

COLOSSIANS 1:9

Years ago I heard a sermon about praying for people we randomly encounter each day. Many of the people we see as we go about our business have no one praying for them. I remember being horrified at the idea of someone going through life without being covered in prayer by someone else. So I have tried to make it a discipline to pray for the person who crosses the street in front of me at a stoplight or for the homeless person begging on the corner or for the obviously harried clerk behind the checkout counter.

One of the ways to perfect this discipline is to listen to nudges from the Spirit about the people you encounter. For example, you may know nothing about the person you see crossing the street, but if you ask God to show you and if you listen to him, often a word or phrase will come to mind. Use that to form a quick prayer for them. Sometimes the need is obvious, like when you see a mom screaming at her kids in the parking lot. You can pray for the safety of the children and pray for peace and goodness in the life of the mother. With practice, we can also learn to hear nudges for needs that may be less obvious.

This was brought home to me very clearly one night at a church potluck. I went back for seconds and found myself across the food table from an elderly lady. I didn't know much about her, but it was suddenly impressed upon me to ask about her son. She jerked her head up from the scalloped potatoes, and with tears in her eyes she told me that her son was not doing well and that she appreciated my asking.

We can pray in confidence for those we don't know, trusting that God knows them and will translate our prayers into his will in their lives.

DAY FIVE

Action Prayer

Hezekiah received the letter from the messengers and read it. Then he went up to the temple of the LORD and spread it out before the LORD.

2 KINGS 19:14

King Hezekiah and the people of Israel were faced with a dire situation. The Assyrians, the most powerful military nation of that time, were intent on capturing Israel. (The story begins in 2 Kings 18:17.) From a human standpoint, there was no way Israel could win. Faced with imminent disaster, Hezekiah went to the temple to pray for God's help and mercy. He took the letter that Sennacherib, the Assyrian field commander, had sent to him and showed it to God—as though God didn't already know what the letter said. Hezekiah then prayed in desperation, as recorded in 2 Kings 19:15-19.

Sometimes when we are faced with a difficult problem, it can help to write out the issue and then lift the paper up to God in prayer. When we literally lay the problem before God, much as we would with a friend or trusted advisor, it can give us a more tangible sense of talking to a real person. It can also help us listen for the help and guidance God longs to give us.

DAY ONE

Community Prayer

They all joined together constantly in prayer.

ACTS 1:14

Somehow Satan has managed to convince many of us that religion is a private thing. We believe that our faith is only between us and God, and that we don't need community to be a Christian. Yet we read in the book of Acts that the early Christians got together constantly to pray, worship, even eat (see Acts 2:43-47). They knew that they would never make it alone.

Besides being an encouragement, praying regularly with others adds the element of accountability. If you are like me, there are some things that just won't happen unless there is someone else depending on me to show up and do it. (I especially need that kind of accountability to overcome my excuses for avoiding regular exercise.) Meeting regularly with a group to pray for your children's schools or for your church or for world issues brings an element of accountability and structure to your prayer life as well as adding power to our prayers. Jesus promises that "where two or three come together in my name, there am I with them" (Matthew 18:20).

Prayer is meant to have an element of discipline. We are invited to bring our thanks and concerns to God at any time and in any situation, but we are also encouraged to deepen our prayer life through regular times of prayer. That can include a weekly rhythm with a group as well as a daily rhythm on our own. This kind of structure helps us overcome the "I don't feel like it" or "I don't feel close to God" mentality that prevents many of us from regularly talking with our Father in heaven.

DAY TWO

Moving to Action

A voice said to him, "What are you doing here, Elijah?" He replied, "I have been very zealous for the LORD *God Almighty. The Israelites have rejected your covenant, broken down your altars, and put your prophets to death with the sword. I am the only one left, and now they are trying to kill me too." The* LORD *said to him, "Go back the way you came, and go to the Desert of Damascus. When you get there, anoint Hazael king over Aram."*

1 KINGS 19:13-15

This passage always makes me shake my head. Here is Elijah, hiding out in a cave to escape being killed by Jezebel, and God gives him a laundry list of kings that need to be anointed (see verse 16)! I know I would be a bit upset if I had barely come through a harrowing experience but after complaining to God all I got was a list of things that needed to be done for other people. I wouldn't enjoy having a good pout interrupted like that. In fact, I would feel as if God had not heard my prayer.

This passage knocks the false foundation of "God is here for my agenda" out from under us. While God is intimately concerned about and involved in all the details of our lives, he views them always within the context of "thy kingdom come, thy will be done on earth as it is in heaven."

Sometimes when we are feeling most sorry for ourselves, the word we need from God is to get out and do something for somebody else. In that act of obedience, we will ultimately find the answer to our prayer for our own needs.

DAY THREE

Praying for Children

Pour out your heart like water in the presence of the Lord. Lift up your hands to him for the lives of your children.

LAMENTATIONS 2:19

While we must always be careful not to take Scripture verses out of context, sometimes phrases leap out at us and urge us to make them our prayer. The portion of the verse above is from a longer passage in which Jeremiah is weeping over the destruction of Jerusalem and urging the people to pray literally for the lives of their children. For some of us, that is what we are doing if we are praying for an ill or seriously injured child.

But if we understand the greater context—Jerusalem lost her protection from God because the people did not take God's commandments seriously—then we can see how all of us need to pray for the welfare of the children in our own culture. While we may not know children who "faint from hunger at the head of every street," as the rest of this verse says (though there are children going to bed hungry every day, everywhere in the world), the children we see could be fainting from a lack of truth or goodness or godly models in their lives. The starvation of the soul is as critical as the starvation of the body.

Using the disciplines of meditation and study, we can come to recognize the subtle lies of our culture and the spiritual danger that our children are in. One way to protect them is to significantly limit their TV watching because that does more to form a child's character than most of us realize. Another way to protect them is to spend as much time with them as possible, affirming them in every way possible. Use Luke 2:40 to pray for a child you know. Ask God to bless him or her in the areas mentioned in that verse.

DAY FOUR

Covering the Family Tree

David divided the Levites into groups corresponding to the sons of Levi: Gershon, Kohath and Merari.

1 CHRONICLES 23:6

Following this verse are many verses and many chapters listing more names and descendants. It doesn't make for inspiring reading—unless you are looking for an unusual name for your baby—and I confess I used to skim those sections quickly.

Until, that is, I discovered what it means to pray for family—not just the nuclear family, but the extended family and those brought into the family through adoption and marriage. And I discovered it means praying not just for the usual kinds of things we pray for regarding our children, but praying for the generations to come. It means praying that decisions made today will lead to godliness and righteousness in future generations, and that the negative impact of previous generations will be muted or rendered ineffective in our children's lives today.

Suddenly I viewed those lists not as endless unpronounceable names but as people through whom God worked faithfully for generation after generation after generation. It made me think about relatives long dead who may have prayed for me when I was a young child, possibly affecting the decisions I made as I grew and matured. It made me think about grandchildren and the need to begin praying for spouses for my children even when they were too young to even think of marriage.

I began to see my name as one in a long list that stretches before and after me. I began to marvel at the ways God has worked and is still working in just my little family tree, let alone all the family trees of the world. It certainly impacted the way I came to pray for my family!

DAY FIVE

Meditation Guides Prayer

Now when Daniel learned that the decree had been published, he went home to his upstairs room where the windows opened toward Jerusalem. Three times a day he got down on his knees and prayed, giving thanks to his God, just as he had done before.

DANIEL 6:10

When talking about the spiritual disciplines it is hard to define where one stops and another starts. They are meant to be used together, and each discipline strengthens and informs the other disciplines. This is true with the discipline of meditation and the discipline of prayer. Meditating on God's Word, creation and the world around us is meant to lead us into prayer.

A good way to deepen spiritual formation in young and old alike is to meditate on various heroes of the Bible and then use those heroes and their stories as the basis of praying for character development.

For example, Daniel was a young Israelite man who was captured with the rest of his people by Nebuchadnezzar, yet he and his three friends were determined not to lose their faith in God in the culture they were forced to live in. Many of us know the story of Shadrach, Meshach and Abednego, but there are other vivid stories in the book of Daniel and throughout the Bible (like the book of Esther) that can capture a young person's heart and imagination as much as any modern action adventure. By thoughtfully reading through these stories, alone or with a child, you can begin to think about what aspects of the hero you would like to have for yourself (or for your child). This in turn can lead to a time of praying for that characteristic to be a part of your life or the life of the child.

Since God often gifts our children differently than we are gifted, follow their lead on what they would like to pray for to be developed in their character. It may not be what you would pray for, but the Spirit deals with each of us as individuals.

The Discipline of Fasting

WHAT WAS YOUR PHYSIOLOGICAL RESPONSE to the title of this chapter? Did your stomach knot? Did any muscles tense? Maybe you couldn't detect any particular response. For most of us, though, I suspect there was not a sense of "Oh, goody!"

The discipline of fasting seems to elicit two responses in people: fear or a sense that it is no big deal since they skip meals all the time. Neither one has any place in this discipline.

The discipline of fasting is meant to be one of joy and freedom. The basic definition of fasting for a Christian is "saying no to otherwise normal activities for the sake of intense spiritual focus." The Christian discipline of fasting has nothing to do with weight loss, political manipulation or asceticism for the purpose of punishment.

Fasting is traditionally associated with food, but it isn't limited to food. Fasting can be a time of denial of anything that allows us to avoid God, such as exercise, novels, TV, entertainment, shopping and conversation. In and of themselves none of these things are bad, but when they get in the way of our worship and prayer life or keep us from serving others, then we need a time of doing without them in our lives so that we can reevaluate our priorities.

Many people panic when you ask them to give something up. A desire to hoard immediately washes over them. They fear that they will never have access to the item again or that if they give up food for a time, they will die. (If you have *any* kind of medical condition, check with your health-care provider before beginning a food fast.)

On the other hand, some people are so paranoid about gaining weight that they skip meals all the time. These people need to fast from their attitude toward food and eat regular, healthy meals with joy and thanksgiving.

The discipline of fasting will expose the true priorities of your life. If you want to know what really motivates and drives you in your daily life, engage honestly in the discipline of fasting. Arthur Wallis's book *God's Chosen Fast* (1968) is an excellent discussion of all aspects of biblical fasting, from the why to the nitty-gritty of how.

This discipline is one of the two disciplines that have the most potential as tools for freedom for many Christians (the other is the discipline of confession). If rightly used, the discipline of fasting can untie age-old knots of bondage that have kept you from having a free and joyful spirit in Christ. Remember, Jesus was at his strongest, not his weakest, after forty days of fasting in the wilderness. That is why he was able to so effectively dispatch Satan's temptations. We too can find tremendous strength in times of adversity if we have trained well in the discipline of fasting. It is worth the fight and hard work to learn this discipline so that you can rid yourself of the sleeping demons hidden deep within your soul beneath layers of idolizing food and material possessions.

Each week choose one or two suggested activities from the list below to help you practice this discipline:

For Anyone

- Since its earliest days the church practiced fasting on Wednesdays and Fridays. Find a way to begin training in this discipline. Start slowly—by skipping lunch on those days for example—and build up to longer fasts. Obviously, if you have a medical condition, check with your doctor. Consider a bread and water fast or a fast from sweets or coffee if you can't fast from food completely. Just do something for some period of time.
- Eat smaller portions at mealtimes for a week. The next time you are at a fast-food restaurant, don't supersize the order. Don't have seconds at dinner.
- Eat only when you are hungry, and stop when you are full. When you are tempted to grab a snack out of boredom or loneliness, pray instead for those who have little or no food, or for a situation that you are concerned about.
- Pick a day to fast. If someone notices and asks why you are not eating, carefully explain what you are trying to accomplish. Be aware of how

your words and actions might impact the other person, especially if it is a child asking.

- Keep a journal on your fast days. Write down attitudes and emotions that rise to the surface when you have no food to keep them pressed down. Focus your prayer time on those issues while you are fasting so that you may truly benefit from this discipline.
- Find an organized race or walk to participate in. Train regularly, learning to stretch, to walk or run properly and to cool down. Have plenty of water and good shoes. While you are training physically, meditate on the training we can do for our souls, such as by fasting.
- Find an area in one of your relationships where you can let go a little bit more. Maybe someone doesn't need as much help as you give with homework or the sales report. Work on being a silent presence, inviting requests for help but not offering help in advance.
- Fast from needing to be right for a day. If someone offends you, ignore it. As much as possible, don't point out to anyone how wrong they were in a situation.
- Fast from mental and physical activity for fifteen minutes a day. Rest in God, reminding yourself that you are not in charge of keeping the universe running smoothly.
- Fast from adding any new activity into your schedule for a month. Pray for God to guide you into a good balance in your life.

Especially with Children

- Identify areas where there are potentially dangerous distractions from keeping God front and center. It could be an obsession with clothes or video games or relationships or food. Commit to a fast from those things on Wednesdays and Fridays for the next eight weeks.
- Get out one suitcase and think about what you would put into it if you knew you had to flee from a fire, a famine or a war situation. Meditate on what it would be like to lose everything else.
- Adopt a child through an aid organization. Talk about ways that your child could get involved, such as writing letters to the child, earning money to help support him, learning as much as possible about her

country and why there may be issues of poverty and famine there.

- Go to a farm or a farmer's market. Talk to the farmer about what it means to grow food or raise animals for food. If possible, pick your own produce and then eat that food for dinner. Many children have no idea where their food really comes from.

DAY ONE

What and Why

The grace of God that brings salvation has appeared to all. . . . It teaches us to say "No" to ungodliness and worldly passions, and to live self-controlled, upright and godly lives in this present age, while we wait for the blessed hope—the glorious appearing of our great God and Savior, Jesus Christ.

TITUS 2:11-13

These verses sum up the reason for the discipline of fasting. The whole point of saying no to an otherwise normal activity is for the sake of waiting well for Jesus' glorious appearing. Christian fasting is not for weight loss, political manipulation or punishment; its whole point is to make us better disciples of Christ.

Fasting often brings out the worst in us. In our hunger we uncover a spoiled child within that demands what it wants when it wants it under threat of throwing a temper tantrum. We discover we use treats to cover up greed and a naturally selfish nature. We discover that we aren't as nice as we think we are.

Jesus invites us to embrace the blessed hope that the best is yet to come. Jesus invites us to wait for the true joy that he has promised, not getting sidetracked by what we put in our mouths or use to medicate painful thoughts. The tension is always, can we trust him to fill the emptiness we create in ourselves through fasting with something even better?

DAY TWO

Impact on Others

Food does not bring us near to God; we are no worse if we do not eat, and no better if we do. Be careful, however, that the exercise of your freedom does not become a stumbling block to the weak.

1 CORINTHIANS 8:8-9

During Lent I usually give up something (often involving sugar) in an attempt to stop and think about all Jesus gave up for me. Because temptations around food are such an area of struggle for me, I play all kinds of games with the rules I lay down for myself during that time of fasting. One year my little games did damage to another person.

I had been asked to bring dessert to a dinner party. Since we are commanded to not make a big deal of our fasting (see Matthew 6:16-18), I said yes to the request, but I didn't think it through very clearly. To me dessert means something with sugar or chocolate, so I brought a rhubarb pie instead of a less sugary alternative like fresh fruit. And while Lent isn't meant to be a time of rigidity, I knew that God was calling me to get a grip on some out-of-control eating habits by cutting out sugar for six weeks. But because I did not go to God in prayer over what to bring for dessert during a fast time, I was not a good witness of the goodness a Lenten fast can be.

It somehow came up that I had given up sugar for Lent. I joked that the pie didn't count because rhubarb is a vegetable, right? The problem was that my hosts were struggling to give up alcohol for Lent, which they consumed a lot of. They saw my cavalier attitude toward the pie and started making their own rationalizations for why they could break their fast, too. So they had another glass of wine. I was so ashamed at having become a stumbling block to their fast.

My salvation is not dependent on whether I eat or don't eat sugar during Lent. I will, however, have to give an account of how I struggle to walk closer to Christ and whether or not I make it more difficult for someone else to do the same.

DAY THREE

The First Sin

When the woman saw that the fruit of the tree was good for food and pleasing to the eye, and also desirable for gaining wisdom, she took some and ate it. She also gave some to her husband, who was with her, and he ate it.

GENESIS 3:6

Not eating when you are hungry is a foreign idea to many people. Yet if we look at the entire story surrounding today's verse (see Genesis 2:1–3:24), we can see that there is a larger issue at stake here: that issue is obedience to God. God gave Adam and Eve everything they needed for life and fulfillment. He asked them to trust him in one issue, and that was not to eat from the tree of life. Why? I'm not sure we will ever really know this side of heaven, but that was the way God set things up.

Today when we choose to fast from food for a period of time, we are seeking to draw closer to God, to stand in raw obedience and dependence on him alone. Are we saved by this practice? No. But it can certainly be an eye-opening experience that shows us all the other things in our lives we depend on besides God.

Just as Adam and Eve hid from God after they had eaten from the forbidden tree, so we many times hide from God by covering up the promptings of the Holy Spirit with food. For example, God might be asking us to look at anger issues in our life, but we assume we are cranky because we are hungry. In reality, we use food to keep our true angry self somewhat pacified. When we take away the food crutch, we are able to look at how much anger drives our responses, and then we can turn to God for forgiveness and help.

Regular fasting can help us hear God's call in our lives more clearly.

DAY FOUR

Trust Issues

The LORD will guide you always; he will satisfy your needs in a sun-scorched land and will strengthen your frame. You will be like a well-watered garden, like a spring whose waters never fail.

ISAIAH 58:11

This verse is part of a passage detailing what the Lord considers to be a godly fast (see verses 1-12). The imagery is striking. God is inviting us to be an oasis for people who are trapped in a "sun-scorched land" existence. Part of learning to be that oasis involves letting God guide us through fasting. In fasting we take away the clutter and props we use to avoid the real issues in our lives. When we can face those issues and gain better control over them, we can then help those who are still lost in their own desert.

Fasting helps us ask, do I really believe God will satisfy my needs despite the seemingly barren landscape of my life? Do I believe that I can live as a well-watered garden in the midst of the desert? Do I even want to be that spring whose waters never fail for those who are dying of thirst for a word of truth from God?

As Christians we believe we should answer yes to those questions. But in our heart of hearts, do we really long for that kind of relationship with the living Lord? Fasting from food and other activities for periods of time helps us discover our real answer to that question.

More on Training

Do you not know that in a race all the runners run, but only one gets the prize? Run in such a way as to get the prize. Everyone who competes in the games goes into strict training. They do it to get a crown that will not last; but we do it to get a crown that will last forever. Therefore I do not run like a man running aimlessly. . . . No, I beat my body and make it my slave so that after I have preached to others, I myself will not be disqualified for the prize.

1 CORINTHIANS 9:24-27

I live in an area where a big 10K race is held every Memorial Day. While there are professional athletes from around the world who participate in it, there is also a race where thousands of amateur athletes can run or walk the same course the professionals compete on. People come from all over to participate or watch, and the town is consumed with the race for days.

One year I decided that I would walk the course. I was just beginning to regain physical fitness after years of being out of shape. I trained for the race by walking some every day. Well, I am here to tell you that walking some every day is not the same as a 10K race. I made it to the end, but I was very sore for several days afterward, not to mention discouraged at how poorly I did compared to the lean bodies running past me. I resolved to be more dedicated and regular in my walking from that point on.

Fasting is one discipline you must train in. The spiritual benefits only come after the mechanics are down pat. If a crisis hits, you will not fast and pray as effectively if you have not trained in fasting. You will be too consumed with your hunger. It would be like the people who enter that Memorial Day race with no training and collapse along the way.

DAY ONE

Depending on God

Who among you fears the LORD and obeys the word of his servant? Let him who walks in the dark, who has no light, trust in the name of the LORD and rely on his God.

ISAIAH 50:10

When we were teaching our children to drive, we gradually had to let go of the impulse to give them constant verbal instructions. At some point we had to trust that they were getting the hang of it and would make the next turn without us talking them through every step it. The first night that our oldest daughter took the car by herself with her brand-new driver's license was a hard moment for my husband and me. We wanted her to grow up and be independent, yet we were terrified thinking about all of the horrible things that could happen to her with her new freedom.

Letting go of growing children can be a serious faith crisis for some of us. Do we really believe that God loves them more than we do? Do we really believe God will work in their lives without us hovering over them? Do we hover over other family members or coworkers because we are afraid they won't do it right—meaning the way we believe it needs to be done?

One of the issues the discipline of fasting addresses is the issue of trusting God. What kinds of things do we depend on to help us feel better when we are nervous or afraid? Alcohol? Food? Television?

Just as we are called to trust our children, our family members, our friends more and more over time, so we are called to trust God. Fasting can help us develop that trust.

DAY TWO

Rule of Hospitality

Then John's disciples came and asked [Jesus], "How is it that we and the Pharisees fast, but your disciples do not fast?" Jesus answered, "How can the guests of the bridegroom mourn while he is with them? The time will come when the bridegroom will be taken from them; then they will fast."

MATTHEW 9:14-15

There are inappropriate times to fast. Hospitality nearly always supersedes fasting. For example, I was doing my usual sugar fast for Lent one year. Our family had been invited to visit an older couple for the afternoon. They had gone to a great deal of effort to set a dessert table complete with tablecloth and flowers. They offered us several kinds of homemade cookies and gourmet ice cream.

If I had said, "Oh, no thank you, I gave up sugar for Lent," it would not have had any spiritual benefit for me (instead it would be bragging and calling attention to my fast), and it would have been an insult to their hospitality. So I graciously accepted the dessert, choosing my least favorite ice cream flavor and cookie. They had no idea I was breaking my fast, and I kept it to a minimum with choices that weren't my favorites.

Here is another example. Some Trappist monks were guests at a convent. As the visiting monks sat eating their steak for dinner, one of the nuns said, "Isn't your order vegetarian?" The monks said yes and kept eating. They clearly understood Jesus' command in Luke 10:7 to "stay in that house, eating and drinking whatever they give you," even though it meant breaking the rule of their own monastic order.

As Christians we always need to be in training with this discipline. Part of that training is knowing when to accept the gift of food despite a fast.

DAY THREE

The Second Coming

So then, let us not be like others, who are asleep, but let us be alert and self-controlled.

1 THESSALONIANS 5:6

Most of us have had the experience of eating way too much and then wanting to do nothing more than lie down in pain. Continually overindulging in food leads to health problems, and continually overindulging in entertainment and material possessions leads to faith problems. We begin to forget that God is to be the center of our lives, and not all the treats and luxuries we long for.

Jesus warns us in Matthew 24:42-44, "Therefore keep watch, because you do not know on what day your Lord will come. But understand this: If the owner of the house had known at what time of night the thief was coming, he would have kept watch and would not have let his house be broken into. So you also must be ready, because the Son of Man will come at an hour when you do not expect him."

Fasting keeps us lean and prepared for the coming of Jesus. We've all heard of people who dropped dead without warning. Let us use fasting from food and other things that distract us from keeping our eyes on Jesus to teach us to stay alert and self-controlled. We never know when Jesus will call us home.

DAY FOUR

Learning Humility

Starting a quarrel is like breaching a dam; so drop the matter before a dispute breaks out.

PROVERBS 17:14

In the parking lot of a fast-food restaurant, I saw two men in a loud, ugly, foul-mouthed shouting match over a driving infraction one of them apparently committed. It went on and on, and I was afraid it would become physical. The really horrible part of the scene was that in the back seat of one man's car there were two small children taking in every gesture and word of the encounter.

For some of us, a fast from the need to be right at all times would be even harder to do than a food fast. Walking away from an insulting or infuriating situation could be harder than skipping lunch. Yet doing that could be more revealing as to what is really driving our thoughts, words and deeds.

How much better it would have been if these men had known how to fast from the need to always be right. I shudder to think what those children learned that day.

DAY FIVE

Needs Versus Wants

Godliness with contentment is great gain. For we brought nothing into the world, and we can take nothing out of it. But if we have food and clothing, we will be content with that.

1 TIMOTHY 6:6-8

I walked into a store where plastered on the wall in large letters was this statement: "Do you need it? No. Do you have to have it? Yes." The blatancy of these words took my breath away. I know that the whole goal of advertising is to get us to buy something regardless of whether or not we need it, but seeing that message spelled out in those large letters stopped me in my tracks.

The problem for many of us is that we don't have a clear sense of what our needs are compared to what our wants are. We have bought the lie that more is better, and in doing so we have come to believe the insidious lie that everything we have, we need.

One year the western part of the United States endured a terrible drought that sparked many fires. As we left home for a vacation, I put together a small pile of computer disks and photographs with instructions for the house sitter to grab those items in the event of an evacuation notice. I struggled with the thought that in the event of a major fire, all I would be left with was the cat and two boxes of possessions.

Fasting is a tool to help us regain a biblical perspective on what is really necessary for life. By temporarily letting go of the food, activity or possession we think we need, we can begin to see how all too often we make the things that are meant to be merely supportive the focus of our lives.

DAY ONE

Fasting from Franticness

Yet the news about him spread all the more, so that crowds of people came to hear him and to be healed of their sicknesses. But Jesus often withdrew to lonely places and prayed.

LUKE 5:15-16

I was all aflutter inside. I had a zillion e-mails, most of them requiring thoughtful responses, and then the computer went down. An important item had been misplaced and was possibly lost completely. I had lots of things to do at church, plus several big writing projects to work on, not to mention that Christmas was coming and everything that goes with that. I was completely frustrated. So many things needed to be done, yet I was unable to do much of anything.

I decided that the best thing I could do at the moment was pray about my concerns and frustrations, eat something healthy and pet the cat. I couldn't find what was lost and I couldn't fix the computer, but I could focus on settling myself down. Amazingly, as I withdrew from activity and let myself rest in God, I found I was able to get a new perspective on things, set some priorities and return my breathing to normal. And in the mercies of God, what was lost eventually turned up, and the computer came back to life—all without my frantic attempts to keep the universe under control.

Sometimes Jesus walked away from a lot of sick and hurting people so that he could keep himself centered on God and settled in body, mind and spirit. Don't we need to do the same?

DAY TWO

Chaos Versus Calm

Now the earth was formless and empty, darkness was over the surface of the deep, and the Spirit of God was hovering over the waters.

GENESIS 1:2

So begins the story of God bringing order out of chaos in the creation of the world. Even today God continues to work in the formless, empty darkness of our lives to bring the order of his kingdom to birth in them.

Years ago I copied down a quote by French theologian François Fénelon: "When we notice in ourselves eager desires for something in the future, and when we see that our temperament carries us too intensely to all that must be done, let us try to restrain ourselves from hurry, and ask our Lord to stop the haste in our hearts and the agitation of our behavior, since God has said Himself that His Spirit does not dwell in confusion." Ouch!

While we could talk about this idea under the discipline of simplicity, it also involves the discipline of fasting. We cannot live a healthy life if we stuff our calendars with unlimited activity. One of the ways to partner with God in bringing order out of the chaos of our lives is to say no to (fast from) doing more activities than we can sanely accomplish in a day or week. We need to fast from the idea that we will miss out on something if we don't say yes to everything! Jesus himself walked away from some people and situations to keep the priorities of prayer and the kingdom of God first in his life.

We are finite. We cannot do everything, we are not called to do everything, but we are to "seek first his kingdom and his righteousness" (Matthew 6:33).

DAY THREE

Sowing Good Seed

Listen then to what the parable of the sower means: . . . The one who received the seed that fell among the thorns is the man who hears the word, but the worries of this life and the deceitfulness of wealth choke it, making it unfruitful.

MATTHEW 13:18, 22

It isn't how we start out in our Christian walk that counts, it is how we finish. God takes us where we are and embraces us with grace and forgiveness. But that is only the beginning. We are called to grow in that grace and forgiveness so that at the end of our life we are very different people than when we first said yes to God. We can never retire from an active pursuit of holiness.

I have encountered many young adults who were on fire for God. They were ready to go anywhere and do anything for the kingdom. But twenty years later, some of them are not even sure they believe in God. They are consumed with mortgage payments, car payments, careers and college bills, and issues of aging. The call of God in their lives seems so remote and youthfully idealistic. Sometimes their involvement with the church is perfunctory and aimed more at making sure their children are exposed to a wide range of ideas than at real, meaningful faith commitment.

How did this happen? For some it was traumatic experiences they could never quite overcome. For others it was a day-to-day ignoring of the "weeds" growing in their souls, until one day they woke up and realized the weeds were stronger than the original seed of faith planted years ago.

In addition to food, we can fast from activities that dominate our lives and draw us away from God. Sometimes fasting from TV or exercise or entertainment or shopping is more insightful than fasting from food. The weeds quickly become apparent, and we might be shocked at the depth of their root systems.

DAY FOUR

Standing with the Poor

The King will reply, "I tell you the truth, whatever you did for one of the least of these brothers of mine, you did for me."

MATTHEW 25:40

One day it hit me that my carrying a little extra weight on my body was a sin. It meant that I was using even more of the world's resources while living in a culture that already consumes an excess of those resources. My overeating, wasting food and eating less-than-healthy food options was a slap in the face for the hungry and malnourished.

Suddenly my goal to lose weight was more than just for looks and health; it became a statement that I wanted to consume less so there would be more for others. That did not make losing weight any easier, but it did help motivate me at times when I was tempted to cave in and eat some extra empty calories or skip my daily exercise.

In today's verse we get the ending of Jesus' parable of the sheep and the goats. The sheep (the believers) were surprised to find out that all of their small and hidden kindnesses were actually given to Jesus, just as the insensitivities of the goats (the unbelievers) to those around them wounded Christ himself.

This parable always stops me in my tracks. The little things count, for good and for ill. Everything I do or don't do, including the way I eat, has an eternal consequence for me and an impact on others.

DAY FIVE

Healthy Eating and Fasting

Train a child in the way he should go, and when he is old he will not turn from it.

PROVERBS 22:6

When dealing with the discipline of fasting, we must remember to model goodness for the sake of the children in our lives. We must not be obsessive about food (either eating or not eating) because we are in danger of passing that obsession on to children. We must not allow growing children to do complete food fasts, since it is not healthy for them.

While children need to learn proper self-denial, the discipline of fasting must be handled in such a way that eating disorders or pathologies related to deprivation are not created. Do *not* attempt to teach this to your children while you are still getting a handle on this discipline yourself. You can share your struggle with this concept as appropriate, but do not attempt to have children participate until you yourself understand the difference between healthy and unhealthy self-denial.

Having laid out this important warning, let me now say that fasting is easier to learn when you are young than after years of unbridled self-indulgence. If we can instill in our children the idea of giving up certain things on a regular basis, they will be well equipped to use fasting with prayer as a powerful tool when they mature.

Here are some ideas for how children can fast in a healthy way. Perhaps they can fast from sugar on Wednesdays and Fridays. Or maybe one day they can fast from sugar and another day they can fast from computer games or videos. If this practice has become a household routine, it is easier to say, "No, you can't have a cookie; it's Wednesday. How about an apple?" You can replace the time spent on computer games or watching TV with a family read-aloud time.

Remember, these disciplines are meant to become holy habits. Start small but start early. Most importantly, start.

DAY ONE

Feasting and Fasting

This is a day you are to commemorate; for the generations to come you shall celebrate it as a festival to the LORD. . . . *Celebrate the Feast of Harvest with the firstfruits of the crops you sow in your field. Celebrate the Feast of Ingathering at the end of the year, when you gather in your crops from the field.*

EXODUS 12:14; 23:16

These verses are only samplings of the many places in the Bible where God commands his people to stop work and celebrate. We need to remember that feasting is also a part of the rhythm of the discipline of fasting. We say no to earthly things for a while so we can better say yes to the things of God. Or to put it another way, we fast from temporal things so we can feast on eternal things.

For example, the church year seasons of Advent (the four Sundays before Christmas) and Lent (the six weeks before Easter) are times to fast and reflect on God's work in humanity and our relationship to that work. Then we are to fully celebrate Christmas (traditionally, December 25 to January 6) and Easter. Even today in the Eastern churches, fasting is forbidden for the week after Easter because it is to be a time of rich feasting in celebration of Christ's resurrection after the long, strict Lenten fast.

Our culture urges us to gluttony in the days before Christmas, but the church invites us to prepare our hearts for the Christ child through fasting. The concept of a Lenten fast is more culturally accepted but not well understood. In Lent we are invited to a "spring cleaning" of our bodies and minds as we walk with Jesus to the cross. It is difficult to fully embrace the radical goodness of Easter morning if we are already full of ourselves. You cannot fill with God what has been filled with earthly things.

"Then the angel said to [John], . . . 'Blessed are those who are invited to the wedding supper of the Lamb!'" (Revelation 19:9). Will we be hungry for that feast when it arrives?

DAY TWO

Fasting and Prayer

On that day [the people of Israel] fasted and there they confessed, "We have sinned against the LORD."

1 SAMUEL 7:6

As we age, many of us find that bad habits and sins persist in staying with us. It seems like no matter what we do to change our attitude or our behavior, we remain stuck. Sometimes we are not even sure why we continue to respond poorly in certain situations; it just seems to flow out of us like a volcanic eruption that can't be stopped.

The combination of fasting with prayer for a specific situation has a powerful track record throughout the centuries. The book of Esther in the Bible tells how Queen Esther saved her entire race from genocide through prayer and fasting. Barnabus and Saul (later renamed Paul) were set aside for ministry through the prayer and fasting of an entire church (see Acts 13:1-3). And the elderly prophetess Anna was privileged to see the baby Jesus after spending years praying and fasting (see Luke 2:36-38).

Our fasting and praying for a situation can move mountains in our own life or the life of another. However, we must train regularly in the mechanics of fasting so that when we need to fast and pray for a situation, we are truly able to focus on God and not on our stomach. It is a mystery, and yet by clearing an empty space in our body we allow God to fill our spirit more fully.

New Testament Fasting

When you fast, do not look somber as the hypocrites do, for they disfigure their faces to show men they are fasting. I tell you the truth, they have received their reward in full. But when you fast, put oil on your head and wash your face, so that it will not be obvious to men that you are fasting, but only to your Father, who is unseen; and your Father, who sees what is done in secret, will reward you.

MATTHEW 6:16-18

In this section of the Sermon on the Mount, Jesus gives a new teaching on an old practice that he assumes his followers will continue. There are two kinds of fasting spoken of here: one is the obvious abstention from food, and the other is the command to fast from drawing attention to how spiritual you are. For some of us, the latter is more difficult than the former. We will do great acts of service and piety as long as someone else knows how much we are "sacrificing for the Lord" and will let others know of our sacrifice.

Jesus asks us to decide where we want the reward to come from (note the implication that there will be a reward for our efforts). Do we want it to come from our peers? Or do we want it to come from our Father in heaven? We can't have it both ways.

Fasting is an inward discipline that will eventually show its fruits in our public life, but as soon as the fasting itself becomes visible, we have lost the spiritual benefit. Fasting for political change or for weight loss is not the same as the discipline of fasting for spiritual growth. Other kinds of fasting have their place, but their rewards are quite different from the rewards for fasting to mature as a Christian.

DAY FOUR

Becoming a New Creation

Yet on the day of your fasting, you do as you please and exploit all your workers. Your fasting ends in quarreling and strife, and in striking each other with wicked fists. You cannot fast as you do today and expect your voice to be heard on high.

ISAIAH 58:3-4

In Bible times, fasting two days a week was a normal part of a religious Jew's life, and many in the church continue that practice today. Unfortunately, many of us have gotten away from fasting, and in so doing we have cut ourselves off from a powerful tool to use in our Christian walk.

However, as the prophet Isaiah pointed out to those who were following the form of fasting without living the meaning of it, fasting is meant to mature us into people who live and work for justice in all of society. Fasting is meant to rein in our selfish desires and greediness. Fasting is meant to draw us into "the peace of God, which transcends all understanding" (Philippians 4:7), a peace that is not dependent on the circumstances around us.

Many of us have the idea that when we become crabby on a fast day it is because we are hungry. In reality we are crabby because we have a spirit of greed or entitlement or lust or anger in us that we keep under control with food. When we fast, whether full or partial food fasts, we also are to fast from arguing, greed and unjust practices to those around us.

DAY FIVE

Just Do It

Have nothing to do with godless myths and old wives' tales; rather, train yourself to be godly. For physical training is of some value, but godliness has value for all things, holding promise for both the present life and the life to come.

1 TIMOTHY 4:7-8

I was given a beautiful crown-of-thorns plant by my mother-in-law. She had had one as a child, and it had been trained to grow in the shape of a crown. After several years of letting mine grow straight up, I decided to guide it into a crown shape. I put stakes in the pot and began to tie down the long spiky branches into an oval. For months I worked with that plant, and all I got for my effort was a lot of thorn pricks. Finally I untied all the branches and let it grow the direction it was already headed.

While it is true that the earlier we start incorporating the spiritual disciplines into our lives, the easier it will be to make them a natural part of our faith walk, in the mercies of God, it is never too late for anyone to start walking closer to God. We have to be careful that we don't throw up our hands and say, "I'm too old to change." That is not true, even with a tough-to-learn discipline like fasting.

Even if we are closer to the end of our life than its beginning, we must remember that in God's perspective, our entire life on earth is the "introduction" to our eternal life. Death is a beginning more than an ending. So even as we grow physically older each day, we can continue to nurture and shape our spirits to be more like Jesus who is able to take the prickly thorns of our soul and mold them into a beautiful shape. Fasting can help us get a clearer perspective on what that means in practical ways.

The Discipline of Study

THE DISCIPLINE OF STUDY is a close cousin of the discipline of meditation. The discipline of study gives us the foundation for much of what we are called to focus on in the discipline of meditation.

For Christians the first priority in this discipline is the study of the Bible. After that comes the study of materials related to our faith: devotionals and writings of Christians from all times and all places. Then comes the study of creation, other people, current events, history, art, music, works of fiction, movies. In short, everything around us is available for study, in which we ask, how is God at work here? What does this say about God? Is it a true statement or a distorted one? Why or why not?

This discipline also includes the consistent, intentional memorization of Scripture. When we have large portions of the Bible tucked away in our minds and hearts, we can use those passages whenever we need them. For example, instead of fuming while waiting in a long line, you can think about a passage of Scripture you have memorized and meditate on what it is saying to you as you stand in that line.

For people who don't consider themselves academic or who never liked school very much, this discipline can sound dreadful, overwhelming or even frightening. You may not think of yourself as a scholar, or maybe you have learning disabilities that prevent you from easily learning material through reading. If that is the case, ask God to guide you to a different way of studying the Bible and his work in the world and in creation. Maybe you can listen to an audio version of the Bible while driving or cooking dinner. Or get a series of taped lectures given by solid Christian teachers (such as those available through the bookstore of Regent College in Vancouver, British Columbia, which can be accessed online). Maybe your church library has audio resources on various topics by Christian speakers; ask your pastor for good suggestions. Or when you go on vacation, take an audio guided tour of an art museum or a nature area that could give you more insights into God's hand at work in the world and creation.

This discipline can be likened to reading a murder mystery. Clues to the identity of the murderer are usually left throughout the book. How good are we at picking up on those clues before the last chapter? That is what God has done in the world: he has left clues about his work and his plan for all creation. As it says in Romans 1:20, "Since the creation of the world God's invisible qualities—his eternal power and divine nature—have been clearly seen, being understood from what has been made, so that men are without excuse." The discipline of study invites us to become better at finding the clues of God's work in the world.

Again, the discipline of guidance is critical here. We must be careful to process our conclusions with other Christians so that we don't get off the path of God's kingdom and end up out in left field. The discipline of worship is also important because in regular worship we are reminded of who God is—the God we are supposed to be looking for in all of these areas of life and faith. So let us take the advice of wise King Solomon and seek wisdom ourselves, applying our hearts to gain understanding (see Proverbs 2:2).

Each week choose one or two suggested activities from the list below to help you practice this discipline:

For Anyone

- Read a good murder mystery, such as one in the Brother Cadfael series by Ellis Peters, and see if you can figure it out before the end. Then use those same skills to look for God's work in the world as you read the newspaper and the Bible or as you talk to others.
- Pick a passage of Scripture and focus on how it applies to you only. Don't allow yourself to apply it to anyone else.
- Remember a time in your life when you faced a big test. Maybe it was for your driver's license or for a professional license. How did you prepare for that test? How might you apply the same concepts to your faith?
- Read a biography of someone you don't know much about, like Amy Car-

michael or Saint Francis of Assisi. What do you find inspiring about the person's life? What do you find odd? Do you sense God calling you to something while you read about this person?

- Do you know God, or do you know about God? One way to gain both kinds of knowledge is to read a short Bible passage and then read any commentary you can find about it (like in a study Bible or another Bible-study resource). Then spend the rest of your devotion time listening to what God may be saying to you about what you read in that passage.
- Pick one of your favorite worship songs or hymns and study it. First speak the text out loud. Then hum the tune. Does the music support the meaning of the text? If not, what is the tune's message?
- Read one of the shorter books of the Bible, like Ruth, Philemon or Jude, straight through. If you have access to a commentary or a study Bible, read the notes associated with that book. Then spend the week focusing on a few verses of the book here and there, a kind of rechewing the initial larger portion of ingested material.
- What are your favorite Bible verses? Memorize one today. What clue does it give you about becoming better at imitating Jesus?
- If you know someone who is in school, ask her what she is learning. Don't make this a "Did you do your homework?" question, but try to engage him in what it is he is actually learning. Don't argue with her, but make it a respectful discussion. Share what you know about the subject, but don't be afraid to say what you don't know about it. Pray with him for wisdom and guidance in seeking God's truth in this subject.
- If it's been a long time since you studied in a school environment or studied to take a professional exam, look for a new opportunity today. Find a Bible study, a community-college course, a lecture series, a community-service club or a new hobby that will require you to think, write and speak about something new.
- From your daily news source, pick an issue facing local, national or international leaders. On a three-by-five-inch card, write down three points to pray about. Carry the card around with you today, praying as often as you can for the kingdom of God to come into that situation.

Especially with Children

- Get a book about indentifying flowers, animal tracks, shells, constellations or trees. Spend fifteen minutes every day learning one new thing from the book. At the end of the time, thank God for the wonders of creation.
- Look at a secular magazine advertisement or TV commercial. Can you articulate its message in one sentence and effectively communicate it to someone else? What is the Christian response to that message?
- Sit down as a family or with friends and talk about your similarities and differences. Listen to others when they tell you, "I hate it when you . . ." Ask them how they would like you to change whatever it is. This exercise can be very eye-opening (and humbling); you often discover that what other people hear you say is not what you think you are saying.
- Listen to a different kind of music than the kind your church usually uses in worship. If possible, learn about the piece from the liner notes or the Internet. Can you imagine using that style of music regularly in worship? Why or why not? What does that style of music say about what the people who wrote it believe about God?

DAY ONE

The Occasional Checkup

Examine yourselves to see whether you are in the faith; test yourselves. Do you not realize that Christ Jesus is in you—unless, of course, you fail the test?

2 CORINTHIANS 13:5

The discipline of study invites us to look at a variety of sources, like Scripture and devotional books, history and current events, and human relationships to see where God is at work. Another profitable area of study is ourselves. For those of us who have been Christians for a long time, it is easy to get complacent with our faith commitment. We have our routines of worship, private devotions and service that we continue year after year. And those are not necessarily bad things.

However, it is good to periodically ask ourselves if we still are growing in our relationship with God and gaining a deeper understanding of the faith. One way to assess yourself is by using the basic tenets of the Christian faith as outlined in either the Apostles' Creed or the Nicene Creed. Go through the creed point by point and ask yourself if you still believe it. Make an appointment with your pastor or an accountability partner to talk about any misgivings you have that maybe you didn't have before.

Like a houseplant, we sometimes need new soil and a new pot. That doesn't mean abandoning what we believe, but it might mean reading a new devotional book or trying a new system for reading the Bible or getting into a study group with other Christians.

DAY TWO

Integrity in Living

Do your best to present yourself to God as one approved, a workman who does not need to be ashamed and who correctly handles the word of truth.

2 TIMOTHY 2:15

When we read and study to increase our knowledge and understanding of the living God, we must do so with an attitude of humility and repentance. As we read the words, we must let them read us so to speak. We must never use the discipline of study as a purely fact-finding mission. We must use it to be transformed by those words.

Negative examples of lives that don't match knowledge include health-care professionals with unhealthy lifestyles, counselors whose personal lives are a mess and financial managers who can't control their own debt load. Such people have not let the words they preach transform their own lives.

As we study God in Scripture, books and in his work in the world around us, we must ask ourselves how his hand is moving in our lives and how we may be called to respond to him. We must learn to handle the word of truth correctly by taking what we see and hear, and through prayer learning to use it for good first in our own lives before applying it to others.

Fear Has Its Place

The fear of the LORD is the beginning of wisdom; all who follow his precepts have good understanding. To him belongs eternal praise.

PSALM 111:10

In the first semester of my freshman year in college as an organ major, I encountered a phenomenon called juries. These are the final exams for private music lessons. At the appointed hour, you come to the appointed place with all the other organ students. When your name is called, you play the piece you and your instructor agreed upon while your peers listen and the faculty grades you.

At my first jury I was very nervous. I liked my organ professor and I loved playing the organ, but my fear of juries drove me to be more diligent in my practicing than I otherwise would have been. That fear helped me gain wisdom in practicing and following my teacher's instructions with more care.

If we seek to know God in Jesus more deeply, and all that that means for our lives, we will be filled with love and joy. We will also be overwhelmed and nervous, if we are honest. That is the beginning of true wisdom.

A Bigger Picture

Ezra had devoted himself to the study and observance of the Law of the LORD, and to teaching its decrees and laws in Israel.

EZRA 7:10

The book of Ezra tells the story of a Jewish man in exile in Babylon (modern-day Iraq). It tells of his return to Jerusalem, where the temple was being rebuilt against great odds. God blessed Ezra's journey with speed (it only took him four months to get from Babylon to Jerusalem!) because Ezra yearned to share what he knew about God with the people of Israel. Ezra was focused on learning and teaching God's law, and God honored that focus.

Many people live their lives by default, meaning they live based on whatever happens to come their way. While we don't want to be so driven that we can't be flexible, we also don't want to come to the end of our lives and realize we haven't been very intentional about anything. When we commit to regular study of the Bible and readings from Christian writers, past and present, we begin to see a picture of what God may be calling us to. Ideas and situations we hadn't thought of for ourselves may become possibilities after reading about them in the lives of Christians throughout the centuries.

DAY FIVE

Lifting Faith Weights

They confronted me in the day of my disaster, but the Lord was my support.

PSALM 18:18

We live in an old mountain cottage that was originally a summer sleeping cabin. Over the course of a hundred years, the original little house has been added on to and winterized.

A couple of years after we moved in, my husband was doing a thorough check of the foundation and supports under the house. Since the house basically sits on the ground, this was a crucial inspection. He pulled the outer wood off the base of the thirty-foot north side and discovered only five wooden supports, none of which were truly at right angles, and several of which had dry rot! It is a wonder that whole side of the house hadn't collapsed.

In the discipline of study we seek to strengthen the supports of our "faith house." We seek to have a knowledge of God that will support us in times when we don't feel God's presence in our lives. We seek to have truths ready to counter the lies of "dry rot" that come to us in subtle and not-so-subtle ways every day. We do this primarily through regular reading and memorization of the Bible. We don't want to come to a difficult time in our lives and discover our faith supports aren't strong enough to hold us up.

DAY ONE

Co-creators with God

Now the LORD God had formed out of the ground all the beasts of the field and all the birds of the air. He brought them to the man to see what he would name them; and whatever the man called each living creature, that was its name.

GENESIS 2:19

We went to pick out a kitten from a litter that was only eight weeks old. We found a darling little white cat with blue eyes that appeared to be a female. When we picked the cat up three weeks later after we returned from vacation, we discovered she was a he! We could not accurately assess the gender of an eight-week old kitten, but with age, things were much clearer. All of our expectations had to be changed, including the name we had picked out for a female cat.

In the discipline of study we are invited to learn more about the world and God's creative process in it. We are invited to express our own creativity and to enjoy God's creativity as we see it in nature. In learning about plants, animals and inorganic materials, we can see some of the ways God fits everything together. We can get a better perspective on how much God loves us as we see our place in the created order.

DAY TWO

Godly Knowledge

This is what the LORD says: "Let not the wise man boast of his wisdom or the strong man boast of his strength or the rich man boast of his riches, but let him who boasts boast about this: that he understands and knows me, that I am the LORD, who exercises kindness, justice and righteousness on earth, for in these I delight," declares the LORD.

JEREMIAH 9:23-24

On our first tour of Israel, we had a very knowledgeable and experienced secular Jewish guide. Our heads were filled with information about the numerous sites we saw each day. In our group was an elderly woman traveling with her two daughters. She was a strong Christian but not well educated.

As our group sat in the place where tradition says Jesus was abused and tortured by the Roman soldiers before being led out to be crucified, our guide was giving lots of good information. Suddenly Mama, as everyone called the older lady, began to pray. The power of the Holy Spirit poured through her simple though not always grammatically correct sentences, and you could have heard a pin drop when she finished. Included among the tear-stained faces of the listeners was our Jewish guide.

I think all of us in the tour group learned that knowledge is secondary to the power of the Holy Spirit at work in the lives of those who are open to it.

DAY THREE

The Power of Music

I will sing with my spirit, but I will also sing with my mind.

1 CORINTHIANS 14:15

When I am teaching church musicians how to choose music for worship, I talk about the theology of the text and the theology of the tune. Many understand the former but not the latter. The theology of the tune refers to the message of the music by itself, without the text. In my classes we talk about how a text can be good and a tune can be good, but they may not be good together.

My classic example is the camp song "They Hung Him on a Cross." The tune is a very upbeat melody, complete with hand clapping, but the words tell about how Jesus was hung on a cross "one day when I was lost." The theology of this tune completely negates the impact of Jesus' death on the cross for our sin. Words about the Resurrection would be much more appropriate to this tune.

As music combined with text is a more powerful medium than the spoken word alone, it is important that we pay attention to texts and the tunes they are paired with. For example, some rap songs have words that glorify abuse. The words combined with the rap music have an uncanny way of going deeply into minds and hearts to subtly transform people's thoughts about that issue. I will never forget the time I was in a store many years ago and heard Madonna's "Material Girl" playing in the background. I was horrified to realize how quickly I remembered the words to that song because the tune was so catchy.

While all genres of music have good and bad examples in them, it is important that what we believe about God be carried to our innermost thoughts through music that supports our theology, especially in times of worship.

DAY FOUR

Faith-Filled Study

Their minds were made dull, for to this day the same veil remains when the old covenant is read. It has not been removed, because only in Christ is it taken away. Even to this day when Moses is read, a veil covers their hearts. But whenever anyone turns to the Lord, the veil is taken away.

2 CORINTHIANS 3:14-16

As a Christian we must approach studying the Word of God from a position of faith in Jesus, even if we don't understand everything written in Scripture. In the early church, new members had to be baptized first (i.e., say yes to faith in Christ) before receiving full instruction in the faith and being allowed to stay in the gathering place for the entire worship service. It was only after baptism that new Christians could sit through the part of the service in which Holy Communion was given.

To the early church faith was an assumed prerequisite for the words of Scripture making sense, and it should be to us as well. Even with faith there are things that fall into the category of mystery. This is why trying to explain a difficult passage of Scripture or a doctrinal issue like the Trinity to unbelievers is often very frustrating and sometimes impossible.

We all know people who have gone to church their whole lives and yet have no understanding of the Christian faith. They say things like "It doesn't matter what you believe so long as you believe in God." Or "All paths lead to God." Or "I believe in the words of Jesus but not Saint Paul." Or "I don't like the God of the Old Testament, so I ignore all of that." After years of hearing, they seem to have no understanding of the faith the church has taught since its beginning.

For some it is because they have never really allowed Jesus to become Lord—ruler—of their lives. For others it is due to poor teaching by their clergy. As in the passage above, it is still possible to have a veil over our minds and hearts that distorts the clarity of the words of Scripture. Let us regularly ask God to take that veil away.

DAY FIVE

Plans and Purposes

The plans of the LORD stand firm forever, the purposes of his heart through all generations.
PSALM 33:11

It was early June, and school had just ended for the year. We left on a family vacation to the area around Moab, Utah. It was already so hot that the hand lotion I left sitting in the tent all day was painful to use. We had hoped to do a lot of exploring in that area, but everyone was miserable. So we abandoned our plans and set up camp near a mountain lake in Colorado for several days. We had not done our homework very well on the temperatures around Moab in June, and as a result we were disappointed at losing the site-seeing opportunities we had originally hoped to have.

In the discipline of study we are invited to get to know the Lord's plans, especially through reading Scripture and commentaries on it. As we get to know better what God's plans and purposes are, we will begin to have a small glimpse of his big-picture plans and desires. Then we will be less likely to be caught unprepared regarding a godly response to situations in the world and in our neighborhood. This doesn't mean that we can turn to Scripture to find out how to proceed with every detail of our daily lives, but we will learn broad principles within which God invites us to make plans.

Jesus warns his disciples to be students of God's plans: "Watch out that no one deceives you. Many will come in my name, claiming, 'I am he,' and will deceive many. When you hear of wars and rumors of wars, do not be alarmed. Such things must happen, but the end is still to come" (Mark 13:5-7).

By having a sense of what God ultimately wants to happen, we can begin to know more fully how to pray and how to plan.

DAY ONE

Digestion

[The Lord] said to me, "Son of man, eat what is before you, eat this scroll; then go and speak to the house of Israel." So I opened my mouth, and he gave me the scroll to eat. Then he said to me, "Son of man, eat this scroll that I am giving you and fill your stomach with it." So I ate it, and it tasted as sweet as honey in my mouth.

EZEKIEL 3:1-3

All of us have favorite foods, things we look forward to eating. Often these foods are associated with special occasions like birthdays, Christmas or the Fourth of July picnic before the fireworks. When we eat these foods, a whole host of sensations and emotions floods our being. Those sensations start in our mouth and move all the way through us, including into our minds and hearts, as we think about the last time we enjoyed the flavor and texture of that food.

In today's passage God told Ezekiel to eat the scroll that contained the words of the Lord and to fill his stomach with it. Ezekiel found that it tasted sweet as honey. Those words from God became an intimate part of his being; they went into his very core.

In the discipline of study and its companion, the discipline of meditation, we are invited to take the Word of God and ingest it into our minds, hearts and souls. God's Word is to become an integral part of our very being. We can compare it to a cow chewing its cud: the cow takes in a lot of grass and then rests and rechews it a little bit at a time so the food will move properly through its system to nourish its body. (This is a good visual example to use if you are trying to teach this discipline to children.) We can do the same with the Bible.

DAY TWO

Life and Death

Consider him who endured such opposition from sinful men, so that you will not grow weary and lose heart.

HEBREWS 12:3

Lent, the period of the church year between Ash Wednesday and Easter, is a very hard time for many people because of its focus on the increasing conflict between Jesus and the religious leaders of the day, his arrest, crucifixion and death. Many people quite honestly would prefer to skip over that whole season. Some avoid Lent entirely and go right to the Resurrection. I know of one pastor who thought being marked with ashes on Ash Wednesday reminded people too much of death, so he used glitter instead!

The problem with this attitude is that it lessens our ability to stay strong and hopeful. Focusing on the depressing and even gruesome events of the crucifixion may seem like an odd way to find hope and strength in our lives, but if we believe the writer to the Hebrews, it is a valid reality. The important point of the above verse is that we should consider (think about, study, meditate on) Jesus, including everything that he suffered.

It is like learning to rock climb or water-ski. We need to watch the instructor and imitate that person's every move as we heed his or her instructions. Our first time out may not be very successful or even particularly fun, but if we stick with it and carefully watch our guide, soon we will begin to gain some proficiency of our own.

The same is true of our Christian walk. Each of us has hard things in our lives. Yet if we watch how Jesus handled the difficult events and people in his life, we will begin to gain proficiency in those things ourselves as we imitate him.

DAY THREE

Real Priorities

Great are the works of the LORD; they are pondered by all who delight in them.

PSALM 111:2

Christians are persecuted with varying degrees of severity in China. It is not legal to own a Bible, gather for worship with others or share the gospel with anyone under eighteen years of age. Bibles are scarce, and while there are organizations committed to smuggling them in, the shortage is acute. People have to share Bibles or copy portions of Scripture by hand in order to have God's Word. In some places, when a pastor is able to get some Bibles for his underground congregation, they only go to people who have memorized all of Psalm 119, which has 176 verses. Only those who are the most committed to learning Scripture get a precious copy of the Bible, so studying and memorizing God's word becomes a significant priority.

Whether or not people are persecuted for their faith, it usually isn't hard to discern what is really important in their lives. Just look at how they spend their time and money! That is a more accurate indicator than anything they might say about the priorities in their life.

If someone who didn't know you were to look at your calendar and your checkbook, what would they see are the true priorities in your life?

If we truly love God, if we want to know more about him and his will for our life and for the world, then we need to ponder Scripture on a regular basis. It must become a priority for us. It can also be a way to stand with the persecuted church around the world if we pray for it each time we open our Bibles.

Focusing Well

Do not conform any longer to the pattern of this world, but be transformed by the renewing of your mind. Then you will be able to test and approve what God's will is—his good, pleasing and perfect will.

ROMANS 12:2

How many times have you seen someone imitate someone else? Maybe it was a Hollywood celebrity imitating a politician, or a teenager imitating a teacher, professional athlete or famous rock star. Whatever the case, the imitator had to study the other person enough to know how they speak, use their hands and facial muscles, and stand.

Such imitations can often be humorous, but they point to a deeper issue: we eventually become what we focus on, intentionally or unintentionally. Whatever we (adults and children) spend the most time listening to, watching, concentrating on or memorizing will ultimately shape our personalities and behaviors in profound ways, for good or for ill.

There are many benefits to memorizing Scripture. One of them is that it causes us to focus intentionally on God's Word. There are many good systems for learning to memorize Scripture, even long passages. These are the basic steps:

1. Start small. Begin with a short, familiar passage, and commit it to memory. Don't allow yourself to paraphrase or skip words. Memorize every word in its proper order. Practice by writing it down without looking and speaking it out loud to yourself in a mirror.
2. As you move to a longer passage, break it down into shorter sections one or two verses long. Use the suggestions in step one to learn each section.
3. As you begin each new section, add the previous section(s) to your practice of writing it out and speaking it out loud.
4. If possible, find an audio version of the Bible or record yourself reading the passage on tape to listen to while you are in the car or cooking dinner.

It is worthwhile to learn as much of Scripture as you can. Not only will it be there for you to use in any situation; it will also help form you into the image of Christ.

DAY FIVE

Hard Questions

The first to present his case seems right, till another comes forward and questions him.

PROVERBS 18:17

November 15 is the day the Western church has set aside to remember Saint Albert the Great (1206-1280), or Albertus Magnus, as he is sometimes called. He was born in Germany and became a Dominican monk. Universities were just coming into being, but Saint Albert was a remarkable person who studied every field of knowledge that was known at the time, garnering a reputation as a great teacher. He wrote thirty-eight large volumes on logic, mathematics, ethics, plants, animals and astronomy, in addition to his Bible studies and sermons. He was the first to study the mountain ranges of Europe.

As impressive as all this is, what is most important about Saint Albert is that he stood against the prevailing fear that knowledge and study would destroy Christianity. His strong faith coupled with intense study paved the way for a new age of scientific exploration. He believed that by understanding more about God and creation, we would love God more.

Sometimes it seems that fear of study is still prevalent among Christians. It's as if we are afraid that a question will come up that is too big for God to answer. Or worse, a question will be raised that will finally annihilate everything we believe about God.*

If we really believe God created the universe and all that is in it, then we can ask hard questions knowing that all of the answers ultimately rest in God. If we are honestly seeking truth—not just looking for an excuse to avoid God through asking questions—then we will be guided to the answer as we move toward God.

*See chapter 15 of *The Great Omission* by Dallas Willard (San Francisco: HarperSanFrancisco, 2006).

DAY ONE

Study in Community

The Lord said to Moses, "Send some men to explore the land of Canaan, which I am giving to the Israelites. . . . So they went up and explored the land. . . . When they reached the Valley of Eshcol, they cut off a branch bearing a single cluster of grapes. Two of them carried it on a pole between them. . . . They came back to Moses and Aaron. . . . There they reported to them . . . : "We went into the land to which you sent us, and it does flow with milk and honey! . . . But the people who live there are powerful, and the cities are fortified and very large. . . . We can't attack those people; they are stronger than we are."

NUMBERS 13

When the Lord had Moses send the spies into the Promised Land, I'm sure he wanted them to come back with an exciting report for the people of Israel. The land was so fertile that it took two people to carry one cluster of grapes! Yet what the spies saw (except for Caleb and Joshua) were people who were big and powerful and lived in walled cities that looked impenetrable. They did not see the goodness of the land or remember the history of God leading them out of slavery in Egypt by parting the Red Sea, feeding them in the wilderness with manna and giving them a system of worship and government so they could lead good, productive lives. The spies were so focused on what they couldn't imagine doing as human beings that they forgot what they could do as the people of God.

When we study the Bible, creation, human relationships or anything else, we must have an accountability group around us to keep our focus in the right place. Only Caleb and Joshua lived to see the Promised Land because only they could see God's ability to work beyond the facts on the ground.

DAY TWO

Knowing Our Culture

Preach the Word; be prepared in season and out of season; correct, rebuke and encourage—with great patience and careful instruction.

2 TIMOTHY 4:2

One Friday night my pastor husband and I wandered into a local bookstore. After we were there a while, I was surprised to see him reading a secular magazine, one that focuses on self-fulfillment at the expense of others and doing whatever feels right at the moment. "Why are you looking at that?" I asked.

"Because," he said, "I need to know what people are being taught by the culture."

One of the interpretations of today's verse is that we need to be grounded in the Word of God so we can speak as well to people we are not comfortable with as those we are comfortable with. Sometimes I know I am an ineffective witness for Christ because I really don't understand where the other person is truly coming from. I don't watch or read a lot of what our culture produces, but many people do, and what we focus on the most is what forms us. Many people, especially children and young adults, come to church with a lot of cultural formation imprinted on them. And then we wonder why they aren't impacted more by the good news of God in Christ! We must learn how to respond to all of that cultural imprinting.

While I am not advocating that we spend a lot of time reading less-than-uplifting magazines and books or watching a lot of junky TV and movies, at some point we have to study these things so we are able to tell others how God offers a different and even better perspective on life.

Always Learning

You, then, who teach others, do you not teach yourself?

ROMANS 2:21

As I hit middle age, it became apparent that I needed to be more intentional about exercising or I was going to gain weight and lose mobility. So I began to attend an exercise class at the local recreation center. The woman who taught it had been in the fitness business for decades, and she taught a number of different fitness classes each week.

One day after class, the instructor said something about a fitness center where she went for her workouts. I was incredulous! After all the teaching she did each week, why would she need to go to a fitness class? But she reminded me that teaching fitness classes was not the same as having her own concentrated workout.

Music teachers also need to do their own practicing, school teachers and medical personnel need continuing education credits to stay current—you get the idea. Even a stay-at-home parent needs continuing education of some kind just as much as any other profession. Everyone, including parents, who teaches anyone else, informally or formally, needs to keep their mind sharp through some kind of mental exercise.

The discipline of study says that we become what we focus on, so we need to be intentional about that focus.

DAY FOUR

Current

I urge, then, first of all, that requests, prayers, intercession and thanksgiving be made for everyone—for kings and all those in authority, that we may live peaceful and quiet lives in all godliness and holiness.

1 TIMOTHY 2:1-2

When we traveled in the Hashemite Kingdom of Jordan, I was impressed with many things, including the way Jordanians expressed love and admiration for the late King Hussein as well as his son, Abdullah, the current monarch. They spoke in glowing terms of both men. Pictures of King Hussein and King Abdullah were plastered everywhere: bus stop shelters, hotel lobbies, inside and outside of shops, at the entrance to tourist sites. As we were coming from a country where cynicism about political leaders is a national sport, this was an amazing phenomenon to encounter.

One illustration of the discipline of study depicts a Bible in one hand and the newspaper in another. As Christians we are meant to be aware of current events locally, nationally and internationally so that we know how to pray for God's will in those situations. We are called to pray for our leaders' success so that we might live quiet, godly and holy lives, doing the work of the kingdom of God, a ruler we are invited to love and admire at all times.

DAY FIVE

Knowing Personality Types

Every year [Jesus'] parents went to Jerusalem for the Feast of the Passover. When he was twelve years old, they went up to the Feast. . . . Jesus stayed behind in Jerusalem, but they were unaware of it. . . . After three days they found him in the temple courts, sitting among the teachers, listening to them and asking them questions. Everyone who heard him was amazed at his understanding and his answers. When his parents saw him, they were astonished. His mother said to him, "Son, why have you treated us like this?" . . . "Why were you searching for me?" he asked. "Didn't you know I had to be in my Father's house?" But they did not understand what he was saying to them.

LUKE 2:41-43, 46-50

Any parent who has more than one child knows how different they can be in their thinking, attitude and learning style. We had one child who loved school, but the other struggled to get through because of boredom and a kinesthetic learning style. One child talked about every detail of everything, and one said only the bare minimum in response to many questions.

Jesus, the perfect Son of God, must not have been easy to raise, as hinted at in the above passage. Mary and Joseph obviously did not understand why Jesus had to be in his Father's house when they had just spent the last three days anxiously looking for him. Luke leaves a lot to the imagination when he reports Mary's words on finding Jesus: "Son, why have you treated us like this?" I'm not sure those would have been my words!

It is important for us to study theories of personality and learning styles. It took time and intentional reading for me to learn how to approach the same subject with each child because each one heard words and voice inflections in very different ways. To avoid unnecessary battles, I had to learn how each of my children approached life, and it was not in the same way I did! I had to work to understand the way they thought and felt and processed situations in order to be the best parent I could be to them. In the mercies of God, that study reaped rich rewards.

The Discipline of Simplicity

MAYBE THIS DISCIPLINE CONJURES UP romantic images of earlier eras or fantasies of simpler times that we sigh about but feel we can never regain. Let me encourage you: the discipline of simplicity can be practiced at any economic level because it is first of all an inner attitude toward possessions.

Sometimes people who have very little economic wealth are obsessed with acquiring more. This characteristic is the opposite of the discipline of simplicity. And the reverse can also be true: people with a lot of wealth can fully engage in the discipline of simplicity if they hold that wealth lightly, as belonging first of all to God.

The discipline of simplicity also deals with the way we use our time and the way we use words. It is an overall attitude of contentment and gratitude manifested in a visible way of living that includes not trying to do too much or have too much. It is a way of speaking that lets our yes be yes and our no be no, as Jesus commands in the Sermon on the Mount (see Matthew 5:37).

Poverty in and of itself does not indicate a life of simplicity. Spending all of your time trying to keep body and soul together because of unemployment, or going from agency to agency for help tends to make for a complicated life.

In the discipline of simplicity, we seek to have adequate housing, clothing, food and transportation for the needs of the season of life we are currently in. If we can afford more than what we truly need, we give that extra money to help others. We also seek to have a balanced rhythm in terms of work, play and rest, and we strive to say what needs to be said simply and in a straightforward manner.

In short, through the discipline of simplicity we seek to live a life that is pleasing to God, life-giving to ourselves and has an element of availability to others. We can live a life of goodness, joy, peace and balance if we will engage honestly with this discipline.

Each week choose one or two suggested activities from the list below to help you practice this discipline:

For Anyone

- What are the needs for the season of life you are in right now? How much income do you need to support those dependent on you? How much living space? How many cars? If you have more than you truly need, what can you do to help someone who may be below their "adequate needs threshold"? If you have less than you need, how might you restructure your finances to meet your needs?
- Go through your purse, wallet or briefcase. Look at each item and ask yourself how necessary it is. Continually carrying heavy bags around eventually does damage to our bodies.
- Next time you are asked to do something you don't want to do or can't do, simply say no. Fight the temptation to justify yourself to the other person.
- How many of your conversations are about time or possessions? Are they conversations that express gratitude, or are they arguments? Spend time praying about the right use of time and possessions for the season of life you are in right now.
- Each night write down in a notebook three blessings from that day. Refer to the list when you are struggling with feelings of not having enough.
- Examine any thoughts and comments you made today that involved comparing your possessions with those of someone else. What does this tell you about your basic attitude toward wealth and possessions?
- Make a list of everything you do. Is there enough time to do what you have committed to doing and still have some restorative time alone and with your family? If not, find a way to drop or at least postpone an activity.
- Look at the next celebration your family will be hosting. Is it something you look forward to doing? Does it take you days to recover from and weeks to pay off? What can you do differently that would bring more joy and peace to all involved?

- If the thought of not having enough creates a knot in your stomach, then you may be dealing with the demon of fear. Find a trusted friend or a professional to help you discover why you are so afraid of not having something. Pray for the ability to trust God's good provision as you begin to loosen your grip on all the stuff you have hoarded in fear.
- Do something to help someone today, and let go of the expectation for a reward or thank-you. If they offer, encourage them to do something for someone else.
- Be content today in everything: your meals, your clothes, your car, your job, your home. When you are tempted to think, *If only I had . . .* or *I wish . . .*, stop and give thanks to God for what you do have.

Especially with Children

- Set up an age-appropriate allowance for your children to learn wise decisions regarding the use of money. It could be a small amount for a younger child to use on a vacation, or it could be a yearly clothing allowance for an older child. Make sure they understand that when that money is gone, you will not give them any more until the next vacation or the next year. Learning good financial habits can also include the hard lesson of how to make do when you haven't managed the money well.
- Give something you own to someone in need, especially if you haven't used the item in the last six months or more.
- Look at the tags on your clothes to see where they were made. Get out an atlas and find where the country is located. Get a book about that country or look it up on the Internet. Pray for that country and for the people who made your clothes.
- Plan a time of restful play. It could be blowing bubbles in the park or collecting rocks or shells or leaves on a walk. Spend an hour or so coloring with crayons. Show that the activity is important by putting it on the calendar along with all of your other activities for the week.

DAY ONE

Enough Is Enough

Keep falsehood and lies far from me; give me neither poverty nor riches, but give me only my daily bread. Otherwise, I may have too much and disown you and say, "Who is the LORD?" Or I may become poor and steal, and so dishonor the name of my God.

PROVERBS 30:8-9

Many people mistakenly think that to live simply one must have a small log cabin and grow all their own food. While that may be God's call for some people, the only thing that image does for most of us is make us feel guilty for what we do have.

The heart of the discipline of simplicity is found in the verse above: we need a good balance of wealth to care adequately for our daily needs and the needs of those we are responsible for, but no more. Once we have reached that adequate threshold, we are invited to share the rest with others to further the kingdom of God. Someone once said that if you want more, desire less.

In my community many decent homes are knocked to the ground and replaced with a huge structure. Some are ten thousand plus square feet and will house only two or three people! The discipline of simplicity invites us to look at that scenario and ask, what would a reasonable amount of space be? The answer could be ten thousand square feet; the answer could also be a whole lot less.

We are asked to assess our needs for the season of life we are in, and that season will change as kids come and go, as we care for aging parents, etc. We cannot be judgmental about someone else in this discipline, as what your neighbor needs will not be the same thing you need. Our standard should be based on the call of Christ in our lives, not keeping up with the Joneses.

DAY TWO

Drowning in Stuff

After this, Jesus traveled about from one town and village to another, proclaiming the good news of the kingdom of God. The Twelve were with him, and also some women who had been cured of evil spirits and diseases.

LUKE 8:1-2

My daughter has never packed lightly for anything. Her suitcase for a week at summer camp would weigh somewhere around fifty pounds, in addition to her sleeping bag, pillow, camera, and other miscellaneous jackets and hats that wouldn't fit into the suitcase. After a while the handle began to rip off the bag because it had been crammed to capacity so many times.

I wonder what Jesus' entourage looked like as he traveled around Israel. There were at least thirteen men and several women in the regular group, plus those who followed along for part of the time. Sometimes there were even large crowds traveling with them (see Mark 6:30-44). How did they pack? And who carried all of their stuff? They were not wealthy, though we know that the women mentioned by name in the rest of Luke 8:2 supported Jesus and his disciples, so they weren't destitute either. Were they each allotted one suitcase and a carry-on?

Humor aside, we need to note that Jesus never let anything detract from his focus of preaching the good news of the kingdom of God. He trusted God to provide, allowing material possessions to serve him and his disciples rather than the other way around.

The question for us is, which of the possessions and activities in our lives are keeping us from following Jesus fully?

DAY THREE

Speaking Simply

Simply let your "Yes" be "Yes," and your "No," "No"; anything beyond this comes from the evil one.

MATTHEW 5:37

Mary asked me to teach Sunday school. Because I was just beginning to learn about the discipline of simplicity, I wanted to respond carefully, acknowledging her need but aware that I was committed to serving the church in another way at that time. So I simply said, "I'm sorry, but I'm not called to teach Sunday school." There was a moment of silence on the other end of the phone line, and then Mary said something I will never forget: "Thank you for being so honest." In so many of her calls that evening, she had gotten lots of excuses as to why they couldn't do it now, but maybe later because they were so busy right now, etc., etc., etc. She was so relieved to get an honest, straightforward answer, even though it was no, that she hung up feeling encouraged!

The discipline of simplicity deals with all aspects of our lives, including our conversations. When we say more than is necessary to answer a request for assistance, we begin to tread on the dangerous ground of saying things that may not be entirely true so as to justify our unwillingness or inability to help, or make the other person feel better. We feel obligated to come up with some invincible excuse that will make it OK to reject the request and still be likable to the other person.

Let your yes be yes and your no be no. If you don't want to or aren't able to do it, simply say so. You will be doing everyone a favor.

DAY FOUR

Fighting over Having

Better a little with the fear of the LORD than great wealth with turmoil.

PROVERBS 15:16

We all know this too familiar sad story, either from personal experience or from reading about it: a couple supposedly has everything—a large house in an upscale neighborhood, healthy children and tons of money. Everyone who knows them thinks they really have it made, and truth be told, many harbor some jealousy because of their seemingly easy life. Then we hear that the couple is breaking up, fighting over custody of the children and dividing up the money and possessions. Sometimes even sordid tales of abuse and neglect come to light.

Today's verse is one that we easily assent to in principle but often have a hard time grasping emotionally. It sounds so romantic, like a good TV special, but when it comes right down to it, many of us want to make sure we have great wealth and not just a little. We really do envy those who have many possessions.

We need to ask ourselves if our attempt to gain great wealth is causing turmoil in our lives and relationships. And if it is, is it really worth it?

DAY FIVE

Count Your Blessings

The boundary lines have fallen for me in pleasant places; surely I have a delightful inheritance.
PSALM 16:6

Many of us are familiar with the old hymn "Count Your Blessings." It encourages us to name our blessings one by one. For those of us who are "glass half empty" kinds of people, it is especially important that we keep a written list of all of our blessings and look at it regularly. While there is much sadness in the world, there is also much to give thanks for. We need a way to keep that positive perspective.

When my husband first entered the ministry, our children were quite small. We lived in a tiny duplex and had few material resources. Since I was at home all day, I often had time to make a mental list of everything I felt was missing in my life. Then my husband would come home and share about the people he had visited who had cancer or who were dying or who were having serious marital problems. Focusing on all the good things that I had in my life and gratefully acknowledging all the struggles our family was not facing would cause me to stop whining.

It takes purposeful training to keep our focus on all that we do have, to affirm that our glass is more than half full.

DAY ONE

Visible Simplicity

Naaman's servants went to him and said, "My father, if the prophet had told you to do some great thing, would you not have done it? How much more, then, when he tells you, 'Wash and be cleansed'!"

2 KINGS 5:13

Take the time to read the whole story of Naaman in 2 Kings 5:1-19. It is a powerful story about following obvious, simple directions. Like Naaman, many of us aspire to do great things for God but have a hard time doing simple acts of obedience day in and day out.

We could each make quite a list of examples of small acts of disobedience we routinely engage in that seem inconsequential and yet are symptoms of a spirit of pride and arrogance: safety issues in the kitchen, routine maintenance appointments, taking medication properly, eating and exercise issues—the list could be endless. Why do we think we are above these simple acts of obedience?

Naaman had come a long way. He wanted Elisha to razzle-dazzle him back to health. The simple command to go and wash was an insult to Naaman's position as commander of the army for the king of Aram. And yet the simplicity of it healed Naaman's soul as well as his body. He may not have come to confess God as Lord of all (verse 15) if he had been distracted by a big display of hocus-pocus on Elisha's part.

The kingdom of God is simple enough for even a child to participate in. We don't have to make our spiritual life complicated in order for it to be authentic. In fact, the simpler it is, the more effective it can be.

DAY TWO

Who Is Blessed?

Jesus looked at [the ruler] and said, "How hard it is for the rich to enter the kingdom of God! Indeed, it is easier for a camel to go through the eye of a needle than for a rich man to enter the kingdom of God." Those who heard this asked, "Who then can be saved?' Jesus replied, "What is impossible with men is possible with God."

LUKE 18:24-27

I was talking with someone about a young couple who had "had" to get married because the girl was pregnant. I asked this person how the couple was doing and was told that it seemed like they were fine because the pictures of their house showed nice furniture in it. The implication was that if they had a nice house with nice furnishings, then of course everything was fine.

We are often tempted to look at the material possessions of those around us and assume that the more and the better their possessions, the better off they are. In the culture of the Bible, it was assumed that those who were rich were blessed by God and those who were poor were somehow being rejected by God because of sin. Many of us today also have that assumption.

We need to be careful that we don't do the reverse and spiritualize poverty or vilify wealth, as some do. (For an excellent discussion of this issue, see the chapter "Is Poverty Spiritual?" in Dallas Willard's book *The Spirit of the Disciplines*.)

One focus for our prayers should be our fundamental attitude toward wealth or the lack thereof. For example, we may find ourselves discouraging our children's interest in a certain occupation because they can make more money in another field. External circumstances are not a trustworthy indicator of blessedness or giftedness.

Sane Schedules

I planted the seed, Apollos watered it, but God made it grow. So neither he who plants nor he who waters is anything, but only God, who makes things grow.

1 CORINTHIANS 3:6-7

The following words of E. Lee Phillips continue to bring me up short: "Lord, do not let us do more if in doing less we might do it better."* Talk about a lone voice in the wilderness of a culture that cries, "More, more, more!" Today's verse reminds us that God created us to work in community, and each of us is given a different task to do. God has promised that there will be enough gifts to cover the needs of the community; we don't have to do it all ourselves.

We all know people who are grossly overcommitted in their lives. Keeping a good balance regarding an appropriate number of things to be involved in during a particular season of life can be tough when there are so many activities to choose from.

I once knew a woman who wanted to work a full-time job, have young children at home, work part time at her church, be on denominational and local church committees and do a program of study that had a significant element of accountability associated with it. When I knew her, her work in the study program was suffering. When that fact was pointed out to her, she became angry and was insulted that someone was implying that maybe she couldn't do it all!

What would you have said to this person? How does your family handle a great opportunity that comes up when the calendar is already full? The discipline of simplicity speaks to our calendars as well as our possessions.

*As quoted in *For All the Saints: A Prayer Book For and By the Church*, vol. 3, comp. and ed. Frederick J. Schumacher with Dorothy A. Zelenko (Delphi, N.Y.: American Lutheran Publicity Bureau, 1998), p. 94.

DAY FOUR

Simple Celebrations

I know what it is to be in need, and I know what it is to have plenty. I have learned the secret of being content in any and every situation, whether well fed or hungry, whether living in plenty or in want.

PHILIPPIANS 4:12

One of my summer neighbors had just wrapped up a birthday party on her porch. All the kids in the immediate neighborhood had been invited to celebrate her young son's birthday. Paper products, cake crumbs and wrapping paper were everywhere. It was a mess, but she said this was nothing compared to what she would have had to do back home. There she would have felt the need to put together a carnival for thirty children and a cocktail party for their parents to socialize at while the birthday party was going on. I was exhausted just listening to her describe it!

Later I thought back to the times when I have gone overboard on a celebration: too many gifts, too many guests, too much food. Here are some good questions to ask when planning a party or a celebration: Is it possible to celebrate the event well without a major production costing lots of energy and money? What is a reasonable celebration for a younger child? An older child? A teenager or young adult? When is it appropriate to go all out?

The discipline of simplicity invites us to keep a perspective that is not dictated by the neighborhood we live in or the groups we associate with. We are encouraged to do activities that bring joy to everyone involved, including the person who has to plan it, host it and clean it up. It is okay to celebrate in a way that honors our particular time constraints, economic realities and energy levels.

DAY FIVE

A Good Rhythm

Then, because so many people were coming and going that they did not even have a chance to eat, [Jesus] said to them, "Come with me by yourselves to a quiet place and get some rest."

MARK 6:31

Does the activity level of this verse describe your household? Do you often find yourself feeding the kids in the car between activities or napping in the car during the piano lesson or soccer practice? Do you ever allow yourself to make an appointment in your daily planner so you can be alone with Jesus for a while?

I live in an area that has a very active summer community. There is something going on all the time, somewhere, with someone. I have a friend here who entertains out-of-town family and friends all summer long. I have never known another place where so many people are fed and housed that didn't have a AAA-approved rating sign hanging out front!

My friend and I maintain perspective in the midst of all of the comings and goings by sitting somewhere quiet and sipping iced tea. We use the time for rest and refreshment, to catch up on each other's lives and to hold each other accountable regarding all of the choices we need to make each day.

The discipline of simplicity has no prescribed rule for the use of time, only a humble realization that none of us can do it all. We must have a good rhythm of activity and rest in each week. If Jesus and his disciples did it, then it is OK for us to do it too.

DAY ONE

Fear of Nothing

In the morning there was a layer of dew around the camp. When the dew was gone, thin flakes like frost on the ground appeared on the desert floor. When the Israelites saw it, they said to each other, "What is it?" For they did not know what it was. Moses said to them, "It is the bread the Lord has given you to eat. . . . Each one is to gather as much as he needs. . . . No one is to keep any of it until morning." However, some of them paid no attention to Moses; they kept part of it until morning, but it was full of maggots and began to smell.

EXODUS 16:13-16, 19-20

Years ago I heard the story of a couple who had lived through the Holocaust. Even years after that experience, their freezers, refrigerators, cupboards, pantries and basement shelves were packed with food. Because of what they had endured in the concentration camp, they were determined to never be without an abundant supply of food again.

Maybe you know someone who lived through the Great Depression. Often those people (and their children) have trouble throwing anything out. They still remember the era when too many had too little, and every scrap and crumb needed to be put to good use.

In today's Bible passage, the Israelites had some among them who didn't believe God would send the next day's manna. Maybe they had had too little for too long in Egypt. Or maybe they were naturally distrustful or greedy. For whatever reason, they were going to grab all the food they could while it was there, but the next day their hoarded stash was full of maggots. They had to learn that God would "Give us this day our daily bread" in a literal way that most of us do not have to do.

Fear is a powerful emotion, and it doesn't go away overnight. But it is not a good reason to grab and collect unnecessarily. The bigger issue is, do we believe God will provide what we need *today?*

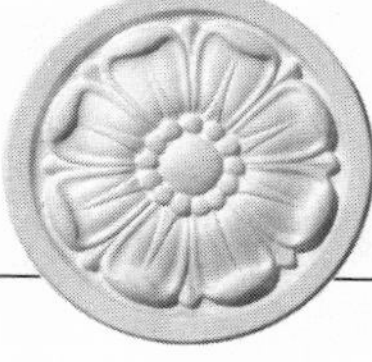

DAY TWO

Dying Well

God said to [the man], "You fool! This very night your life will be demanded from you. Then who will get what you have prepared for yourself?" This is how it will be with anyone who stores up things for himself but is not rich toward God.

LUKE 12:20-21

An older woman was dying of cancer, and she was regretting that she had so little time left on earth. When her daughter asked her what she would like to have more time to do, the reply was "Clean out the closets."

This woman had hoarded stuff all her life. You couldn't walk into her house without navigating through the piles. Her closets and cupboards were stuffed to unusability. In the last days of her life here on earth, the thing that occupied her thoughts was the stuff she had never gone through and gotten rid of when she had the chance. Not only that, her family was going to be left with the task of sorting through all of those possessions in their grieving state.

Today's reading comes from a parable Jesus told. The rich fool in the parable thought he had it made with all of his stuff, yet that very night he was going to have to give up the one thing none of us can ever hang on to—his life. Like the dying woman, he had spent a lifetime focused on the accumulation of things but spent little or no time on accumulating a character that was rich in the things of God. The former would be lost at death; the latter would have lived on into eternity.

If you were to die tonight, would God say to you, "Well done, good and faithful servant" or "You fool"?

DAY THREE

Pay It Forward

Give, and it will be given to you. A good measure, pressed down, shaken together and running over, will be poured into your lap. For with the measure you use, it will be measured to you.

LUKE 6:38

In the movie *Pay It Forward,* the concept of doing something good for someone else is presented in an unusual way. The idea is that when someone does something for you, instead of thanking them or repaying them, you "pay it forward" by doing something good for someone else. In the movie, this kindness is usually done to complete strangers: a young reporter whose car is totaled is given a car by a stranger who had two. A homeless person who had been helped by someone saves a woman about to jump from a bridge. It is interesting to see the chain of goodness wind through the story. Some of the characters that pay it forward find themselves on the receiving end of someone else paying it forward.

The above verse may be loosely paraphrased as "pay it forward." I have found this concept to be a good way to deal with a spirit of greed. When we have been especially helpful to someone, we may secretly hope to be rewarded in some way.

However, if I adopt the spirit of paying it forward, then I let go of the desire to be thanked and rest in knowing that someone else down the line will benefit from the goodness I have shared. The discipline of simplicity includes letting go of who owes you a thank-you.

DAY FOUR

Godless Clutter

On the evening of the fourteenth day of the month, while camped at Gilgal on the plains of Jericho, the Israelites celebrated the Passover. The day after the Passover, that very day, they ate some of the produce of the land; unleavened bread and roasted grain. The manna stopped the day after they ate this food from the land; there was no longer any manna for the Israelites, but that year they ate of the produce of Canaan.

JOSHUA 5:10-12

Many of us hang on to things long after we should have let go of them: clothes we haven't worn in months, books we haven't looked at in years, dishes we quit using when the kids were little. Yet if someone were to suggest that we get rid of these items, many of us might defend the need to keep them with the cliché, "Oh, but I might need that some day!"

Where is the balance between hoarding and saving for future use? Unfortunately, there is no simple answer because what is one person's clutter could be another person's research materials. This is where an objective person, like an accountability partner, can help us determine the real reason we are hanging on to something we haven't used in years.

A guiding principle can be found in today's Bible reading. The Israelites were provided manna for food as they wandered in the wilderness. When their wandering days ended, so did their need for the manna. And as soon as that need ended, God cut it off. The people needed to learn to eat the produce of the land. If the manna had continued, they may never have transitioned from being a nomadic people to a settled people, a call that came from God.

Sometimes our possessions hold us back from taking the next step in faith. It is like taking the training wheels off of our children's bikes when they are old enough to ride without the extra help; we sometimes need to step out in faith and let go of something so we can grow into the next phase of our calling in Christ.

DAY FIVE

A Good Balance

Set your minds on things above, not on earthly things.

COLOSSIANS 3:2

The Renovaré Spiritual Formation Bible gives this definition of the discipline of simplicity: "The inward reality of single-hearted focus upon God and his kingdom, which results in an outward lifestyle of modesty, openness, and unpretentiousness and which disciplines our hunger for status, glamour, and luxury."* This is a tall order for any of us to tackle, but it can be especially tricky when working with children and teenagers.

I met a man who had grown up during the Depression having very little. He spent his whole life trying to give his children all the material advantages he'd never had, but in order to do so he worked multiple jobs, so he never had much time for relationships. While the kids grew up with lots of stuff and opportunities, the family eventually fell apart because there was no cohesion.

The tension in this discipline is between giving our children enough so they don't grow up feeling deprived and giving them so much that nothing has any meaning.

My husband and I had good success with this by giving our children yearly clothing allowances, beginning in eighth grade. It gave them freedom in a controlled circumstance, helped them understand how expensive designer fashions are and motivated them to find age-appropriate jobs in the summer. Sending our children on mission trips to local and foreign sites also helped them see firsthand what daily life is like for others who have less. Those trips helped them appreciate the intangible good things (such as love and kindness) as well as the material blessings of our family.

We adults must model this discipline in very transparent ways in order to help young people grasp what it means to live on God's economic scale, not the culture's.

**The Renovaré Spiritual Formation Bible* (San Francisco: HarperSanFrancisco, 2005), p. 2313.

More Is Never Enough

Whoever loves money never has money enough; whoever loves wealth is never satisfied with his income.

ECCLESIASTES 5:10

Some people are never satisfied. The Irish saint Columbanus is reported to have said, "The man [or woman] to whom little is not enough will not benefit from more." We all know people like this. Give them an all-expenses-paid trip to an exotic destination and they complain about the view from their hotel room. Take them to a place of beautiful scenery, and they complain of being tired from all the traveling. Show them another culture with all of its marvelous characteristics, and they hate the food and the bathrooms. These kinds of people always find something wrong because they are looking for perfection on earth, a quality that is simply not available in this life.

The verse above reflects the human condition of always wanting more, of never being satisfied or content. One way to practice the discipline of simplicity is through a spirit of contentment. This is so contrary to the culture around us that people are bound to take notice. We can strive to be sincerely thankful for all of the little things in life. Sure, there may be struggles or things we wish were different or needs or wants we would like to see met, but we are invited to keep them from becoming our defining reality.

When we respond in peace and joy to the question "How are you?" we can be a witness to others of God's goodness in all things.

DAY TWO

Simple Leadership

The king, moreover, must not acquire great numbers of horses for himself or make the people return to Egypt to get more of them, for the LORD has told you, "You are not to go back that way again." He must not take many wives, or his heart will be led astray. He must not accumulate large amounts of silver and gold.

DEUTERONOMY 17:16-17

No matter how far up the "prestige heap" we may move, we are not to do things that will cause our heart to be led astray. It doesn't make any difference if you are the king or a lowly servant: we are called to use material possessions for the good of others, not solely to improve our status.

We all know people who drift away from the church because they are consumed with too many leisure activities and hobbies, too many vacation opportunities, too much upkeep on multiple houses, too many possessions.

God warned the kings of Israel not to go back to Egypt (the place where they were enslaved) to accumulate more things. God brought the people of Israel into a place of freedom, and they were not to long for the material possessions in the land of their former bondage.

A modern-day equivalent is the credit-card debt many people enslave themselves with. It leads to worry, fear, fractured relationships and hearts that are led astray from God. Despite what all the advertisements say, slavery to things, and the debts created in attaining them, is not worth it in the long run.

In the discipline of simplicity God invites us to say no to "great numbers" and "large amounts." We are invited to say yes to a goodness that doesn't force us to go back into Egypt to get it.

DAY THREE

A Direct Focus

Whatever was to my profit I now consider loss for the sake of Christ. What is more, I consider everything a loss compared to the surpassing greatness of knowing Christ Jesus my Lord, for whose sake I have lost all things.

PHILIPPIANS 3:7-8

It was the first week of the semester when a fire struck a condominium complex that housed primarily college students. Some lost everything. One woman had just brought everything she owned in life, including collections she had started as a young child, to her condo; hers was one of the ones totally destroyed. While there was an outpouring of help and support from the college, aid agencies and the community, many students lost valuable textbooks, computers, and mementos that could never be replaced.

What would you lose if your home burned down? What would happen if you lived your life, as Saint Paul suggests, as if everything had already burned down? Paul has just finished giving his resume in verses 4-6, and it is quite impressive, but he says it counts for nothing. Knowing Christ is all that matters. It is as if Paul burned down his house, handed back his awards and spit on all of his work and learning up to the point of meeting Jesus on the Damascus road (see Acts 9).

While most of us aren't called to live that radically in practice, we are all called to live that radically in spirit. We are to live in such a way that no matter what we gain or what we lose, we don't care as long as we know Jesus.

DAY FOUR

Both/And

What I mean . . . is that the time is short. From now on those who have wives should live as if they had none; those who mourn, as if they did not; those who are happy, as if they were not; those who buy something, as if it were not theirs to keep; those who use the things of the world, as if not engrossed in them. For this world in its present form is passing away.

1 CORINTHIANS 7:29-31

Eugene Peterson, a well-known pastor and author, has a saying: "Lord, teach us to care and not to care." When I first heard him say it, I found it hard to understand; but the above verse could easily be summed up by his statement.

Saint Paul is writing to a church, urging them to keep their eyes focused on Jesus and eternity. We are not to get so wrapped up in the emotions, relationships and stuff of this world that we lose the next world. "Teach us to care and not to care." Teach us, Lord, to be your people regardless of the condition we find ourselves in: married or single, sad or happy, rich or poor.

Paul said it another way in Philippians 4:11-12: "I have learned to be content whatever the circumstances. I know what it is to be in need, and I know what it is to have plenty. I have learned the secret of being content in any and every situation, whether well fed or hungry, whether living in plenty or in want."

Can we say the same thing? Can we care about people and situations and material possessions in a way that doesn't allow them to possess us? The discipline of simplicity invites us to this kind of freedom.

The Real Cost

Do not trust in extortion or take pride in stolen goods; though your riches increase, do not set your heart on them.

PSALM 62:10

I assume that most of us don't use extortion or theft to acquire our material possessions. However, I also assume that most of us feel pride if we manage to improve our lot in life through hard work and sound financial planning.

Let me suggest a way that most of us do actually take pride in "stolen" goods without even realizing it: we buy cheap clothing that is often made in other countries by poor people who work in miserable conditions. I realize that it is important to find ways to clothe our families well yet inexpensively, especially when children often seem to outgrow their clothes before you can get them home from the store. But we need to realize that in many cases we have stolen health and fair wages from others in order to do so.

I have become increasingly aware of how expensive such clothes really are in terms of the pollution of the factories to other nations' water and land, as well as the toll on life and health these factories exact from their workers. This is one of those issues most of us would rather not think about because we feel we can do little or nothing about the problem; all it does is increase our guilt load.

We have the option to not buy clothing and shoes from companies that exploit their workers (check the Internet for current information on this issue; you can start by searching for "exploitation of garment workers" using a search engine such as Google). This might be a difficult option for some of us. But all of us can pray for the people who made our clothes. Look at the tag of the garment to see where it was made, then pray for those who made that item and for the country they live in. Pray for God's goodness, justice and mercy in their lives. Pray that your heart will not be set on increasing your own wealth at the expense of others.

The Discipline of Solitude

SOMETIMES IT FEELS LIKE SPLITTING hairs when talking about the different disciplines. This is just such an example because the discipline of solitude is closely related to the discipline of meditation. In both there is the possibility of hearing God's voice, though in the discipline of solitude it comes more as a byproduct of resting in the presence of God, whereas in the discipline of meditation it comes from actively listening to what God has to say to you through Scripture or a piece of artwork. Solitude is often a prerequisite to the discipline of meditation.

This is a discipline that is hard for many in our culture because technology can keep us on call twenty-four hours a day if we choose to be available. The question we have to ask ourselves is, do we use our technology, our entertainment options, our church work to avoid being with God?

The discipline of solitude involves finding a quiet place so we can be more aware of God-with-us (Emmanuel). But it also involves learning to quiet our minds and thoughts. Ultimately the goal is to have a place of stillness and peace deep in our hearts at all times, a deep abiding awareness of the presence of God in us. The visual image here is that of an anchor at the bottom of the ocean, holding firm while the storm rages around the ship at the surface.

The hardest part of this discipline is learning to be internally quiet. Most of us can find a quiet place somewhere, but our minds still jump from thought to thought. Many have described our minds at such times as a tree full of monkeys. Often when we first start this discipline, all the thoughts and feelings we have not allowed ourselves to process due to excess busyness or the daily constant noise come flooding in. We must find a way to deal with those things first if we hope to be able to simply rest in God's presence and let him fill us.

Then it is from that deep inner well of peace and solitude where we have regularly sat with Jesus that we can draw a word to speak into the lives and situations we find ourselves in each day.

Each week choose one or two suggested activities from the list below to help you practice this discipline:

For Anyone

- Commit to spending fifteen minutes a day in quiet. Eliminate as much noise as you can. Sometimes it is helpful to do a "mindless" activity with your hands like knitting or to look at flowers or flowing water. Give your mind permission to be free from distracting thoughts or worrying about your to-do list. Ask God to fill you with his presence. (Variation: Sit in silence with God about an issue that grieves you. Trust that God knows all about it. Wait to feel his presence in your pain.)
- Before commenting on any situation you hear about today, listen for God's voice about it. If you aren't sure you have heard God correctly, stay silent. If appropriate, seek counsel from a trusted Christian friend or accountability partner.
- If you are experiencing a spiritually dry time, remain faithful in prayer and to your tasks. Consider that now may not be the time to find a new church, a new job, new friends. At least for a while stay put, commit to prayer and obedient discipleship and trust that God is burning off the dross in your soul.
- Each night at bedtime commit your life, your family, your work to God, acknowledging that no one is ever guaranteed tomorrow. If you wake up worrying in the middle of the night, picture God holding in his hands everything you are concerned about.
- Set aside a precise time every day for solitude and prayer, even if it means walking out in the middle of something else to keep that appointment with God.
- Ask God to help you stop hiding from him. If you are afraid of God, admit it. Sometimes learning to listen to God involves first asking him for the desire to listen.
- Be careful of your words today. Take note of the small talk and opinions

that you express or that others express. Are those words furthering God's kingdom, or are they godless chatter?

- What is an area of your life where things seem to be at a dead end? Can you name any bits of refreshment or sustenance in it? Thank God for those small assurances that he has not forgotten you, and trust that God has you set aside for a time so that you will be better prepared for the next step.
- When you are tempted to speak negatively about something or someone, find a way to praise and thank God instead.
- When praying, build in a time of silence. Imagine putting the person or situation you are praying about into God's outstretched hands, and then wait to sense God's presence in that person's life or situation.

Especially with Children

- Without censoring their feelings, teach children appropriate ways to communicate. Teach them that all feelings are real, but not all should necessarily define behavior. Help them review situations in which they had an inappropriate outburst. Role-play to model other ways they could have handled their verbal outburst.
- Look at your family's daily and weekly schedule. Are there regular times when each of you can be quiet for a while? What does each person need to do to have at least a little bit of solitude in each day?
- When you pick up your child from school or a music lesson or a sports practice, turn off the radio, cell phones and iPods. Use the time to talk about what transpired in each other's days.
- Learn the Jesus Prayer: "Lord Jesus Christ, Son of God, have mercy on me, a sinner." It can quiet your mind so you can sense the presence of God. It is also useful when you are afraid or facing temptation.

What It Is

Be still, and know that I am God.

PSALM 46:10

What is the difference between the discipline of solitude and the absence of noise? Simply put, through this discipline we develop a more profound awareness of the presence of God, using stillness to help us. Many of us have sat in extended times of silence on retreats or in Taizé worship services and felt nothing. We were aware of small environmental noises and our own thoughts, but sensing the presence of God did not happen.

Solitude is a discipline because it is not mastered quickly or without intentional practice. For some people being alone and quiet is tantamount to a death sentence. For others it is something they do easily but not necessarily to experience the presence of God.

We begin the practice by sitting in silence. Sometimes it can help to commit to fifteen minutes a day, doing something like petting the cat, doodling aimlessly or knitting. Through these mindless activities, we seek to let go of the endless chatter in our minds and the need to be in constant control. We seek to open ourselves to the movement of God's Spirit.

We have to distract ourselves, almost like a parent tries to distract a toddler who is clinging to a toy in the store and won't take no for an answer. If we are that parent, we have to find a way to distract the child from that toy so we can get out the door with a minimal amount of fuss.

So it is with our minds. We need to focus on a soothing activity, tricking our minds into letting go of planning and fretting so we can become aware of the presence of God.

An Ancient Prayer

But I have stilled and quieted my soul.

PSALM 131:2

We begin the discipline of solitude by finding a place of external quiet, but we don't progress in the discipline until we can find a place of internal quiet. It does no good to be sitting quietly if our minds are all aflutter.

But unlike turning off the radio or TV, it is not so easy to turn off our minds. Plus we are not turning them off totally to join in some kind of cosmic mindlessness, but rather we are seeking to silence the inner noise so that we can sense the presence of God.

Here are some mental images to help you visualize this discipline. Imagine that your mind is a dining-room table piled high with papers and projects. Your goal is to clear a space for yourself and a dinner guest. Or think of your mind as a jungle of thoughts that you must transform into a quiet garden where you can meet with God.

One of the tools that Christians throughout the centuries have used to help them create that inner quiet space for God is the Jesus Prayer, which can be said over and over: "Lord Jesus Christ, son of God, have mercy on me, a sinner." This is like outshouting the enemy. By repeating the name of Jesus over and over, we are able to send the demons of distraction and chaos fleeing. We can provide a space for Jesus to come and fill with his presence. We can still and quiet our soul, as the psalmist says.

DAY THREE

Listen First

Peter said to Jesus, "Rabbi, it is good for us to be here. Let us put up three shelters. . . . (He did not know what to say, they were so frightened.)

MARK 9:5-6

One of the purposes of the discipline of solitude is to be regularly sensing God's presence so that you will have the right thing to say when the occasion arises. Right after a traumatic event people often don't know what to say, so they just start talking. You can observe this on TV newscasts when people are interviewed after a devastating storm or accident.

Another reaction people have is to do something—anything. Peter had just seen the Lord transfigured before him. He was scared to death, so to cover his fear, he started talking about something he could do. Words and actions seemed preferable to waiting quietly on the mountain with Jesus.

When we encounter a situation that requires a response, such as a friend who has just experienced the death of a loved one, we are invited to stop first, quiet our minds and listen for God's voice instead of immediately talking and doing something.

For example, taking food or sending flowers to a grieving friend is not a bad response. But if we wait in silence before we act, we may sense God moving us in a direction that may meet an even deeper need, one we may not have been aware of if we had rushed into action.

DAY FOUR

There Is a Season

There is a time for everything, and a season for every activity under heaven: . . . a time to be silent and a time to speak.

ECCLESIASTES 3:1, 7

My friend, who is a petite, blond woman, was driving through a rough neighborhood. It was hot, and she had the window of her car rolled down. She stopped at a red light, and a car roared up next to her with two men in it. One of them was obviously trying to hustle her. After listening to a few of his attempts to engage her in conversation, she turned and looked him straight in the eye. "Jesus loves you," she said calmly. The guy was flummoxed. "Jesus loves me?" he said hesitantly before the car roared off as the light changed to green.

One of the goals of the discipline of solitude is to develop a rhythm of speaking and silence so that we know when each is appropriate in a given situation. In reading the Passion story in the Gospels, we see that at times Jesus answered his accusers, and at times he remained completely silent. He entrusted himself, reputation and all, to God's care, speaking when the Spirit moved him and remaining silent at other times, even when he could have defended himself and his mission on earth.

My friend could have completely ignored the hype from the men in the car, but it was a time that she felt compelled to give them a different response than they had probably ever gotten. At least for a moment it changed their thought pattern.

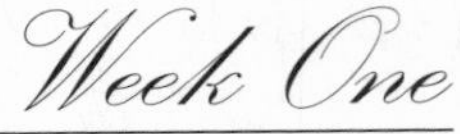

DAY FIVE

Communicating Appropriately

Do not let your mouth lead you into sin.

ECCLESIASTES 5:6

My father claims I must have been vaccinated with a phonograph needle because I love to talk. Apparently when I was a toddler I could not keep quiet in church. I often had to be taken out because I talked constantly at stage-whisper level. I still love to talk. When I have something to process, I need to talk it out with someone so I can hear what my ideas and feelings sound like out loud.

Naturally, my talking has gotten me into trouble over the years. As I have grown in grace, I have learned to be quiet at times. I have learned, often the hard way, that my need to process verbally is not always done well with others. Many times I have silently prayed the Jesus Prayer *(Lord Jesus Christ, Son of God, have mercy on me, a sinner)* over and over in situations where I was in danger of misspeaking. I have silently prayed *Jesus, Jesus* at times when I knew I needed to be quiet because I was in danger of speaking in anger or frustration.

While it is important that all of us, adults and children, find expression for our full range of thoughts and feelings, it is equally important that we learn to express those thoughts and feelings in appropriate ways. Letting every thought burst out of our mouths in raw form is only going to get us in trouble. Learning when to keep silent is a critical life skill that we should learn as early in life as possible.

DAY ONE

A Hard Place

It was Preparation Day (that is, the day before the Sabbath). . . . So Joseph bought some linen cloth, took down the body, wrapped it in the linen, and placed it in a tomb cut out of rock. Then he rolled a stone against the entrance of the tomb.

MARK 15:42, 46

If we take seriously the discipline of solitude, God will begin to strip us of our dependence on his blessings. God will seem to withdraw from us, and we will come to know whether we love God or just his gifts. This is called the dark night of the soul, and it is usually marked by a time of spiritual dryness.

The Saturday between Good Friday and Easter Sunday is a prime example of this state. The disciples could do nothing because it was the Sabbath. The Sabbath laws were ironclad at that time. The disciples had to sit in misery with all their hopes and dreams dashed, waiting for Sunday morning. Wouldn't it have been tragic if they had broken the Sabbath laws, run to the tomb on Saturday to finish the burial rites and missed the Resurrection on Sunday? They were blessed for remaining faithful to what they knew, and in that faithfulness God lifted the stone from the tomb and their hearts. We too are encouraged to wait in quiet during hard times, reminding ourselves of what we know about God and trusting him with the unknown.

How many times have we or someone we know mistaken God's work of pruning in times of spiritual dryness as a need to find a new church, a new job or a new spouse? While sometimes a change is what God is leading us to, at other times we need to wait while God takes us to a new level of faith and trust in him. This is where godly counsel becomes critical. We need someone to help us discern if we are being called to stay where we are and wait for God to prune the dead wood in our lives, or if God is using this spiritually dry time to move us in a new direction.

DAY TWO

Waiting Faithfully

All this happened to us, though we had not forgotten you or been false to your covenant.

PSALM 44:17

Psalm 44 is a good psalm to pray through if you feel like your faith is dust. If you believe you have been faithfully following Christ and yet everything seems flat and meaningless, you may be in the dark night of the soul. This is that purifying state where God invites you to a deeper level of faith, though at the moment it feels like God has moved to another universe.

One dark period I went through included an inability to play the organ, an instrument I had studied and practiced for years. My faith is intertwined with music, but God was weaning me away from the idolatrous elements of that connection. Music was in danger of becoming my god. For some months I really couldn't coordinate my hands and feet well. The joy was gone, and it was a dry, unfocused time in my faith.

Then one day, with the help of friends, I sensed that the fog had lifted. The gift that had been taken away was restored. Shortly thereafter I entered graduate school as an organ major, but I went with a new perspective. I had learned to hold my gift lightly, trusting its use (and non-use) to God. Later I went for twelve years without being able to play the organ regularly because of circumstances I was in at the time, but I was at peace with it because of what I had learned in that dark night of the soul.

Living Knowing Death

Then, because so many people were coming and going that they did not even have a chance to eat, [Jesus] said to them, "Come with me by yourselves to a quiet place and get some rest."

MARK 6:31

For many of us, when we hear Jesus extend this gracious invitation, we say, "I'll be there as soon as I finish ______." We feel that if we don't continue with the activities we are involved in, civilization as we know it will cease to exist—or so we arrogantly think. (The discipline of simplicity can be helpful in learning the discipline of solitude.) What if we don't get a chance to finish whatever it is that we use as our excuse for not spending time with God? He could call us away from this life at any time, leaving things unfinished and with us having wasted opportunities to know the God of eternity better.

In some monasteries there is always an open grave in the cemetery. It is a constant reminder that death is imminent for each of us, the end of all our labors here on earth, and so we need to keep our work in perspective.

One way we can incorporate this idea into our lives is to envision your bed as your grave as you go to sleep each night. Don't think of it in a gruesome, frightening way but in the sense that sleeping is very much like death. In committing ourselves to God's hands during sleep, we can also remind ourselves that we believe God will care for us, our loved ones and our projects while we are not able to.

People often react very strongly to this idea. For some it is just a creepy thought. You may think you'll never be able to sleep again if every time you lie down you envision your bed as a grave. But people who have learned this practice also have a solid confidence in God. They have the deeply joyful knowledge that they are so important God sent Jesus to die for them, coupled with a realistic view that life will go on after they die. They know that God is ultimately the sustainer of all our work, and our work is in his hands whether we finish it or not.

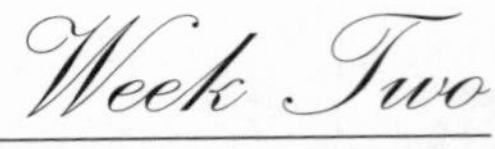

DAY FOUR

Being Quiet

Jesus often withdrew to lonely places and prayed.

LUKE 5:16

As Jesus' fame spread, he often withdrew from situations, even though there were still unmet needs. This is the opposite of what we might expect from someone who was trying to get his message across to the most people in the shortest amount of time. But the model for us as Jesus' disciples is that the more we are involved in day-to-day demands, the more time in solitude and prayer we need.

Too many of us keep going until we drop. We feel we can't walk away from everything "just to pray." We worry that we won't get it all done. And that is precisely the point: we are not supposed to get it all done. We are called to do what we can while growing in faith ourselves. All else is idolatry. We would do well to heed Saint Paul's warning in 1 Corinthians 9:27: "so that after I have preached to others, I myself will not be disqualified for the prize." People who are raising or teaching children have a specialized preaching ministry that requires good care of their own faith and discipleship.

The discipline of solitude is an inner reality with an outward manifestation. If the inner reality is there, it will be evidenced in the outward manifestations. Those manifestations include the ability to know when to speak and what to do. It is evident to others whether we have an interior faith life that is rich or poor whenever we open our mouth.

Praying Without Words

When you pray, do not keep on babbling like pagans, for they think they will be heard because of their many words.

MATTHEW 6:7

I used to think that I had to lay everything out for God so he could make his decision as to whether I would get a yes or a no to my prayer. One day it dawned on me that this showed a lack of faith. While I certainly am invited to process anything and everything with my heavenly Father, it is for my sake, not his. God already knows far more about the situation than I do. I can simply lift up a name or a face in silent prayer, and God knows the needs. Because I am such a verbal person, this was a revolutionary idea.

From everything I've read, it seems that the greatest masters of Christian prayer use fewer words as they move deeper into relationship with God. Those who know God intimately spend more time in quiet, listening prayer than they do in laying out verbal petitions. They have come to know God at such a level that words don't need to be exchanged. They love the silence that God fills so fully with his presence.

In corporate worship, spoken prayers for the community gathered together are important. As individuals, though, we are invited to say less, trusting that God has gotten to the situation ahead of us.

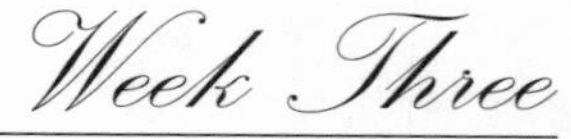

DAY ONE

Whither Can I Flee?

Where can I go from your Spirit? Where can I flee from your presence?

PSALM 139:7

This entire psalm describes a situation that has been repeated over and over again in the history of humanity, starting with Adam and Eve in the Garden of Eden after they ate the forbidden fruit (see Genesis 3): someone does something wrong, intentionally or unintentionally, and they try to hide from the person they have to answer to. Children do it, spouses do it, friends and coworkers—we all try to hide, to cover up the mess. We especially try to hide from God when we know we have disobeyed him in some way.

The discipline of solitude can be frightening because in seeking to quiet our minds and focus on God, we have to come out of our hiding place. A woman once shared with me that she was afraid to listen for God's voice in her life because she was afraid he would send her to some remote mission field she had no interest in going to. When she learned that the call of God in our lives works hand in hand with our giftedness and interests, she began to enjoy listening for the voice of God during her prayer time.

We have to ask ourselves, are we afraid of hearing God? Do we avoid silence so we can avoid God? Psalm 139 tells us that no matter where we go in the world or in our minds, God is there.

DAY TWO

Saying Nothing

Turn away from godless chatter and the opposing ideas of what is falsely called knowledge.

1 TIMOTHY 6:20

Talk shows are good examples of what this verse warns against. People say anything they want about any situation. It makes no difference if their statements are true or false, based on fact or fiction—if someone says it and really believes it, then it is true for them. Nothing is absolute, everything is relative and everyone's opinion is valid.

Unfortunately, God's Word and wisdom have also been subject to this kind of discussion. Some of us Christians have even bought into the idea that if we feel something about God or really believe it, then it is OK. "I know God will let my dog into heaven because I really want it there." "As long as you believe in God, it doesn't really matter if you go to church or not." "She has to be in heaven; she was such a good person."

Godless chatter can even be about the things of God. We should be very careful when we feel we are especially wise about a matter being discussed. That pride goes before a fall is still true (see Proverbs 16:18).

DAY THREE

Illness Leading to Health

There remains, then, a Sabbath-rest for the people of God; for anyone who enters God's rest also rests from his own work, just as God did from his.

HEBREWS 4:9-10

Years ago I saw a magazine ad that showed a nurse in the traditional white uniform and cap, and she had a big smile on her face. The reason for the smile, apparently, was that by taking the medicine being advertised, this nurse could work even though she had the flu. That ad always bothered me. Shouldn't a medical professional encourage people to stay home and rest when they are sick?

Today's verses point to an eternal Sabbath rest that will happen for God's people someday but that can be enjoyed in small increments now. We know from the creation story in Genesis 1 and 2 that God rested after he finished his work. One thing that set the Jewish nation apart as the people of God was the observance of the Sabbath laws found in Leviticus, Numbers and Deuteronomy. Even the early Christians kept the Sabbath, with the day of rest (or "stopping" as the Hebrew can also be translated) gradually being moved to Sunday to honor the day Christ rose from the dead.

Why do we today think we don't need that rest? Why do we view it as a badge of honor to go to school or work when we are sick? Will civilization as we know it really come to an end if we take a vacation or a sick day?

If we want to model God's kingdom at work in the world, we need to embrace with joy a Sabbath rest, a day of stopping our regular routine. In the discipline of solitude, we can begin to sense how God might want us to do that in the midst of our impossibly full lives.

DAY FOUR

Waiting Patiently

For God alone my soul waits in silence; from him comes my salvation.

PSALM 62:5 NRSV

Icons are windows into a deeper issue. In religious use, icons portray spiritual truths through highly symbolic visual images. They were originally made to help people who couldn't read learn about Bible stories and the things of God. Today there are many books and Internet sites devoted to religious icons and their history and meanings. These resources would be a good choice of subject if you are looking for something to do in the discipline of study.

I have been interested in this kind of ecclesiastical art for a long time, so I was surprised when I read about an icon called Christ of the Holy Silence. At first I thought, *God speaks to us. Why would someone portray Christ as silent?* But when I saw the icon, I realized that it showed Christ before Pilate. The holy silence was Christ's utter dependence on God during those trying last hours of his life here on earth. The Holy Silence icon is meant to help us understand that at times we may need to be totally quiet and wait for God, trusting that our hope in him will not be disappointed.

This can be a powerful message in the midst of a noisy world that has to comment on everything. Sometimes there truly is nothing to say, and we are better off being quiet, trusting God to take care of our reputation and the situation we find ourselves in.

Quiet Hours

I was advancing in Judaism beyond many Jews of my own age and was extremely zealous for the traditions of my fathers. But when God . . . called me by his grace . . . I went immediately into Arabia. . . . Then after three years, I went up to Jerusalem to get acquainted with Peter.

GALATIANS 1:14-15, 17-18

Today's verses are from Saint Paul's account of what happened to him after he met Jesus on the Damascus road. It is interesting to note how long he remained hidden after that event. If it had happened today, he might have been tempted to start a church the next day and share his tale with everyone who would listen. But he didn't; he went to the desert, that place the church has traditionally held to be the place you go to face the demons of your life.

This is an important story for all of us, especially children, to understand. So much is instant in our culture, but it takes time to deepen in wisdom and understanding. As our children grow, they need to have their own mini versions of desert experiences—times of solitude when they can reflect on their day or a big decision they have to make regarding college or a relationship. They need to grow up seeing that the discipline of solitude is a tool that will help them more accurately reflect God to others.

Saint Paul was a powerful witness to others right after his conversion on the Damascus road and his baptism, as we know from the rest of the story in Acts 9:18-31. But he became an even more powerful witness by spending three years out of the mainstream, learning who God was and unlearning habits and thought patterns that were no longer true to the message he would be preaching all over the world for the rest of his life.

The discipline of solitude may first teach us how to rest and balance busy schedules, but its completion is found when we more deeply reflect God to others.

DAY ONE

Stop Wrestling and Listen

I sat alone because your hand was on me and you had filled me with indignation. Why is my pain unending and my wound grievous and incurable?

JEREMIAH 15:17-18

The prophet Jeremiah had a miserable life, as far as I can tell. He lived during one of the worst periods in Israel's history; civilization as he knew it really was coming to an end. And he had the job of repeatedly telling the people that it was all their own fault. This did not make him very popular, to say the least. He was being used mightily by God, but it was not easy for him.

It came to the point where God's hand seemed to be so heavy on Jeremiah that there was no one to even process his misery with. He sat alone, in silence, and asked God his questions.

All of the spiritual disciplines need to be kept in balance, so what I am going to say next needs to be viewed in light of the discipline of guidance. We live in a highly verbal culture. People make money by going on television and radio talk shows to share their misery and problems. Counselors of all kinds abound—and they do have an important role in the Christian community. But sometimes after processing as much as we can with other people and with qualified counselors, we need to sit alone as Jeremiah did, asking God about our pain and wounds. Then we need to be still long enough to hear God respond.

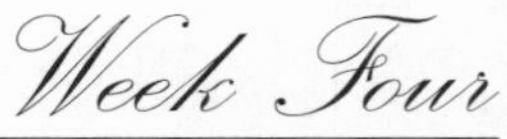

In the Backwater

Then the word of the LORD came to Elijah: "Leave here, turn eastward and hide in the Kerith Ravine, east of the Jordan. You will drink from the brook, and I have ordered the ravens to feed you there."

1 KINGS 17:2-4

It was a dry time for me spiritually. I had chosen to stay home with our children and loved it for the most part, but it meant that I had to put my career, which was also my main creative outlet, on hold for a while. (Daycare was not an option for us financially or for me emotionally.) To be sure, there were days when I felt I was in a wilderness with few oases.

However, it was during that time of setting my music aside that I discovered the spiritual disciplines. I had always been interested in writing, and because practicing the organ in the church's balcony was too dangerous with toddlers, I began to focus my creative energies into writing and speaking and teaching. As I came out of that intense stage of child rearing to a time when I was able to be away from home more, I found that in that wilderness time, God had fed me. The water from the brook and the bread the ravens brought, so to speak, had given a new depth to my music and personality, in addition to another avenue of creativity to pursue.

Sometimes we are afraid to let go of something dear to us, something that may be too difficult to maintain in the current season of life. We may feel that if we let it go even for a season, we will never get it back again.

Elijah certainly thought his ministry was over. How could he serve God in some backwater hiding place east of the Jordan? But as we continue reading the story, we find that Elijah went on from the Kerith Ravine in new strength and faith in God. He kept a widow and her son alive, and he single-handedly confronted the political and religious majority of his time on Mount Carmel. God had fed more than Elijah's body in that wilderness, and God promises to feed us if we will trust him in the backwater times of our lives.

DAY THREE

Listening First

You have wearied the LORD with your words.

MALACHI 2:17

This is a verse that should not be taken out of context. We are always invited to say as much or as little as we want to the Lord. But in this verse the prophet is letting the people know that when they are speaking in the name of the Lord, they had better know what the Lord is really saying. The people Malachi was talking to had been calling good what the Lord calls evil. At some point the day of the Lord will arrive. It will be like a refiner's fire (see Malachi 3:2), a day of judgment that will expose all evil.

For those of us who teach others, this is a fearsome thought. Saint Paul wrote to the Colossians, "Let the word of Christ dwell in you richly as you teach and admonish one another with all wisdom" (Colossians 3:16). And to Titus he wrote: "There are many rebellious people, mere talkers and deceivers. . . . They must be silenced, because they are ruining whole households by teaching things they ought not to teach" (Titus 1:10-11).

The point here is not that none of us should preach or teach, but rather that we who do need to be very sure that we have heard the Lord's voice. This is where the other spiritual disciplines come into play with the discipline of solitude: meditation, study, guidance and confession are especially necessary. When we speak, we want to speak in the same way the Lord would, as much as our sinful human nature allows us to.

DAY FOUR

Close Companions

Though the fig tree does not bud and there are no grapes on the vines, though the olive crop fails and the fields produce no food, though there are no sheep in the pen and no cattle in the stalls, yet I will rejoice in the LORD, I will be joyful in God my Savior.

HABAKKUK 3:17-18

While this verse helps explain the discipline of celebration, it also shows that the disciplines of simplicity and solitude work closely together. In the discipline of simplicity we seek to pare down our possessions, our activities, our words. In the discipline of solitude we learn to limit our thoughts and our conversation in order to sense God's presence more clearly.

People who are in great distress often get to a point where words fail them. There truly is nothing more one can say about the situation. The prophet Habakkuk tells us that even when words fail us, we can express hope, faith and joy in God. Or put another way, when we can't speak positively about life, we can use our language to praise the God of life.

We all know the cliché "If you can't say something nice, don't say anything at all." There is much wisdom in that statement. As Christians maybe we can tweak it a bit to say "If you can't say something nice about your situation, say something good about the Lord of your situation."

DAY FIVE

Growing in the Dark

At that time Jesus came from Nazareth in Galilee and was baptized by John in the Jordan. . . . And a voice came from heaven: "You are my Son, whom I love; with you I am well pleased." At once the Spirit sent him out into the desert, and he was in the desert forty days.

MARK 1:9-13

The latch on the back of my camera was weak, so when I accidentally bumped the button, the back flipped open, exposing the film inside. Needless to say, several pictures were ruined by the premature exposure to the light. There are some things that can only work in the dark, like developing film, growing mushrooms or stargazing. These all need darkness.

The natural instinct for parents is to protect their children from every hurt and pain. We hate it when they are rejected by friends or left out of a game. We want them to be as loved by others as they are by us. In today's verse, though, God the Father says that Jesus is his Son whom he loves, but then he immediately allows him to be driven into the desert to face physical, emotional, mental and spiritual hardships for the next forty days. It doesn't seem right, does it?

Yet when Jesus comes out of that experience, he is clear about who to call as disciples, he knows exactly what he is dealing with in driving out demons, he is able to heal many and he knows when to walk away from the needs of people to spend time with God (see the rest of Mark chapter 1).

Jesus was the divine Son of God, but he was also fully human. If he needed those solitary tough times to strengthen his character and refine his mission, why do we think our children should be protected from every hurt and rejection that comes their way? We need to love and support our children, but we need to let them experience those dark, lonely times to strengthen their character and refine the call of God in their lives.

The Discipline of Submission

LET ME BEGIN BY SAYING what the discipline of submission is not. This discipline has nothing to do with being a doormat. It does not encourage putting up with abuse of any kind. Instead, this discipline stems from the knowledge that we are loved by God and the value that we have because of his love. It is a discipline of strength, of knowing who we are in God's kingdom. Then in that knowing we are invited to let go of the need to always have our own way.

This discipline is exactly what Jesus modeled at the Last Supper. He fully knew who he was, what was going to happen in the next three days and why; yet he served his disciples by washing their feet (see John 13:3-5). We must keep our eyes on Jesus and look at how he practiced the discipline of submission if we are to have any hope of rescuing it from the negative associations our culture has given it.

The discipline of submission is also the best route to a spirit of true humility. You cannot become humble by focusing on humility. We learn humility through acts of service, such as letting others go first. The discipline of service is a close companion to the discipline of submission. It is also a mirror of the discipline of simplicity. There, we learn to hold material possessions lightly; here we learn to hold issues lightly.

The root word of *humble* also gives us the word *humus,* or earth. In the discipline of submission we become so firmly rooted in the soil of God's love that we are able to live in an attitude of service and humility, full of joy and peace. We know who we are, and we can let others be who they are. There is no envy or competition; we have nothing to prove because Jesus has proved it all for us in his death and resurrection.

I invite you to explore this discipline from a new perspective. As you begin to know more deeply the love of God that is the foundation of this practice, you will discover "the way of the towel" that Jesus modeled.

Each week choose one or two suggested activities from the list below to help you practice this discipline:

For Anyone

- Submit to someone else's schedule today. Focus on your inner attitude as you let someone else dictate the pace of an activity.
- Commit to daily exercise and good eating habits. Submit to being a good steward of your body.
- Carry through on a chore or project today. Fulfill every aspect of it and do it right—no shortcuts! Carry the task through to completion.
- Pay attention to your feelings when you are given advice or instruction, especially if you didn't ask for it. If you are resentful, suspect a root of pride and pray for deliverance from it.
- Practice not justifying your every action today. Whenever possible, do things without explaining them to someone else. Pay attention to how this makes you feel.
- Ask God to help you live in forgiveness, especially if you are struggling with feeling awkward or uncomfortable around someone you have wounded in the past but who has forgiven you.
- Read Jeremiah 32 and put yourself into the story as a citizen of Jerusalem during that difficult time. What would have been your reaction to Jeremiah's purchase of the field? Where do you need to "buy a field" today in your life's circumstances?
- What is an area where you are counting on or angling for a specific outcome? Is it the area of study or focus in your child's life? Is it the income level of your spouse? Is it a response from a family member? Write that expectation on a piece of paper. Then either burn the paper or cut it up into small pieces, releasing the person or the situation to God.
- Write down the things you think and say about yourself in the course of a day. If they are negative and self-destructive or arrogantly boastful, rephrase them in a way that reflects God's view of you: a sinner, but one worthy enough for his Son Jesus to come and redeem.

- Is there an area where you need to step out in faith? Pray for the gift of courage, and then submit to God's call in your life, trusting that he will lead you safely through.

Especially with Children

- Have a formal dinner with your children at home or in a restaurant. Teach them how to use utensils properly, how to speak and act at the table, how to dress appropriately for the occasion. Help them understand that their behavior impacts others and that it is not OK to do whatever they want whenever they want.
- Do your children, spouse, friends know how much you love them? How much God loves them? Don't assume they do. Spend some time exploring this issue with your loved ones, seeking if necessary to correct any false notions they may have about their intrinsic worth.
- Do the small acts of service your community expects: clean up after your dog, respond to phone calls and e-mails, don't litter even with small things like gum and cigarette butts, etc. If you feel resentment in any of these small acts, look at the deeper attitude of pride or arrogance behind those feelings.
- Don't allow your children to argue over every thing. Teach them gently but firmly to do what they are told without backtalk or sulking. If they don't understand why they have to do something, teach them to ask respectfully; then give them an honest answer, but help them learn to respect authority, starting with you as their parent. Romans 13:7 does not imply blind, unthinking compliance but assumes a godly attitude in us who follow Christ.

DAY ONE

A Foundational Truth

For God so loved the world that he gave his one and only Son, that whoever believes in him shall not perish but have eternal life.

JOHN 3:16

This verse is the foundation of the discipline of submission. Why? Because when we approach submission firm in the knowledge that we are loved immeasurably by God, we protect ourselves and our families from the idea that putting up with violence is a form of godly submission.

In his book *Spirituality*, Thomas Hopko writes, "Humility does not mean degradation or remorse. It does not mean effecting some sort of demeaning external behavior. It does not mean considering oneself as the most vile and loathsome of creatures. Christ Himself was humble and He did not do this. . . . Genuine humility means to see reality as it actually is in God. It means to know oneself and others as known by God—a power . . . greater than that of raising the dead! The humble lay aside all vanity and conceit in the service of the least of God's creatures, and to consider no good act as beneath one's dignity and honor."*

We need to know God's rich love for us and teach it to our children, showering them with love (not material possessions) and being honest but lavish in praising them. We need to teach them respect for all people and all of creation. We need to help them understand that at the foot of the cross, the ground is level and no one is intrinsically better or worse than someone else in God's eyes. Our behavior is important, but our worth to God is not based on behavior. Behavior reflects what we believe about God, ourselves and the world.

The discipline of submission, and its resultant humility, comes out of the powerful knowledge that God loves us unconditionally and that Jesus is the only trustworthy model of humility. We need to do everything in our power to make sure our children know that.

---

*Thomas Hopko, *Spirituality* (New York: The Department of Religious Education, The Orthodox Church in America, 1976), p. 73.

DAY TWO

Stepping into the Flood

Now the Jordan is at flood stage all during harvest. Yet as soon as the priests who carried the ark reached the Jordan and their feet touched the water's edge, the water from upstream stopped flowing.

JOSHUA 3:15-16

When God led the Israelites out of Egypt, he promised to give them their own land. When they reached the edge of the Promised Land, the children of Israel sent spies to scope things out, but all of them except Caleb and Joshua reported it would be impossible to defeat the current residents of the land. God was so frustrated at the Israelites' lack of faith that he sent them back into the wilderness to wander for forty years until the generation that had come out of Egypt had died off. (Read the whole story in Numbers 13 and 14.)

After the forty years had passed, the Israelites were ready to trust God's leading and his plan for them as a nation. They prepared to enter the Promised Land, but in front of them lay the Jordan River—at flood stage. When God had led them out of Egypt, he held back the waters of the Red Sea so that they could cross over on dry ground. This time God told Joshua that the waters would part only after the priests carrying the Ark of the Covenant—that powerful symbol of God's presence—stepped into the flooding water. They would need to show their faith in God in a concrete way by stepping into that raging flood.

Many of us have faced similar challenges: choosing between two different medical procedures or deciding whether to take a new job in a different location. Sometimes God stops all the obstacles so we can begin to move forward. At other times we are called to step into the flooding waters, trusting that they will part when we take that step. This calls for courage, a quality that we should be praying to develop in our character.

DAY THREE

Was It Really God Speaking?

See, I am sending an angel ahead of you to guard you along the way and to bring you to the place I have prepared. Pay attention to him and listen to what he says. Do not rebel against him; he will not forgive your rebellion, since my Name is in him.

EXODUS 23:20-21

The rugged individualism that has become a source of pride in America has seeped into our Christian faith, forming a major heresy: the belief that "God speaks to me" apart from Christian community. Lone Ranger Christians believe that because they heard a voice, God has spoken, and no one can say a word against it. Many of us can tell of tragic consequences that resulted from such claims.

In today's passage we are reminded that God plants messengers (the meaning of the word *angel*) all around us. They come in many forms, but all of them need to be verified. We are to use the Christian community to help us discern God's call in our lives. This takes humility and requires that we share with others the thoughts, ideas and messages we believe have come to us from God. If the community verifies that the message is from God, we are to follow without hesitation. This, too, takes humility and faith that we have been equipped for what we have been called to.

DAY FOUR

Prideful Attitudes

Then [Jesus] said to them, "Give to Caesar what is Caesar's, and to God what is God's."

MATTHEW 22:21

We all know people who are constantly looking for a loophole. Sometimes those loopholes become nooses, such as when they lose property in a tax war with the IRS or they waste time and money fighting a deserved traffic ticket. These people never seem to understand that trying to wriggle past every boundary in society can cause havoc in their lives. They always hope that next time at least, they'll beat the system.

The discipline of submission calls us to play by community rules, whether we agree with them or not. Acts of submission that many of us feel we are above doing include taking the grocery cart back to the cart corral, being on time, using our numbered offering envelopes at church and respecting publication deadlines for things like school and church newsletters.

One area that I have struggled with is driving the speed limit. I would push the envelope by trying to do too many things before I needed to be somewhere, so I'd leave later than I should have and then I'd speed to make up that time. I would even go through yellow lights when they were "pink," as a coworker described it, in my attempt to race across town. It was only after I got a speeding ticket—which I still tried to justify to the unsympathetic officer—that I came to realize the arrogance of my attitude.

The refusal to submit in small ways can indicate a deeply rooted pride that says, "I am above everyone else's rules." Such an attitude doesn't reflect the spirit of Christ. Instead of defying what we may disagree with, we can work toward change while complying out of honor and respect for others.

DAY FIVE

Jesus Is the Model

Then Jesus went with his disciples to a place called Gethsemane, and he said to them, "Sit here while I go over there and pray." . . . Going a little farther, he fell with his face to the ground and prayed, "My Father, if it is possible, may this cup be taken from me. Yet not as I will, but as you will."

MATTHEW 26:36, 39

It's one thing to submit when we don't particularly like something, such as seeing a movie that isn't our favorite but that our spouse or child chooses. But what about submitting when everything in our being is afraid? What if we feel God calling us to do something that will be painful or cause us to be criticized or rejected?

In the garden of Gethsemane Jesus knew real fear about what was going to happen to him. He knew what was coming, and while he had lived a life of perfect obedience so far, his humanity wanted to shrink back from the coming horrors. He faced a real temptation not to submit to what God had called him to do.

The highest goal of our lives should be obedience to God in all circumstances. This is not easy or perfectly attainable in this life, but Christ gives us hope. Like him, we can pray for courage and a spirit of complete obedience. God gave it to him—and he will give it to us.

DAY ONE

In and Out

When Simon saw that the Spirit was given at the laying on of the apostles' hands, he offered them money and said "Give me also this ability so that everyone on whom I lay my hands may receive the Holy Spirit." Peter answered: "May your money perish with you, because you thought you could buy the gift of God with money!"

ACTS 8:18-20

These three verses are from a story in which a popular magician named Simon is displaced when Philip preaches the kingdom of God to the Samaritans. Philip baptizes Simon, who then follows Philip around Samaria. The miracles and signs the Holy Spirit was doing through Philip impressed Simon very much.

The problem was, Simon was not yet inwardly transformed. He wanted the same power Philip, Peter and John had, so he offered to give them money for their secret gift. He saw that they had a power greater than what he had access to, but he had not yet let the message behind those signs and miracles seep down into his soul. He was not willing to submit himself to the Lord behind that power.

At times we long for spiritual pyrotechnics in our lives. We want God to fix a problem or avenge an enemy for us. And there are times when God does these things, but usually it is early in our faith commitment. The longer we walk with God, the more we are called to submit to God's quiet, gentle timing of love. This is hard to do, but it demonstrates that our faith is grounded in God, not in displays of power.

DAY TWO

An Apple a Day

Therefore, I urge you, . . . in view of God's mercy, to offer your bodies as living sacrifices, holy and pleasing to God—this is your spiritual act of worship.

ROMANS 12:1

In my teens and twenties, I could eat anything I wanted and never seemed to gain weight, even without regular exercise. Then I hit my forties. At first I refused to accept my aging body. "I'm not going to age gracefully! I'm going to fight it tooth and nail!" became my joking battle cry. Except that I really wasn't joking. I felt like I was just getting it together, coming into my own, but now the rules had changed and my body was falling apart. This was not fair. Suddenly I had to start exercising and watching what I ate. I had a new set of physical rules to submit to.

I have wanted to keep the above verse in a purely spiritual realm, but God has been impressing upon me that there is a physical side to this passage too. I am not a witness for God's goodness if I am overweight and out of shape. I am not a good steward of his gifts to me if I am too tired or unhealthy to use them for others. And it is selfish of me to not take care of my body for years and then expect others to care for me later when I develop health problems.

While I am not called to look like the front cover of a magazine, I am called to look like a child of the Creator.

DAY THREE

Our Greatest Possession

You hate my instruction and cast my words behind you.

PSALM 50:17

I discovered that I had dropped one of my favorite alpaca wool gloves in the grocery store. I was in a hurry and hadn't put them in my coat pocket but carried them in my hands with several other items. In spite of immediately retracing my steps and asking twice at the service desk, I couldn't find the glove anywhere. Even though the other glove was perfectly good, it was useless without its mate. A moment of carelessness on my part, and a good pair of gloves was ruined.

In our brokenness because of sin, there is no way we can perfectly follow every word of God. We will inevitably ignore some of God's good commands and rationalize away others. However, we are called to be intentional and deliberate in the things that God has instructed us to do. Just as we lose gloves or other items through haste and carelessness, one moment of sloppiness and "dropping" one of God's commands can bring frustration and loss in our lives.

We must choose to follow what we read in our daily devotions and hear proclaimed in worship. We are to carefully carry those words around with us into the everyday situations of our lives, making sure that nothing is lost through carelessness.

DAY FOUR

A Sign of Pride

Listen to advice and accept instruction, and in the end you will be wise.

PROVERBS 19:20

I live in a mountainous area with lots of wildlife. We regularly see deer, coyote, fox, mountain lions and bears. In late July the bears begin a feeding frenzy to gain enough weight to last them through their winter hibernation. Every year the park rangers put out warnings about tying down trash, bringing in bird feeders and not leaving pet food outside. They don't want the bears to become "dumpster bears" because too many then end up being destroyed.

I really liked my bird feeder and always resented having to bring it in at night during this season. So I pushed the limit with taking it down. I would leave it out when we would leave home for the evening, thinking it would be fine until we got home well after dark.

Then one day a bear took the bird feeder down at two in the afternoon, while I was sitting on the patio just a few feet away, chatting with a friend. It was at that point that I decided to submit to the laws of nature and the wise advice of the park rangers. I put the bird feeder away for several months until the bears went into hibernation.

This wisdom was again reinforced when later in the fall a bear tried to break in through our front door because it smelled salmon in the kitchen. God's laws are for a purpose, and sometimes he uses his creatures to remind us of that fact.

DAY FIVE

Obey First

For this very reason, make every effort to add to your faith goodness; and to goodness, knowledge; and to knowledge, self-control; and to self-control, perseverance; and to perseverance, godliness; and to godliness, brotherly kindness; and to brotherly kindness, love. For if you possess these qualities in increasing measure, they will keep you from being ineffective and unproductive in your knowledge of our Lord Jesus Christ.

2 PETER 1:5-8

We are called to have a childlike faith, meaning we are to relate to God as children relate to adults: trust him even when we don't understand. For example, young children don't ask a lot of questions about personal hygiene; they simply know that they have to brush their teeth, bathe and wash their hands before eating. Later they progress in knowledge of why those activities are necessary. Some of them may go on to become health-care professionals and can give their parents even more reasons and technical explanations for the necessity of personal hygiene.

So it is with our faith. We are called to follow and obey God and then add understanding to that obedience as we are able. This goes against what our culture and even some Christians teach. We are told that something must be fully understood before a decision can be made. As Christians we must always remember to trust and follow God first, even when we can't give thorough explanations for everything God asks us to do. Knowledge may come with time.

DAY ONE

Our Reputation

When [Jesus] was accused by the chief priests and the elders, he gave no answer.

MATTHEW 27:12

I am always quick to defend my actions to someone else. Whenever I feel like I am misunderstood, my mouth moves into action. I tell anyone and everyone what really happened or what I really meant to say.

Jesus was probably the most misunderstood person on the planet. He was accused of all kinds of things throughout his ministry. People thought he was a party animal (see Matthew 11:19) or insensitive to those in need (see Mark 1:32-38). And most of them, even his closest friends, did not understand who he really was (Matthew 16:22-23). Yet there were times, like in the passage above, when Jesus remained silent. In that situation he could have said all kinds of things to Pilate, Herod, the chief priests and elders, to his distraught disciples, to the crowds. Yet for much of the Passion story as recorded in the Gospels, Jesus says little to nothing.

In the discipline of submission we are invited to trust God with our reputation. That can be very hard when people assume the worst about us. It is hard to let God move at the right time to reveal the truth and set the record straight. But I know firsthand there have been times I should have let God clarify a situation because my attempts only brought ruin and alienation.

DAY TWO

Tables Turned

Jesus knew that the Father had put all things under his power, and that he had come from God and was returning to God; so he got up from the meal, took off his outer clothing, and wrapped a towel around his waist.

JOHN 13:3-4

Scripture records times when God submits to humanity. In Exodus 32:7-14, Moses talked God out of destroying the people who had made a golden calf to worship in Moses' absence. God would have submitted to Abraham's request to save Sodom and Gomorrah if there had been ten righteous people there (see Genesis 18:16-33). In Deuteronomy 18:16-18, the Israelites told Moses that God was too frightening for them to hear directly, so God submitted to their desire for distance by giving them a prophet to lead them. In John 2:1-11, Jesus submits to his mother's request to help out the wedding party with more wine even though he said that his time had not yet come. In Luke 18:1-8, Jesus tells a parable in which a judge (who represents God) changes his mind because of the persistence of a widow.

In some mysterious way, the God of the universe hears his people and responds in a living relationship that is not predetermined to their requests. Conversely, God never forces himself upon someone who wants no relationship with him. He submits to our refusal to let him be Lord of our lives.

The discipline of submission is actually a discipline of power, as exemplified by Jesus' submission to the disciples at the Last Supper. As we think about Jesus knowing who he was and where he was going while washing dirty feet, it can change our perspective on the word *submission*. It becomes a word expressing strength and a knowledge of who we are and Whose we are.

If the God of all creation can submit to his creatures, surely we can submit at appropriate times.

DAY THREE

Going All the Way

[Jesus] came to Simon Peter, who said to him, "Lord, are you going to wash my feet?" Jesus replied, "You do not realize now what I am doing, but later you will understand." "No," said Peter, "you shall never wash my feet."

JOHN 13:6-8

Peter certainly did not want Jesus washing his feet. He was embarrassed and could not handle the vulnerable feeling that Jesus opened up in him by doing the job of a slave. Perhaps it meant that Peter would have to do the job of a slave, and wasn't he part of the Messiah's intimate group of followers? Isn't the Messiah supposed to rule from a throne, not a wash basin? Peter had trouble submitting his idea of "Savior" to what Jesus was doing that night in the upper room.

Many of us can empathize with Peter. Maundy Thursday is the Thursday before Easter, when the church remembers the Last Supper and when many churches include foot washing in a special worship service. The first time I had my feet washed in church on Maundy Thursday, I found myself shaking. I was surprised by how exposed I felt.

Later as I reflected back on the service, I realized that at a deeper level, I was afraid of the light God wanted to shine deeper into my soul. For me, the foot washing was a symbol of the Holy Spirit asking to come into some of the dark closets of my life, the interior places that are the soul's equivalent of a messy room shut off from the rest of the house when company comes.

While foot washing is not something that should be forced on anyone, it can be a powerful symbol of the discipline of submission, a symbol that God may use to reach more deeply into the dark places of our lives to shine his healing light.

DAY FOUR

You Are Forgiven

The teachers of the law and the Pharisees brought in a woman caught in adultery. . . . Jesus . . . asked her, "Woman where are they? Has no one condemned you?" "No one, sir," she said. "Then neither do I condemn you," Jesus declared. "Go now and leave your life of sin."

JOHN 8:3, 10-11

The last hymn of the service was Charles Wesley's "Oh, for a Thousand Tongues to Sing." It was one I had sung many times, but on that day these words leaped out at me: "He breaks the power of canceled sin." If sin is canceled, I thought, how can it have power? But immediately something I had been forgiven for long ago flashed through my mind, causing the same painful stab in my soul it always does. And it struck me: I had not embraced the forgiveness I had been given! I had not submitted to the grace-filled word of forgiveness and moved on. In fear or pride or disbelief, I was still clinging to a remnant of that guilty act. I had not embraced (submitted to) the freedom Christ offered me.

Don't you wonder what happened to the woman in the verse above? I suspect she had to go home at some point, but did she go right away? Did her husband and family forgive her as Jesus had? Did she leave her life of sin as Jesus commanded her to? Did she submit her life to the grace of an amazing second chance in a society where she would have been stoned had Jesus not intervened?

I can't answer for her, but I can answer for me with the words found in 1 John 3:19-20: "This then is how we know that we belong to the truth, and how we set our hearts at rest in his presence whenever our hearts condemn us. For God is greater than our hearts, and he knows everything."

DAY FIVE

No One Is an Island

Be careful, however, that the exercise of your freedom does not become a stumbling block to the weak. . . . So this weak brother, for whom Christ died, is destroyed by your knowledge. When you sin against your brothers in this way and wound their weak conscience, you sin against Christ. Therefore, if what I eat causes my brother to fall into sin, I will never eat meat again, so that I will not cause him to fall.

1 CORINTHIANS 8:9, 11-13

In elementary school my daughter had a friend who was Muslim. One day my daughter wanted the girl to come over and play after school. I told her that it was the holy month of Ramadan, a time of fasting and prayer for devout Muslims, and we wouldn't be able to have any snacks out of respect for this child. But my daughter came home from school "starving" and ate six or seven snacks while the Muslim girl watched. I tried to encourage them to go play, but my daughter kept saying how hungry she was. Needless to say, the Muslim girl never again wanted to come over to play.

My daughter was not a very good example of the discipline of submission because she was insensitive to her friend's fasting. As Saint Francis of Assisi is reported to have said, "Preach the gospel at all times, and when necessary, use words."

In today's verse, Saint Paul explains the discipline of submission by saying that meat is meat, but if a weaker brother sees that you got it from the temple of an idol, his faith in Christ may be severely weakened. In that case, meat becomes a tool of spiritual warfare, and we need to submit our taste buds to the other person's weaker conscience.

It boils down to having good manners and an understanding that our actions don't happen in a vacuum. My daughter and I had a long talk after her friend left.

One: Who Really Counts?

The army of the king of Babylon was then besieging Jerusalem and Jeremiah the prophet was confined in the courtyard of the guard. . . . Jeremiah said, "The word of the LORD came to me: Hanamel son of Shallum your uncle is going to come to you and say, 'Buy my field at Anathoth, because as nearest relative it is your right and duty to buy it.'. . . So I bought the field. . . . This is what the LORD says: As I have brought all this great calamity on this people, so I will give them all the prosperity I have promised them. Once more fields will be bought in this land of which you say, 'It is a desolate waste.'"

JEREMIAH 32:2, 6-7, 9, 42-43

What a crazy thing to do: Jerusalem is besieged, Jeremiah is under house arrest and here he is, buying his uncle's field! If you knew that your land was going to be flooded in a dam project and someone insisted on buying it at full price, you would laugh all the way to the bank.

But this was no foolish land purchase. This was Jeremiah's submission to hope in God's greater purposes. He bought the land at the Lord's command as a sign that while Jerusalem would be sacked and the people would be sent into exile, there would come a day when the Lord would restore the people to the land, and their fields would be bought and sold again. I imagine everyone still in Jerusalem at that point chalked it up to yet another crazy thing this weird prophet was doing. It isn't easy being a symbol for God.

Sometimes we need to practice the discipline of submission with our emotions. While around us it may look like the end of the world, we must submit our despair to the promise of ultimate goodness in God. This does not deny grieving or tears, but it does speak against hopelessness and despair. "You, dear children, are from God and have overcome [evil spirits], because the one who is in you is greater than the one who is in the world" (1 John 4:4).

DAY TWO

Doing Things Right

You shall not steal.

EXODUS 20:15

My children always groan and roll their eyes at me when I tell them that burning CDs or DVDs instead of buying them is stealing. Or that photocopying copyrighted material (like music scores) is stealing. Or that downloading music off the Internet (unless it is a subscription site) is stealing.

Because these are such prevalent practices in our society, few of us recognize them as stealing. And if we are honest, a lot of us don't care. We have the technology to do it, so we might as well save money and use it. We don't care that a lot of people make their living through the royalties and copyright fees on all of the above listed materials. They are nameless people in a long chain from the creative idea to the packaging, and since we think a lot of it is overpriced anyway, we decide to make a "free" copy for ourselves or our friends.

Underneath the issue of stealing of any kind, from burning illegal CDs to robbing banks, is the subtle issue of entitlement: I want it, therefore I am going to take it because I deserve it. Entitlement is a close cousin of pride. It tells me I am entitled to anything I want, and any method I use to get what I want is justifiable.

In the discipline of submission, we seek to expose those deeper attitudes. We seek to live trusting in the good provision of God and with gratitude for all we do have. And we seek to be fair to all who contribute creative, good things to our lives.

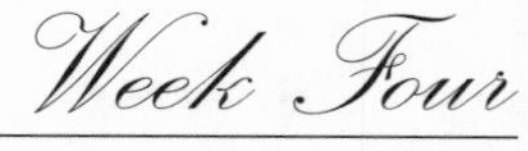

DAY THREE

No Scoreboard

Your kingdom come, your will be done on earth as it is in heaven.

MATTHEW 6:10

An old man went out hunting, the story begins. A rabbit ran past him, collided with a tree trunk and knocked itself unconscious. The old man was so excited that for the rest of his life he stood by that tree stump, expecting another rabbit to come along and knock itself unconscious against it. We laugh at the foolishness of this old man, but how long have we been standing at our own tree stump?

Another way of saying it is this: don't always expect things to go the way you think they should. This is especially appropriate when talking about children. Children are not meant to live the life we couldn't or didn't live. That means they will probably not be gifted in the same way we are, learn the same way we do, be interested in the things we are interested in or choose the same things we would have chosen (or did choose) in life. We could substitute other things here too, such as spouse or coworker. Any time we expect someone to live up to our expectations about something, we are on thin ice.

In the discipline of submission we are invited to let go of our attachment to particular outcomes. That doesn't mean we can't hope or pray or have input in our child's or spouse's or coworker's decision-making process. What it does mean is that we are not to get all wrapped up in the final outcome because we could inadvertenly be working against the coming of God's kingdom into that person's life.

DAY FOUR

Complementary Disciplines

"I am the Lord's servant," Mary answered. "May it be to me as you have said." Then the angel left her.

LUKE 1:38

The spiritual disciplines work in close harmony with one another. One informs and corrects another, and together they help us grow in a balanced way into maturity in Christ.

The disciplines of submission and simplicity are close cousins. The discipline of simplicity teaches us to hold possessions lightly; the discipline of submission teaches us to hold issues lightly. The word *lightly* does not imply a lack of importance but rather that we are invited to live in the reality that God is greater than all of our possessions and issues, that we can "seek first [God's] kingdom and his righteousness, [trusting that] all these things will be given to you as well" (Matthew 6:33).

In today's verse, Mary has just heard that she is to be the mother of Jesus. As an engaged woman, her pregnancy was going to cause all kinds of problems for her and for Joseph, her fiancé. In our culture we tend to forget what an embarrassing position Mary put herself into. While the issue of the Messiah was a huge one for the Jews of that time, no one was quite prepared for his arrival in this way. Imagine running into a young woman you know in the grocery store, obviously pregnant, who tells you she is to be the mother of God but she is still a virgin. Mary's trips to the village well must have become increasingly hard times.

When we engage with the discipline of submission and the discipline of simplicity, we begin to confront how willing we really are to let God have his way with our lives and our possessions. If an angel appeared to you today and asked you to be the Lord's servant in some way that would jeopardize your reputation and your financial status, what would your response be?

DAY FIVE

A Review

For by the grace given me I say to every one of you: Do not think of yourself more highly than you ought, but rather think of yourself with sober judgment, in accordance with the measure of faith God has given you.

ROMANS 12:3

We do not hear good things from our culture about being submissive. Too often being submissive is viewed as a negative quality, where people are doormats for the rest of the world to walk over. Many messages in the media promote an attitude toward life that encourages us to grab something before someone else gets it first.

Being a doormat is not the biblical view of submission. In the Bible submission means accepting who you are as a child of God, with the gifts and talents you have, peacefully acknowledging those areas you are not gifted in. Howard Baker says it this way: "We do not need to think less *of* ourselves but we do need to think less *about* ourselves."*

As Christians most of us know we are not called to be arrogant or boastful, but too many of us feel that in order to be humble, we have to berate ourselves. That is not what God does, and we shouldn't attack ourselves either. We are to be thankful for who we are and what we have been given while joyfully acknowledging when others have gifts that are different or better than ours.

One of the meanings for the word *sober* in the Romans passage above is "not exaggerated or distorted." To think of ourselves rightly is an act of faith in the God of creation, who made us and proclaimed us good (see Genesis 1).

**Soul Keeping: Ancient Paths of Spiritual Direction* (Colorado Springs: NavPress, 1998), p. 93.

The Discipline of Service

THE IDEA OF CHRISTIAN SERVICE is not new to most of us. We know that as disciples of Jesus Christ we are called to serve God and others. In fact, this may seem like an easy discipline and therefore could be a good starting point as you begin your journey through learning the spiritual disciplines.

In doing things for others (which we ultimately do for God, as Jesus tells us in Matthew 25:40), we draw closer to God and to our neighbor, whom we are to love as we love ourselves (see Matthew 22:37-39). However, in making service one of the spiritual disciplines, we look at these large and small acts at another level.

In the discipline of service we learn to see who we are really serving: ourselves or others. This discipline helps us uncover ungodly attitudes in our acts of service, such as a need to get recognition for what we do or a willingness to serve only if it is a big, glamorous event.

The issue of pride may rear its ugly head when we start examining the way we respond to someone who didn't want our help or who didn't acknowledge our help in a way we thought they should have. In this discipline we can let go of needing a thank-you note or our name in the bulletin for things we do for others.

The other issue that may be a surprise discovery here is idolatry; that is, serving God when we should be worshiping God. This is manifested by people who are always doing things for God at church or in other arenas but who often skip worship to do those other acts of service. Any time doing something for God becomes a substitute for worshiping God, there is a spirit of idolatry at work.

Let me invite you to take a look at your heart attitudes and become an even better disciple of Jesus Christ as you seek to reach out to those around you.

Each week choose one or two suggested activities from the list below to help you practice this discipline:

For Anyone

- Serve a meal at a homeless shelter, bring food or clothing to a collection site or sponsor a child in need through an aid organization.
- Find a way to do an act of love for someone you find difficult to love (maybe even a close family member) without denying how you feel.
- Identify an area where you may be overserving. Perhaps your children or coworkers have been telling you that they need space or don't want your help with something. Refrain from asking about the issue or from offering your help. Wait for the other person to seek you out.
- While going about the onerous tasks of your life, pray that those who are doing them in worse circumstances will be blessed. Thank God that you have the strength and resources to do those tasks.
- Find ways to respond to requests for help from people who are begging. Instead of giving them money that could be used to buy alcohol or drugs, find creative alternatives such as granola bars or other snacks that you can keep in the car to hand to someone begging at an intersection.
- Estimate how much time you will spend on a service project. Make sure to spend an equal amount of time in prayer and worship.
- For those of us who are impulsive, let's-do-something-right-now kinds of people, waiting to hear the Lord's voice in a situation can be frustrating, but it is an important part of the discipline of service and keeps us from going off in the wrong directions. Next time you consider rendering a service to someone, stop and listen for God's voice in the situation before you act.
- Become a servant in your conversation by trying to say things in a way the other person will hear. If you have no idea how to do this, find a book that covers the basics of personality types.
- Keep simple food and drink options on hand so that when people drop by to visit, you have something to offer them. Treat unexpected visitors as a gift sent by God, not as an irritating interruption.
- Think of a way that you can smooth over some hurt feelings in your

neighborhood, workplace or family while still maintaining your integrity (that is, not becoming an enabler or codependent). For example, do you need to apologize to your neighbor and replace the flowers your dog dug up, even though it was a hole in their fence that the dog went through?

- Use your position of authority (as a parent, teacher, elected official or top executive) and access to wealth to help someone specifically. Focus on bringing goodness to another person or situation, not on what you can gain from the circumstance.
- Ask yourself who you can serve today through an action that shows you love them even though you can't fix a situation for them. In some cases the "action" may mean not doing anything, if your previous attempts to fix or offer help have only caused alienation and frustration.
- Develop a balanced routine, one that includes good meals and time with friends and family on a regular basis.

Especially with Children

- Find out about the historical Saint Nicholas. Your local library and many Internet sites have plenty of information. Note the differences and similarities between the historical figure and our cultural Santa Claus.
- Identify someone in your neighborhood who may need help. The need does not have to be economic. Maybe they need to be invited for tea or dinner. Maybe they just need a visit.
- Invite a friend over. Help your child make a snack and find something to do or play with that will appeal to the other person.
- The best way to combat faulty motives is to serve anonymously. Find someone your family can help without that person ever knowing who it was.

DAY ONE

The Heart, Not the Wallet

Listen, my dear brothers: Has not God chosen those who are poor in the eyes of the world to be rich in faith and to inherit the kingdom he promised those who love him? But you have insulted the poor.

JAMES 2:5-6

One fall my daughter participated in an exchange program, living in a small village in rural Alaska that was a primarily subsistence culture. The family she lived with made only twelve thousand dollars a year but was generous to a fault. They insisted on paying for everything. They had little, but they treated my daughter very well.

At the same time, another student I knew was in an exchange program and lived with a wealthier family. This family was stingy even with things like toilet paper and light bulbs. They wouldn't even give this student a ride to school, which was a half-hour walk away, but they would wave as they drove past on the way to town!

This is not to say all rich people are selfish and all poor people are generous because we know that isn't true. The point is that our culture encourages us to acquire all we can while ignoring the needs of the people around us. All of us have things we can share with others, regardless of where we are in the economic strata. It is truly a question of attitude and not plentitude.

Small Is Beautiful

This is love: that we walk in obedience to his commands.

2 JOHN 1:6

It was a good lecture, focusing on the need to replace bad spiritual habits with good ones. Now it was time for questions: "What about the need for high risk in the life of the disciple?" The risk that was implied was the kind of self-sacrificing service some people do for the sake of the gospel, in difficult places far from home with no regard for their own safety or security.

It occurred to me that too many of us have the idea that Christian service is better or more authentic if it is hard and dangerous. Somehow we fail to realize it is equally risky to sustain a faithful walk with Christ over the uneventful long haul. While we may at times be called to "something great," more often we are called to the small, seemingly insignificant somethings of the everyday.

"God's will for us is not necessarily arduous in the way we would choose, full of drama and danger; it might be arduous through frustration and tedium."* This was written by a former student of mine who has chosen to spend her life in a Benedictine community, the kind that wears the full habit.

People who have been married a long time know it is the thoughtful, day-to-day living that strengthens the relationship, not the periodic expensive gifts or exotic vacations. So it is in our relationship with God and the acts of service and obedience he calls us to do over a lifetime of walking in faith.

*Hildegard Dubnick, *Auris Cordis 6:1* (Winter 1995-1996), p. 2.

Loving All

[Jesus said,] "But I tell you: Love your enemies and pray for those who persecute you."
MATTHEW 5:44

This is one of those verses that sounds so inspiring and is so hard to do. Loving enemies in the abstract, when they are oceans away, is easier than loving them when they commit acts of atrocity against you personally or against your country. And the people we are called to love don't even have to be bona fide enemies! They can be people with irritating personalities that cause our stomachs to knot every time we see them coming toward us.

The mistake we often make is that we assume love needs to be a feeling. But if we understand love to be an action, then we can do what we don't necessarily feel. Many times my prayer is that Jesus will give me his heart for the person standing in front of me, whom I personally wish wasn't even in the room.

I have had to learn this with a person who has been on my prayer list for a long time. After years of friendship, this person began to slander me for no apparent reason. I tried to reconcile, but finally I started ignoring this person because they were becoming irrational. One day out of the blue this person phoned me requesting some information. Only God knows if there will ever be a true resolution, but that day my prayer was answered because I was able to answer graciously.

DAY FOUR

Backing Off

Martha was distracted by all the preparations that had to be made.

LUKE 10:40

The new sod at the community center was laid just as the drought started. Soon lawn-watering restrictions were being strictly enforced. During a drought grass needs to be left alone to grow tall. It isn't supposed to look neat and manicured; it needs that extra length to survive. But the meticulous groundskeeper at the community center continued to mow the new grass every five or six days as if it were getting a normal amount of rainfall. Within a month, the grass was dead. The groundskeeper's focus on giving the grass what she thought it needed instead of what it really needed kept the new sod from getting a good start.

In the story surrounding today's verse, Martha learns that overservice is as bad as refusing to serve. I suspect Martha was a control freak at some level and wanted everything to be perfect all the time. Jesus warns her that service can become an idol when it is put above a relationship with him.

We need to be careful that the service we want to offer is appropriate to the person or situation. Sometimes not serving is the best form of service. There is a time to mow and there is a time to let the grass grow.

DAY FIVE

Keep Perspective

[Elijah] replied, "I have been very zealous for the LORD God Almighty. The Israelites have rejected your covenant, broken down your altars, and put your prophets to death with the sword. I am the only one left, and now they are trying to kill me too." The LORD said to him, "Go back the way you came. . . . When you get there, anoint Hazael king over Aram."

1 KINGS 19:14-15

If I were feeling as scared and defeated as Elijah was at this point, I don't think I would be pleased to have the Lord answer my fearful prayer with a to-do list of kings that needed anointing (see verses 16-18). Elijah wanted to escape to a faraway place (see verses 3-5), but after giving him a bit of refreshment (see verses 6-8), God called Elijah back into the fray with very specific tasks.

I too have felt frustrated and defeated in projects and service opportunities. I was doing things that I thought would make a difference in people's lives, and yet nothing seemed to work. At times it even felt like people were out to kill the ministry I was trying to build up. Sometimes I would come home, throw the covers over my head and take a nap of resignation.

Yet like Elijah I have also felt the call of God to get up, look at it from God's perspective and keep moving. Often after a hard look sorting out the facts from my feelings in a tough situation, with God's help I am ready to go again.

Service requires that we keep our eyes focused on God, not the immediate outcome.

DAY ONE

Knowing Who We Are

Jesus knew that the Father had put all things under his power, and that he had come from God and was returning to God; so he got up from the meal, took off his outer clothing and wrapped a towel around his waist . . . and began to wash the disciples' feet.

JOHN 13:3-5

It's a fact of human nature that we can more easily rise to the occasion when there is a great need than when there is drudgery to be done day after day. We would all like to be the famous master chef, not the dishwasher in the kitchen. Yet common sense tells us that somebody has to scrub out those secret-recipe lasagna pans.

While service should relate to giftedness, there are things in life that have to be done regardless of whether or not we are gifted in them. Menial tasks can keep us humble and grounded. That truth is behind the rules in many monastic communities: it doesn't matter who you are in the community, everyone takes their turn at the manual labor needed to keep things running smoothly. Even the abbott takes a turn cleaning the toilets.

When I'm scrubbing out the shower, I try to remember the many women of the world who have no home to clean or for whom home is a nightmare. It reminds me that as a child of God, I can be thankful *in* (not for) all things. I can discipline myself to pray for those who are doing the same task I am currently doing but who are in worse circumstances.

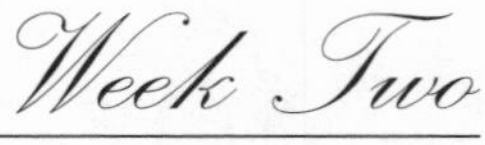

From the Inside Out

All a man's ways seem innocent to him, but motives are weighed by the LORD.

PROVERBS 16:2

My cat had an appointment for his annual shots, and of course he was nowhere to be seen. I pulled out a bit of turkey from the refrigerator and began calling him in my best "here's a treat, kitty-kitty" voice. He thundered out of the closet and down the stairs, meowing expectantly. As soon as he had his treat, I stuffed him in the cat carrier and whisked him off to the vet.

While this is okay for a cat, I am convicted about the number of times I have offered my service to others as "a bit of turkey," expecting to further my own plans and benefit in some way myself. I help at the school garage sale so I can get first dibs on the good items and price them for myself. (In fact, that is exactly how I got my cat carrier!) I help serve a meal somewhere so I can take some leftovers home.

Isn't it all right to gain some good from helping others? Yes and no. The problem is my true motive, not the actual service. When I do something for me under the guise of helping others, I am a liar. While others may laud my selfless act, God sees the real reason I am there.

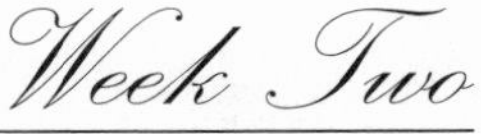

DAY THREE

God Judges

If a man shuts his ears to the cry of the poor, he too will cry out and not be answered.

PROVERBS 21:13

I work at a church that is located in the downtown area. Many needy and homeless people come in looking for various kinds of help. It is easy to get cynical about some of their requests and stories. Some truly are in need of help, but some simply work the system for whatever they can get from it. At times it is tempting to cast aspersions on those people after they leave.

Dietrich Bonhoeffer once said, "How can I possibly serve another person in unfeigned humility if I seriously regard his sinfulness as worse than my own? . . . Such service would be hypocritical."* Jesus never rejected a person who requested help. He often asked hard questions about the request, but he never rejected the person (see for example Mark 10:17-22). What a contrast to the way I often reject people out of hand simply because of the way they look or smell.

I have learned to pray for discernment and for the heart of Jesus when I am asked for money on the street. I try to create ways to meet people's needs without contributing to the purchase of alcohol or drugs. For example, I keep snack items like granola bars in the car. This alternative can be a way to reach out to someone begging at an intersection.

Prayers and actions take time or money; service that costs us nothing should be viewed with suspicion.

---

*Dietrich Bonhoeffer, *Life Together* (New York: Harper & Row, 1954), pp. 96-97.

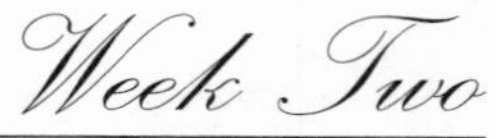

Serving Service

Better is one day in your courts than a thousand elsewhere.

PSALM 84:10

There are two major pitfalls in the discipline of service: the first is service driven by selfish motives. The second is service to the exclusion of a vital faith in Jesus Christ. This latter form of service becomes idolatry because we begin to worship what we do instead of the God in whose name we are called to serve.

Some Christians skip worship services to do a service project, thinking that the latter is a higher expression of faith than the former. Other people spend Sunday mornings running around the church building making sure everything is going smoothly, but they themselves never come in to worship. Any time we make the running of the church a priority over the worship of the gathered community, we are on dangerous ground.

Other examples include people who spend hours protesting an unjust institution or war, who work tirelessly at shelters or projects in Third World countries but who won't spend an equal amount of time developing their prayer and worship life. It is as though they are trying to cut paper with one blade of a scissors.

We need service to help us worship more honestly, and we need worship to help us serve more effectively. The discipline of service is an inner reality with an outward manifestation.

DAY FIVE

Hospitality Versus Entertaining

Who is wise and understanding among you? Let him show it by his good life, by deeds done in the humility that comes from wisdom.

JAMES 3:13

Wisdom does not necessarily lead to "deeds done in humility." Sometimes it leads to wanting to be given honorary degrees and speaking engagements. Sometimes it leads to wanting to be waited on instead of serving others.

Saint Benedict (480-547) was a godly and wise Italian monk. His *Rule*, the book of order for all Benedictine monasteries, is still held in high esteem after fifteen hundred years. Saint Benedict understood well God, people and life in community, thus the rules for governing Benedictine monasteries embody a timeless, godly wisdom.

One of the things Benedict stressed for every monastery was hospitality. All guests were to be welcomed as if they were Christ himself (Rule of Saint Benedict 53:1). In fact, Benedict felt that a monastery would always have guests in it if it was living the rule well.

Hospitality is different from entertaining. In hospitality, the focus is on other people and their needs. In entertaining, the focus is on who we are and what we have. Hospitality involves wisdom (finding out what the other person needs) and humility (a willingness to provide it).

While hospitality may involve acquiring the material possessions needed to feed and house people, those things are meant to serve people rather than impress them.

DAY ONE

Ranking Service

As King David approached Bahurim, a man from the same clan as Saul's family came out from there. His name was Shimei son of Gera, and he cursed as he came out. . . . David then said . . . , "My son, who is of my own flesh, is trying to take my life. How much more, then, this Benjamite! Leave him alone; let him curse, for the LORD has told him to. It may be that the LORD will see my distress and repay me with good for the cursing I am receiving today." So David and his men continued along the road while Shimei was going along the hillside opposite him, cursing as he went and throwing stones at him and showering him with dirt. The king and all the people with him arrived at their destination exhausted.

2 SAMUEL 16:5, 11-14

A fellow committee member became quite impassioned about something. I asked a question that was meant to help clarify the issue, but all it did was throw a verbal grenade into the discussion. I received a very tart response, and it stung. During a break in the meeting, another member of the committee thanked me privately for my question because it was one that needed to be asked.

When we are called to an act of service (sometimes asking a hard question is an act of service), we don't always know if it is right or good. Sometimes we may be met with cursing and stones thrown at us.

In the passage above, King David is fleeing from his son Absalom, who had mounted a successful coupe. David is struggling to discern the will of God in this mess. And then along comes Shimei, who adds insult to injury by cursing David and throwing rocks and dust at his fleeing party. To say that they arrived at their destination exhausted is an understatement.

When Abishai, one of David's men, offers to kill Shimei, David's answer to him shows remarkable faith in the Lord. In the midst of the fear, pain and confusion, David seeks to be a faithful servant of God. He is going to let God deal with Shimei and trust that the Lord will work out everything for good. We are invited to do the same.

DAY TWO

Working Together

Now there was a man in Jerusalem called Simeon, who was righteous and devout. He was waiting for the consolation of Israel, and the Holy Spirit was upon him. It had been revealed to him by the Holy Spirit that he would not die before he had seen the Lord's Christ. Moved by the Spirit, he went into the temple courts. When [Mary and Joseph] brought in the child Jesus to do for him what the custom of the Law required, Simeon took him in his arms and praised God, saying: "Sovereign Lord, as you have promised, you now dismiss your servant in peace."

LUKE 2:25-29

The spiritual disciplines are meant to work together in harmony in our lives. We study them in bits and pieces to learn the mechanics and the ultimate goals for each discipline, but they are meant to function as a seamless whole.

In the passage above, we meet Simeon, who had meditated faithfully on the promises of God such that he was convinced they would come true. One day he heard the Spirit tell him to go to the temple, where he met face-to-face the fulfillment of God's promise: Jesus, the Lord's Christ, being brought to the temple for circumcision.

And from Simeon's faithful meditating on God's promises and listening to the nudging of the Spirit, Simeon rendered a service of prophecy to all who would hear it: "This child is destined to cause the falling and rising of many in Israel" (verse 34).

Simeon was not the only one in Israel waiting for the Lord's Christ, the Anointed One, the Messiah to arrive, but as we know from the Gospel accounts, most people missed his arrival because Jesus did not fit their expectations of what God's promise would look like.

We don't know how long Simeon had waited for this moment. We don't know how long after this event Simeon died. But we do know that Simeon was able to be a faithful servant in the right moment because he had spent time with God, learning to recognize his voice in other situations.

DAY THREE

Speaking Clearly

Though I am free and belong to no man, I make myself a slave to everyone, to win as many as possible. . . . I have become all things to all . . . so that by all possible means I might save some. I do all this for the sake of the gospel, that I may share in its blessings.

1 CORINTHIANS 9:19, 22-23

When I discovered the different theories of personality types, it changed the way I communicated with people. I learned that some people respond well to strong, forthright communication, even if they disagree with you. Others need to have a bit of chit-chat and laughter before you can talk to them about more serious things. Some people are most concerned about keeping the peace; others are concerned about their safety (emotional as well as physical) in particular situations. I am still learning how all of this works, but I've had enough success with it to know it is worth pursuing.

In the verses above, Saint Paul talks about using language that people with differing worldviews can relate to so that the gospel of Jesus Christ may get a fair hearing in all places. Those of us who have raised or taught children know that we need to speak differently to each child, even about the same issue. For example, I could tell one of my children to go clean up her room, and she would comply fairly quickly. But the other needed to be given a window of time by which she needed to complete the task, or else I met with great resistance.

Part of the discipline of service is communicating well. And part of communicating well is knowing who your audience is. Sometimes we can be a hindrance to others and to their reception of the gospel if we do not take the time to learn how they hear.

DAY FOUR

The Reason for Health

Simon's mother-in-law was in bed with a fever, and they told Jesus about her. So he went to her, took her hand and helped her up. The fever left her and she began to wait on them.

MARK 1:30-31

It has always interested me that Simon's mother-in-law began to serve Jesus and his disciples as soon as she was healed of her fever. Her healing was swift and complete, and she gave thanks for that healing by serving Jesus and his friends.

All of us have been gifted by God in many and various ways. Health, talents, life itself are all given to us so that we may be Christ's hands and feet and voice to others around us. When we misuse those gifts or when they are diminished through illness, we are to seek restoration so that we may continue to serve others. We are blessed so that we may be a blessing to others.

Our culture encourages self-indulgence, but self-indulgence is not synonymous with self-care. In self-care we seek to be all that we were created to be so that we may serve those around us. Self-indulgence is a form of hoarding.

The discipline of service also does not mean being a doormat (see the readings in the discipline of submission, which is closely related to this discipline). It includes having appropriate boundaries, knowing when to say yes and when to say no. Godly service means using the fullness of your power and giftedness to help others in appropriate ways for them and for you.

When the illnesses and imbalances of our lives are restored through the power of Jesus, let us give thanks by using our life and our talents in service to God and our neighbors.

DAY FIVE

Conquering Pride

Instead, whoever wants to become great among you must be your servant, and whoever wants to be first must be your slave—just as the Son of Man did not come to be served, but to serve, and to give his life as a ransom for many.

MATTHEW 20:26-28

Our modern idea of Santa Claus is based on a real person. Saint Nicholas, the bishop of Myra (in what is southwest Turkey today), lived in the fourth century. There are many legends about him. One story tells the plight of a poor man with three daughters of marriageable age. He had no money for their dowries, which in that culture was what assured a woman of provision and protection, so their futures looked bleak. Nicholas, who came from a wealthy Christian family, heard about their troubles. Three nights in a row he threw a bag of gold down the chimney of the poor man's house so that each girl would have a dowry, allowing her to marry well, ensuring her future. It is from this story that we get the idea of giving gifts at Christmastime.

In the discipline of service we learn about true service versus self-righteous service. True service really is all about the other person. In self-righteous service, we may be doing something good for someone else, but it is ultimately all about us. We want everyone to know what we did, and we want to be properly thanked for it. We also want to help others in the way we think they need to be helped.

One of the ways to combat that rotten root of self-service is to do acts of service anonymously. When no one knows what you did, you can't be thanked for it. One woman told me she worked on this issue by cleaning up gas station bathrooms. She would strive to leave the facility cleaner than when she went in. Talk about a humbling, thankless job! Doing things like that can help expose ungodly desires for acknowledgment and can help us become true servants, people who are able to do what needs to be done without expecting anything in return.

DAY ONE

Christ Comes in All

Abraham looked up and saw three men standing nearby. When he saw them, he hurried from the entrance of his tent to meet them and bowed low to the ground. He said, "If I have found favor in your eyes, my lord, do not pass your servant by. Let a little water be brought. . . . Let me get you something to eat, so you can be refreshed and then go on your way—now that you have come to your servant."

GENESIS 18:2-5

While on a speaking trip, I had occasion to spend the night at a friend's house. She had a bottle of water for me in the car when she picked me up at the airport. My room had some snacks in it, along with shampoo, a toothbrush and other toiletries, all sitting on a stack of clean towels. I felt so at home that it was hard to leave in the morning!

Even today in remote desert areas of the world, hospitality is given to anyone, even enemies, because the harsh climate can kill someone who has no water, food or shelter. That tradition has been in place since Abraham's time, as evidenced by the verses above. Abraham did not know who his visitors were, but in typical Middle Eastern understatement, the "little bit of refreshment" that he offered them included freshly baked bread and a fatted calf! I know of the people of one West African village who, though they themselves were on the brink of starvation, killed a goat and fixed a feast for a foreign visitor because that is what you do for visitors in that society, even if it means you go without.

I find it hard sometimes to stop in the middle of something to welcome a person who has come to my door. The last thing I want to do is sit and chat while my to-do list is multiplying by the minute. Yet sometimes those interruptions, those people who come unexpectedly to my door or who call on the phone, are the real work that God wants me to do at that moment.

I may not have to kill a fatted calf and bake fresh bread like Abraham did, but a simple glass of iced tea and a cookie can be as refreshing for someone who needs to talk.

DAY TWO

A Kind Word

One of the servants told Nabal's wife Abigail: "David sent messengers from the desert to give our master his greetings, but he hurled insults at them. Yet these men were very good to us. . . . Now think it over and see what you can do, because disaster is hanging over our master and his whole household." . . . Abigail lost no time. She took two hundred loaves of bread, two skins of wine, five dressed sheep, five seahs of roasted grain, a hundred cakes of raisins and two hundred cakes of pressed figs, and loaded them on donkeys.

1 SAMUEL 25:14-15, 17-18

This whole chapter is a lesson in personal relationships. David is on the run from King Saul and is hiding out in the desert. His men are commended by Nabal's shepherds for their protection of them and Nabal's flocks. When David asks Nabal to share with them the feast associated with sheep shearing, Nabal hurls insults at them. David is about to kill Nabal and his household when Abigail shows up. She brings lots of good food as well as an apology for her husband's boorish behavior and lack of gratitude for the help David's men had given their shepherds. David accepts the gifts from her hand, and after Nabal dies (see v. 38), David marries Abigail, saving her from the destitute fate of widows in that culture.

Abigail's apology is telling; she knew what her husband was like, and she knew the danger their whole household was in because they had transgressed that culture's laws of hospitality. Her willingness to take the blame and make restitution with the food kept David from the sin of bloodshed, and it kept her family alive.

It is not always easy to have a servant heart. Sometimes it involves taking blame that isn't yours and trying to make things right that you didn't make wrong. If you have ever had a pet or a child damage someone else's property, you know what I am talking about. (Have a good accountability partner to make sure that you aren't falling into a codependent relationship or continually enabling unhealthy behaviors.)

Abigail's response can be a model for us when we are faced with a difficult situation not of our own making.

DAY THREE

Public Accountability

When you enter the land the LORD your God is giving you and have taken possession of it and settled in it, and you say, "Let us set a king over us like all the nations around us," be sure to appoint over you the king the LORD your God chooses. . . . The king . . . must not acquire great numbers of horses for himself or make the people return to Egypt to get more of them. . . . He must not take many wives, or his heart will be led astray. He must not accumulate large amounts of silver and gold.

DEUTERONOMY 17:14-17

Solomon was a classic example of what would happen when the instructions in today's passage were not followed. Later we read how Solomon accumulated great wealth, lots of horses from Egypt and many wives (see 1 Kings 10:14—11:13). The Lord became angry with Solomon because his heart turned away from God, influenced by the religions of his many wives (see 11:9). Human beings are too easily distracted by wealth and power, so we are commanded not to seek great amounts of either one.

We see this scenario played out throughout the course of history, both inside and outside the church. People are elected to public office or hired to lead others, often with great intentions of serving well. Then they get caught up in the whirlwind of money, sex and power. Not only do they lose their focus, but many times they end up involved in illegal activities that bring about their downfall. In the case of church leaders it also brings great condemnation to the faith.

When we come into a situation where we control lots of money or have a lot of power, we must become increasingly focused on prayer. We must find a group of people who can hold us accountable to God's commandments. We must find ways to keep focused on how we are called to help others with our resources and our influence.

Wealth and power make for heady business, and none of us is immune to being overcome by their dark side.

The Only Option

Dear children, let us not love with words or tongue but with actions and in truth.

1 JOHN 3:18

Sometimes in a relationship the only service we can render is to love the other person. Whether it is a friend or a child in a tough circumstance, a family member in crisis or a neighbor who dislikes you, loving actions may be all we can do.

I am a fix-it person. Whenever my children or friends have problems, I want to swoop in and make everything OK. Many times that is not only impossible, but it's not wise. We may need to let our children, our friends and our family members learn hard lessons, even though it is difficult for us to stand back and watch.

Those of us who have dealt with adolescents know that in their desire to be independent (a healthy quality, by the way), they often do not want help, which they view as interference. In those cases, all we can do, as parents or teachers, is stand back and find ways to love them by the things we do (or don't do) and say (or don't say). This is a form of godly service.

Remember, in self-righteous service, we do things for others because it will make us feel better. In true service, we do things for others because it will make them feel better.

DAY FIVE

God Is Love

No one has ever seen God; but if we love one another, God lives in us and his love is made complete in us.

1 JOHN 4:12

Love is a difficult concept to teach to children in our culture. The message is everywhere that love is a feeling and relationships are over when the feeling is gone. So it is a challenge to teach the biblical model that love is an action and is not dependent on feelings.

The word *love* is so misused: we *love* our parents, and we *love* pizza. We *love* a certain color, and we *love* our new car. It's as if Satan has taken this attribute of God and done everything possible to make it meaningless. It is no wonder that children (and adults) can be so confused about what it means to love someone.

When children grow up, many of them will fall in love, and that is a wonderful gift from God. But those feelings are hard to sustain for decades, and there are times in all relationships when the actions that love requires carry us through, not the here-today-and-gone-tomorrow feelings.

So how do we help children develop a mature understanding of love? Much of it comes from modeling our love in action when our feelings may not be there. We can discuss with them what the loving thing to do may be in a given situation, especially if they were hurt by a sibling or a friend. We can help them understand that loving someone doesn't necessarily mean liking them. Most importantly, we can make sure our children know that God's love is never just a fickle feeling; it is so deeply rooted in action that Jesus came to show us that love.

The Discipline of Confession

THE DISCIPLINE OF CONFESSION is one of the most powerful and yet most feared of the spiritual disciplines. It is powerful because it can free us from guilt and sin to live in the joyous freedom Christ offers in forgiveness. It is feared because we think that out-loud confession of our sins to someone else will diminish us as people and as Christians in that person's eyes. Maybe it is feared because we finally have to admit that we are capable of the evil we have done, that we are not just nice people who made a bad choice.

For many Christians this discipline is practiced in the abstract, through quick prayers of saying we are sorry to God and hoping that he and everyone else will quickly forget about whatever it is we have done (or not done). Many of us also practice it as a group in the corporate confession that begins many of our worship services. While this is an important part of the service, it is not designed to let us off the hook, a kind of "Well, God, everyone here is a sinner, so let's not worry about the specifics."

The discipline of confession is not about appeasing an angry God who will send us to hell if we don't behave. The discipline of confession is about a loving heavenly Father who wants the best for us and is willing to heal us if only we will honestly admit that we are in need of healing. God invites us to come to a place of deep remorse for our sin-filled thoughts, words and deeds. And God in his infinite mercy understands that sometimes it may take us a while to get to that place; that sometimes we can only confess bits and pieces of the sin as we let God have his gentle yet thorough way of cleaning house in the dark recesses of our minds and hearts. As we come to confession, we are invited to be as honest as we can be at that moment, trusting that God will bring the healing and release we need.

It is important to practice this discipline out loud with someone you trust and who is spiritually mature because sometimes that is the only way we will come clean. You can't take a good bath with your clothes on, and you can't cleanse your soul if you are hiding behind all kinds of excuses and rationalizations. In this discipline we are asked to take off our filthy rags, hand them to God through the community he has given us and be given robes of righteousness in return.

Each week choose one or two suggested activities from the list below to help you practice this discipline:

For Anyone

- Ask God for forgiveness for something you did wrong. Name the specific transgression. Thank God that you didn't do something worse, and admit that you are a sinner in great need of Jesus' saving death on the cross.
- Remember a situation in which you were wronged. Write down what should have been done, the excuse given for the wrong and the inexcusable part of the whole mess. Seek to forgive the inexcusable part of the incident.
- If you find yourself mindlessly going through the words and motions of confession every Sunday, work to make those words your own. Then after church find one way to do an act of service for someone else that expresses your heartfelt repentance. (If your church does not have a time of confession, spend time in confession with a mature Christian friend.)
- At bedtime ask for forgiveness for every situation or person you commented negatively on today. Then pray for God to bless that person or situation.
- Fold a paper in thirds. In the left column list three incidents from your past in which you did something wrong. In the middle column list the excuses you gave yourself and others about why you did it. In the right column list the commandment(s) that was broken. Using the right column, confess your past sins to God. Consider doing it out loud with another person present.
- Ask yourself, *What in my life is evidence that I have accepted the message of love and forgiveness Jesus offers to me?*
- Start planning a meaningful observance of Lent. Get a book of Lenten de-

votions from your church's library or your local Christian bookstore. Gather with family members or friends for a structured time of repentance and prayer each week during Lent.

- Memorize 1 John 1:9. Whenever you find yourself wincing over a painful memory, recite it in response to that pain.
- Memorize Psalm 51:10-12 to use at the end of every prayer for forgiveness.
- Keep short accounts with God and with others. That means as soon as you are aware of an offense you've committed, confess it to God and to the offended person (if appropriate). Not only will it stand you in good stead now, but it will help prepare you for that day when you will meet Jesus face-to-face.
- Think of an area in your life where you would like healing in body or mind. Ask God to bring healing to your soul as well as to the area of physical need.

Especially with Children

- Find a way to talk to your child about something he did wrong in the past. Try to ascertain if she is carrying a lot of guilt over that issue. If so, do everything in your power to lift that burden.
- Pray for someone who irritates you. Confess your sin in the situation; then pray for that person as well as a good resolution to the problem.
- Look at your motive behind asking for more. For example, at a meal your motive may be hunger, but it could also be greed or fear that you won't have this food again. Perhaps more time in front of the TV is an excuse to avoid tasks that need to be done. Spend time in confessing these motives followed by a time of thanksgiving for everything you do have.
- If your faith tradition practices private confession, take advantage of that opportunity. If you don't have access to a formal system for confession, create one. Family members or trusted friends can confess sins to each other and then hear words of love and forgiveness spoken by God's people in Jesus name.

DAY ONE

Lessons from Gandhi

You have heard that it was said to the people long ago, "Do not murder, and anyone who murders will be subject to judgment." But I tell you that anyone who is angry with his brother will be subject to judgment.

MATTHEW 5:21-22

Gandhi, the East Indian who struggled with nonviolence against British rule in his country, had a list of seven sins: politics without principles, wealth without work, pleasure without conscience, knowledge without character, commerce without morality, science without humanity and worship without sacrifice. These sins could be described as keeping the letter of the law but not the spirit of the law.

In the discipline of confession we are invited to strip away our rationalizations that say we haven't done anything wrong and acknowledge that we were driven by darker motives. We are invited to be as Jesus was: seamless in our actions and attitudes.

Even though Jesus never broke the law, those who looked at the letter of the law and not its spirit accused him of doing so. Luke 13:10-16 is a good illustration of this. The Jews strictly held the Sabbath law, developing a myriad of rules for what could and could not be done on the Sabbath. As a result, many had lost sight of the gift of the Sabbath as a time for refreshment, for worshiping God and for serving others. They played all kinds of games to get around the Sabbath rules. For example, you could only travel so far from your home on the Sabbath. But if you left your cloak at the end of that distance before sunset on Friday, then that cloak was also considered your "home," so when you got to that point on the Sabbath, you could legally walk further.

The Luke 13 passage records Jesus' healing of a woman on the Sabbath, something the Jews viewed as work, not as the grace of God. Jesus chastises them for losing perspective because of their rules. He was indignant at their desire to be legally correct while forgetting the impact that correctness had on a hurting woman.

Gandhi's list of sins is worth meditating on in light of Jesus' example.

DAY TWO

A U-Turn

Then Jesus began to denounce the cities in which most of his miracles had been performed, because they did not repent.

MATTHEW 11:20

The forecast in the newspaper said the high for the day was supposed to be fifty-three degrees. I left for the two-mile walk to work at 10 a.m. About a block from home, I realized it was colder than I thought it would be, and I probably needed a hat to compliment my jacket and gloves. But I was moving at a fast pace, headed toward a goal, and I didn't want to stop and turn around.

As I walked further, covering my cold ears with my gloved hands, I thought about how often I get the idea that something needs to be done a certain way. I will feel the Spirit nudge me to let it go, look at it from a different perspective and lighten up, but I am at a fast-moving pace toward my goal. Therefore, I often end up plowing into the situation like a bull into a china closet. By the time I am finished apologizing and cleaning up the mess, I realize that it would have been better to turn around and go back to a different way of thinking or acting.

To say "I'm sorry; I was wrong" is hard. It is also freeing because if I can admit to choosing wrongly, then I can choose to do it right the next time. In today's verse, the Greek word for *repent* means "to change one's mind." Some people feel it is a sign of weakness to say they were wrong. In reality, the ability to stop, admit a mistake and go a different direction is a sign of strength.

DAY THREE

True Forgiveness

Forgive us our sins, for we also forgive everyone who sins against us. And lead us not into temptation.

LUKE 11:4

All of us have had hurtful experiences that we remember for a long time. I struggle with the above verse as I think about those occasions when I have been deeply hurt by others. Have I really forgiven them?

There are two things to remember with forgiveness. First, it doesn't mean forgetfulness. We might always remember the incident. The goal is to not let the incident change the way we relate to the person involved. Sometimes even that is not possible. All we can do then is work on letting go of our desire to hurt or humiliate the other person, praying for God to work in his or her life.

The second point is that making excuses for someone is not the same as forgiving them. C. S. Lewis writes, "Even if ninety-nine per cent of [their] apparent guilt can be explained away by really good excuses, the problem of forgiveness begins with the one percent of guilt which is left over. To excuse what can really produce good excuses is not Christian charity; it is only fairness. To be a Christian means to forgive the inexcusable, because God has forgiven the inexcusable in you."*

*"On Forgiveness," quoted in *The Business of Heaven,* ed. Walter Hooper (San Diego: Harcourt Brace, 1984), p. 63.

DAY FOUR

We Become What We Believe

Do not judge, and you will not be judged. Do not condemn, and you will not be condemned. Forgive, and you will be forgiven.

LUKE 6:37

I knew a woman who complained about everyone and everything: her spouse, her children, her parents, her in-laws, her neighbors, her job, her doctor, her church—you name it, she found something wrong with it. She had an underlying expectation that she deserved a good, easy life because she was a good person. She became increasingly bitter that the "bad guys" never got their "due reward." While much of what she said may have been true, her constant focus on the negative began to drive people away.

I tried to hang in there with her, but I would become so depressed after even a few minutes of chatting with her that I began to avoid her too. It became increasingly apparent that she begrudged me my life circumstances and my happiness. My life is not perfect, but I sought to live in gratitude. Her thinly veiled resentment was a complete denial of the struggles and choices I had made to be positive despite difficulties.

I wish I had a happy ending to this story, but I don't. This woman continues her slide into bitter old age, one negative thought at a time. My feeble attempts at trying to get her to be thankful for things have failed. I look at her, read the above verse and shudder. In the meantime, I continue to pray regularly for her, hoping she will someday be able to live in gratitude.

DAY FIVE

Nipping the Bud

You shall not covet your neighbor's house. You shall not covet your neighbor's wife, or his manservant or maidservant, his ox or donkey, or anything that belongs to your neighbor.

EXODUS 20:17

Coveting sounds like such an old-fashioned word. I've even used it as a compliment when a friend has just gotten something particularly beautiful—"Oh, I'm coveting," I purr about the new item. How harmless, right? Wrong!

When I covet (long for, plot how to get, constantly focus on) something, I am in danger of being stingy or ungracious with others so that I can buy whatever it is that I want. I may even fantasize about how to steal the item. Once I found a lovely bracelet when I was on a hike and didn't go too far out of my way to find its rightful owner. It's a well-used path—it could have been anyone, even someone from out of town, right? No one likes to confess these dark whisperings of the mind, but honestly we all have them.

When we covet, we do not trust the God of the universe to provide well for us. If there is something you want, ask God for it. Confess your fears of not having enough. Ask God to open your eyes to the evidence of his generosity in all of creation.

DAY ONE

Confessing Idols

God spoke all these words: "I am the LORD your God, who brought you out of Egypt, out of the land of slavery. You shall have no other gods before me."

EXODUS 20:1-3

Sometimes we think that if we don't have an idol sitting on a shelf in our house that we bow down to three times a day, we have fulfilled this commandment. However, any time we put ourselves before God, we break this commandment. Any time we operate on our own power, apart from the Holy Spirit, we commit idolatry.

I went through a painful incident with a friend I was trying to help. Things were getting worse, and I thought something needed to be done quickly before a window of opportunity was lost forever. Instead of listening for God's ideas and timings, and without consulting others who were familiar with the situation, I did what common sense seemed to dictate at the moment: I gave privileged information to people I thought would help my friend. Instead it all backfired, and we were estranged for a long time.

"You shall have no other gods before me." Sometimes in a given circumstance the idol's name is "control under the guise of common sense." The sooner we name the sin (sometimes the sin of "just wanting to help" is masking the deeper sin of pride or arrogance) and confess its hold on us, the better we are able to follow God's timing in the situation.

DAY TWO

Finding Healing

The LORD God called to the man, "Where are you?" He answered, "I heard you in the garden, and I was afraid because I was naked; so I hid." And he said, "Who told you that you were naked? Have you eaten from the tree that I commanded you not to eat from?" The man said, "The woman you put here with me—she gave me some fruit from the tree, and I ate it." Then the Lord God said to the woman, "What is this you have done?" The woman said, "The serpent deceived me, and I ate."

GENESIS 3:9-13

My children were playing together, but the game was degenerating fast. Voices of frustration were rising, and soon there was crying and the yell, "Mom!" Both children were angry at each other. Both had the look of righteous indignation in their eyes. They each felt justified for the pain inflicted on the other: "I had to hit [poke, kick] her because she did it to me first."

I never bought that excuse. "You are not a victim," was my standard reply. I wanted my children to grow up knowing they were entirely responsible for their responses to others' actions. I did not want them blaming others for their unhappiness. I wanted them to learn to name their own sin in a situation so they could find healing from it and ultimately rise above it.

When we allow ourselves (or our children) to put a spin on wrong actions, we lose the ability to heal from the pain of the incident. For example, when we excuse our wrong behaviors from adolescence with, "Oh, I was just sowing some wild oats then," we lose the opportunity to name the sin as drunkenness or fornication. By naming it for what it really was, we can begin to find healing and forgiveness for it.

This is hard to do, especially if we are used to convincing ourselves that under better circumstances we wouldn't do the same things again. In forcing ourselves to come face-to-face with the true names of our sins, we begin to loosen their haunting grip on us and move into freedom from them.

DAY THREE

Deadly Roots

Then [Jesus] said to them, "Watch out! Be on your guard against all kinds of greed; a man's life does not consist in the abundance of his possessions."

LUKE 12:15

I walked into the grocery store and noticed the employees were wearing party hats. The store was celebrating five years of being in that location, and there were drawings to enter for free gifts. There were lots of free samples and even free birthday cake. I got a free canvas shopping bag and 5 percent off my grocery bill. It was an unexpectedly fun trip.

A week later I was back in the same store, and this time the theme was Mardi Gras. While the employees were wearing colorful beads, there weren't many samples, no freebies and no discount off my bill. I found myself going down aisles I don't usually go down, looking for treats and free things. I actually felt a bit cheated as I left the store.

That is when it hit me: I was experiencing major feelings of greed and a sense of entitlement, a sense that somehow this business owed me more. A small taste of gifting, and I was demanding the same thing every week.

The sad truth is that those feelings were just the tip of a much bigger iceberg of greed and entitlement. As I spent time with God looking at those issues in my life, I realized that after confessing my sin, I needed to begin a litany of thanksgiving for all the good things in my life. "More" is not a song of the kingdom of God.

DAY FOUR

Correct Understandings

This then is how we know that we belong to the truth, and how we set our hearts at rest in his presence whenever our hearts condemn us. For God is greater than our hearts, and he knows everything.

1 JOHN 3:19-20

One of the most important steps in practicing the discipline of confession is an understanding of who God really is: not the God that we equate with our parents or that may have been preached in our childhood faith communities; not the God of modern culture, but God as revealed in Jesus Christ throughout the entire Bible.

When we don't have a balanced view of God, we lose the full power of this discipline. When we emphasize only the judgment of God, we become fearful and seek to hide our sin. When we emphasize only the loving, merciful side of God, we forget how heinous our sin really is. We need to know that we are "poor, miserable sinners," and we need to know that God so loved the world, he sent his only begotten Son (see John 3:16).

There are many times when my heart condemns me. Sometimes I feel overwhelmed and totally unforgivable by anyone, including myself. That is when I must discipline myself to remember who God is. As the verse above says, God knows everything, including all of my shortcomings and failings. But God is greater than my heart, and God's love transcends the sins of the world. Therefore I can stand on solid ground, look God in the eye so to speak and say, "I have sinned. Forgive me." Infinite Love can handle it.

DAY FIVE

Starting Early

Therefore confess your sins to each other and pray for each other so that you may be healed.

JAMES 5:16

It is good to learn from an early age to confess your sins out loud to a fellow Christian and hear the words of forgiveness that Jesus allows us to give one another (see John 20:23). Young children have a hard time keeping a secret, even a secret about something they have done wrong. Their conscience is still fresh, and at some point they blurt out whatever it is they did. Sometimes this is followed by tears, and often there is a huge sense of relief manifested in their little faces and bodies. Children know what a heavy burden guilt is.

When Jesus tells us to become like little children (see Mark 10:15), he meant for us to have a faith that responds to the heavenly Father just as a child responds to a loving parent. Therefore when we are carrying a burden of guilt, we are invited to find a loving adult that we can share that sin with and hear Jesus speak comfort and forgiveness to us through that person.

Some of us are in faith traditions where a system of formal confession is in place. You do yourself and your children a huge favor by taking advantage of that opportunity on a regular basis. For others, though, this is a foreign concept, which is a shame because the discipline of confession can be one of the most liberating forces in our lives. Going to your pastor or a mature, trusted Christian and saying out loud what you did wrong can take a huge weight off your soul.

We must take seriously the healing offered in today's verse, and we must teach children to do likewise by being the mature, trusted Christian they can come to for confession.

DAY ONE

All Have Sinned

Therefore, I tell you, her many sins have been forgiven—for she loved much. But he who has been forgiven little loves little.

LUKE 7:47

This is Jesus' response to the religious elite who thought he should dismiss the woman of questionable character who was pouring costly perfume on Jesus' feet and wiping them with her hair. The religious leaders thought they were better than this woman. They didn't think sin was a part of their lives in any meaningful kind of way. They felt that they stood on ground that was closer to God since they weren't like she was. Hence they had little use for the message of healing and wholeness Jesus offered them. They didn't understand that we don't just commit sins now and then; rather, we are by nature sinners. That's a huge difference in perspective.

When this woman "who had lived a sinful life" (Luke 7:37) came, they couldn't get past the externals of her situation. But Jesus saw her heart. He knew she heard his message of love and forgiveness and that her lavish response was an outward manifestation of the inward acceptance of that message.

I admire this woman who, against all cultural and religious rules and though knowing the enormity of her guilt, publicly expressed her love and gratitude to Jesus. It makes me wonder how deeply I have accepted Jesus' message of love and forgiveness.

DAY TWO

Reclaiming Lent

On the twenty-fourth day of the same month, the Israelites gathered together, fasting and wearing sackcloth and having dust on their heads.

NEHEMIAH 9:1

Can you imagine an entire nation in sackcloth and ashes, fasting and praying for repentance? People walking around crying over their sins and stopping their work in obedience to God's commands? What a sight that must have been. We know from the book of Nehemiah that God blessed the Israelites' work to rebuild Jerusalem, and part of that included rebuilding their faith commitment to the law that God had given to them when they first came out of Egypt.

The closest thing to national repentance we have today is the season of Lent, which starts with Ash Wednesday and ends with Easter. This period of mourning set aside by the church is often poorly understood. While fasting is a common practice during this time, we don't fast to lose weight or to show that we have the willpower to quit smoking. We fast so that we might feast on God. We give up chocolate, TV or trashy novels so that we might gain the divine, the heavenly and the eternal. That makes the season of Lent and its practices of fasting, prayer and almsgiving a significant activity of hope and joy!

What might happen if our whole culture engaged in the forty days of Lent? What might happen if your family or prayer group determined to use Lent as a time for repentance and renewal?

DAY THREE

Having Hope

If we confess our sins, he is faithful and just and will forgive us our sins and purify us from all unrighteousness.

1 JOHN 1:9

I said I was sorry, but the other person was not interested in talking to me, let alone forgiving me. I walked away with a double burden: the knowledge of my own mistake and the realization that the relationship was forever damaged. This is a memory that would cause me to wince whenever I thought about it for years afterward.

Sometimes we only go through the motions of confession, saying we are sorry to God, because deep down we are afraid that God won't really forgive us. When the people around us won't forgive us, it's hard to believe that God will. Yet we have that promise in the verse above: if we confess our sins, God will remain faithful and will forgive us. And he even gives us more than just forgiveness; we will be purified, washed clean, given a fresh start.

Since that happens so rarely in real life, we tend to project our reality onto God. We tend to feel that if our friends and family can't forgive us, neither can God. But that is a lie. Part of the discipline of confession is embracing the forgiveness God promises even if we don't feel forgiven or aren't forgiven by the person we have wounded. But since the word *discipline* comes from the same root word as *disciple,* we must forge ahead in confidence that God has forgiven us and live in that forgiveness even as we may need to make restitution to someone else or find that we have permanently lost a relationship here on earth.

DAY FOUR

Sins Versus Sinner

Then Nathan said to David, "You are the man!"

2 SAMUEL 12:7

In 2 Samuel 11–12, we read the story of David and Bathsheba. In these two chapters David engages in adultery, deceit, murder and lying. Nathan the prophet is sent by God to bring David to his senses. Nathan tells a little story about a greedy rich man stealing the lone, beloved sheep from a poor man, and David is outraged. At that moment God speaks through Nathan to confront David's sin head-on. Nathan had no guarantee how David would respond. To David's credit, he repented.

Psalm 51 is traditionally credited to David as his response to Nathan's confrontation. I have always been intrigued that in verse 4, David says "Against you [God], you only, have I sinned and done what is evil in your sight." Against God only? What about Uriah, Bathsheba's murdered husband? What about the child he fathered who ultimately died? What about Bathsheba herself, who in that culture would have had little recourse against David's advances? Only God was sinned against?!

I think the answer lies in understanding the difference between confessing a sin and confessing to being a sinner. With a sin, we can rationalize that we made a bad choice or that it was a mistake. As a sinner, we confess that any good we do is because of God's goodness and mercy. This is a very humbling thing to admit. We like to think that we're basically good people and that only through poor judgment or cultural pressures do we make mistakes (commit sins).

When we understand that since the Fall, all people are sinful creatures that God loves and redeems, our perspective changes. Our confession might include thanks that we didn't do something worse, since by nature we are capable of great evil. God is ultimately the one offended because through the willful disobedience of our first parents, our nature is now warped from what God created it to be.

DAY FIVE

Confession Without Guilt

If anyone causes one of these little ones who believe in me to sin, it would be better for him to have a large millstone hung around his neck and to be drowned in the depths of the sea.

MATTHEW 18:6

I know of non-Christian adults who shamed their children into stopping their activities at the local church's youth group. I fear for them when I read this verse. But before I can become too smug in thinking I am not condemned here, I have to ask myself: Where have I increased the guilt load for my children? Where have I shamed them instead of correcting them? Where have I held up past sins in front of them long after the issue was supposedly forgiven and resolved? Have I weakened their relationship with Jesus because of these actions and attitudes? The above verse needs to make us adults stop and think carefully about how we interact with children in general.

When we heap guilt upon others, young and old alike, we reinforce a wrong concept of God, one that might take people years to get over—assuming they even want to remain in relationship with a God they think is condemning. We all have a tremendous responsibility to avoid being a stumbling block to someone else's growing relationship with God. Using guilt to get back at someone who has hurt you is a major stumbling block.

DAY ONE

New Hearts

Create in me a pure heart, O God, and renew a steadfast spirit within me. Do not cast me from your presence or take your Holy Spirit from me. Restore to me the joy of your salvation and grant me a willing spirit, to sustain me.

PSALM 51:10-12

After we acknowledge that we are sinners (see verse 5) who have committed sins (wrong words and actions), we are to ask for a change of heart. We are better able to resist sin if our spirit is renewed to a strong level of steadfastness and if we have the joy of God's salvation restored to us. This is similar to knowing that children who come from strong families are less likely to get into trouble.

I know I sometimes miss out on this total restoration and joy that God offers in confession because I stop with admitting what I did wrong and forget to ask for the creation of a pure heart within me. I know my heart won't be totally pure in this life, but it is a goal worth striving for.

Many of the other spiritual disciplines can help in this area: memorizing Scripture and hymns so that deep wells of truth are in my heart, living a simple life so that I don't fall into sin through all the clutter life throws at me, fasting so that I can see who the false gods of my life really are.

The discipline of confession has two sides to it: admitting sin to God and others, and asking for help in developing a willing spirit with a pure heart. One without the other will lead to an unbalanced understanding of what is happening in this discipline.

DAY TWO

Practicing for the Test

I saw the dead, great and small, standing before the throne, and books were opened. Another book was opened, which is the book of life. The dead were judged according to what they had done as recorded in the books.

REVELATION 20:12

I have friends who are elementary-school teachers. Those who teach third through fifth grades spend a part of each year teaching the children how to take the standardized tests required by the state. The students practice filling in the little bubbles and learn how to discern what is being asked of them in each section of the test.

This is a bit like what the discipline of confession is in relation to the verse above. In confession we admit to things we have done or not done, said or not said, thought or not thought. In some ways this is a preparation for the Day of Judgment, that mysterious, final day when we will all have to give an accounting to God of our lives.

There are other places in the Bible that refer to what we do or don't do as being critically important in the end. For example, Matthew 25:31-45 records the parable of the sheep and goats, in which those who are saved did certain things and those who are condemned did not do these things. One must be careful not to take any of this out of context of the overall gospel of Jesus Christ.

It seems that the more comfortable we are coming to God and others in a spirit of confession and repentance, the better we will be able to face Jesus in hope and trust when we do come face-to-face with him at our death.

Like children going to their first standardized testing session, it will be helpful for us to be familiar with the language and spirit of repentance when we come to Judgment Day.

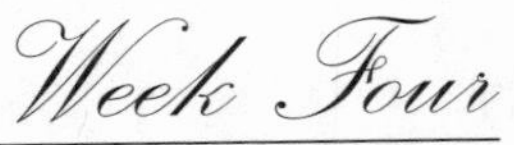

DAY THREE

Insincerity

Then the word of the LORD *Almighty came to me: "Ask all the people of the land and the priests, 'When you fasted and mourned in the fifth and seventh months for the past seventy years, was it really for me that you fasted?'"*

ZECHARIAH 7:4-5

In the movie *The Godfather,* starring Marlon Brando, there is a scene that has always bothered me (that is, it bothers me even above and beyond the general violence of the movie). In the scene, Marlon Brando, who is the fictitious head of a mafia family, is at the baptism of a new grandchild. The scene flips back and forth between the character standing in church as the child's godfather, a wonderful act of faith the family is participating in, and his men out executing people he ordered them to kill. It depicts the height of religious hypocrisy.

In today's verse, God is pointing out the hypocrisy of his chosen people. While they have been fasting and going through the motions of repentance for a long time, they have been denying justice and mercy to others and oppressing the widows, orphans and foreigners in their midst (see verses 9-10).

For those of us in faith traditions where confession is part of the regular Sunday worship service, it too can become hypocritical. The danger is to mindlessly go through corporate confession with the rest of the congregation and think we have it covered. Like Marlon Brando, just because we showed up and recited the words doesn't mean we have engaged in the act of confession. We must use the forms and words to move us into a deeper relationship with God and service to others. If they don't do that, we need to ask God to help us use those words wisely.

True Priorities

Some men came, bringing to him a paralytic, carried by four of them. . . . When Jesus saw their faith, he said to the paralytic, "Son your sins are forgiven. . . . Which is easier: to say to the paralytic, 'Your sins are forgiven,' or to say, 'Get up, take your mat and walk?' But that you may know that the Son of Many has authority on earth to forgive sins . . . " He said to the paralytic, "I tell you, get up, take your mat and go home."

MARK 2:3, 5, 9-11

This story presents a difficult question: is forgiveness for sin more important than physical healing? I've often wondered what the four friends thought. They had carried the man, lifted him up on the roof and then dug a hole through it so they could lower the paralytic down to Jesus. What did they think when Jesus said "Your sins are forgiven"? What did the man himself think?

In the end the man had both his sins forgiven and his body healed, but it does force us to look at what is the higher priority according to Jesus: a relationship with God (since sin is a break in that relationship and forgiveness restores it) versus a sound mind and body. I must admit that if I had been the paralytic or one of his friends, I would have been gravely disappointed in Jesus' first words. These people had come for the healing of a body, but what they got was what the man really needed: healing for sins.

In Psalm 103:2-3, we are told to remember the Lord and forget not his benefits: he forgives all my sins and heals all my diseases. Jesus certainly kept the order given in this psalm when he dealt with the paralytic.

This Bible passage pushes me to look at what is eternal versus what is temporary. My soul will live on; my body will not, no matter how many times it is cured from illness and injury. At some point death will make a mockery of all physical healings. But my soul will be in relationship with God forever. Shouldn't my focus be its healing as well?

The discipline of confession is strong medicine for sick souls. We would do well to use it often.

DAY FIVE

Muddied Waters

You have heard that it was said, "Love your neighbor and hate your enemy." But I tell you: Love your enemies and pray for those who persecute you.

MATTHEW 5:43-44

Apparently neither the Gospel reading nor the Eucharist had much of an impact on me that morning at church. On the way home I was seething about the person who never comes to worship but instead sits out in the narthex and talks the whole time. I had also caught that person sneaking out with something that didn't belong to them and then lying about it.

I was raging inside but struggling to confess to God my sin of anger and a judgmental attitude. Suddenly the Spirit of God spoke to my heart saying, "Pray for this person." I thought, *No way; I'll confess how angry I am and how I am struggling not to judge this person's disruptive, deceitful behavior—but pray for them? That is asking too much, God.*

In typical fashion, the Spirit of God would not let go, so I forced myself to pray for this person. I was still greatly irritated, but I found that my rage dissipated somewhat. I was being asked to take "forgive us our trespasses as we forgive those who trespass against us" out of the abstract and put a face on it.

I don't have a tidy ending to this story. Externally, nothing appears to have changed, but I am better able to let go and trust that God is working in this person's life as well as in mine.

The Discipline of Worship

WHILE OUR WHOLE LIVES are meant to be an act of worship, the discipline of worship deals primarily with the times we gather regularly with our local faith community. As Christians we are called to have a local church and attend it on a regular basis.

Worship is meant to be the highlight of our week, but sometimes it can become a burden in an already full schedule. Too often worship is not the refreshment to our weary souls that it is designed to be. Jesus says, "Come to me, all you who are weary and burdened, and I will give you rest" (Matthew 11:28). Do you associate that verse with coming to weekly worship? Do you find yourself refreshed and rested after worship? Unfortunately, many of us answer no to those questions too many times.

Some of the things that can steal our joy and refreshment in worship are: irritation with someone at church, dislike of the music or style of worship, viewing worship as entertainment and an event we are supposed to get something out of or sheer exhaustion from a too-busy week. In the readings for this discipline, we will begin to address these issues.

Life happens, and we need worship to help us deal with it. Worship is meant to give us hope and a sense of perspective. Worship is meant to give us as a community the chance to praise and thank God as well as mourn for the hard things that happened in the past week. Worship is meant to lift our eyes to the God who made us and loves us unconditionally. Worship is meant to give us language for responding to that God, a language we use not only in worship itself but in everyday life.

The reason worship is considered one of the spiritual disciplines is because many times we don't feel uplifted or joyful when we think of coming to church, so we need to have the discipline of going anyway. God promises that he will be there at that worship service and that he will meet us in the community of our brothers and sisters in Christ to help all of us rise to a new perspective on our lives and the things of this world. The question this discipline asks is, will we be there?

Each week choose one or two suggested activities from the list below to help you practice this discipline:

For Anyone

- Make a commitment to attend church every week. If Sunday morning sporting events and birthday parties have been regular obstacles to going to church, this will take some time to change, but it will ultimately reap rich rewards in your life and your family.
- If your church doesn't sing a wide variety of music, find CDs of other kinds of worship music. If you are used to praise choruses, listen to chant, classical Christian choral music from all ages and a variety of hymns. If you aren't familiar with contemporary Christian praise music, find a CD of that. Use it to praise God for his people in all times and all places.
- Learn prayers and hymns written by other Christians. Get a book from your church's library or look on the Internet for prayers from other cultures and historical times. Use one every night this week at bedtime or mealtime.
- Assess your current faith community using the questions on page 233.
- Which image of Jesus are you more comfortable with: friend or victorious King? Meditate on the other image for the next week.
- Look at your life in its totality. What are areas that are unhealthy? What are areas of great goodness? How do these areas impact your worship?
- Picture God sitting in the pew beside you in church. Does that change the way you feel about being there and your level of participation?
- Lay hands on your checkbook and your calendar. Pray that they may be reflections of the first commandment: "Thou shalt have no other gods before me."
- How do you think you would approach a Sunday morning worship service if you went expecting to be transformed into someone who is com-

plete, finished, healthy? Meditate on that for the next few days, and see how it affects you next time you are in church.

- As a family or with friends, discuss what things are dearest to you. What would it be like to lose those things? Could you still worship God if they were all taken away? Why or why not? Do you know others who have quit coming to church because of a great tragedy in their life that they felt was God's fault? How has that changed their life?
- Are you in worship when the service starts, or are you running around visiting or helping to set up or clean up? If the latter, work to be in worship from beginning to end. Make sure you are not putting service above worship.
- If you had to describe your idea of heaven, what would it be? How does that vision impact what you have to do today? How does it affect your time of corporate worship?

Especially with Children

- Over the next several weeks experiment with what you wear to church. Observe how it affects your worship.
- Encourage children to stand, kneel, pray and otherwise participate in the corporate worship service in the same way adults do. Make it a goal that by early elementary school, they are able to actively participate in all aspects of worship.
- Look at your family's plans for the next weekend. Will you have at least some time where you can focus on worship and keeping the Sabbath holy? If not, can you rearrange the schedule now to make that happen?
- Get a notebook and some colored pencils for your child. Take them to church with you every Sunday. Have your child draw responses to the music, Scripture lessons, sermon, stained-glass windows, etc. Talk about the drawings after church.

Worship Without Ceasing

But you are a chosen people, a royal priesthood, a holy nation, a people belonging to God, that you may declare the praises of him who called you out of darkness into his wonderful light.

1 PETER 2:9 (EMPHASIS ADDED)

Being crowned Miss America must be an exciting experience, but being Miss America must be tedious at times. When the winning contestant is chosen to wear the crown, there are expectations that come with it, such as how she will act, dress and speak, and that she will make all the public appearances the pageant committee sets up for her. She is not chosen just for one moment of glory but for a year-long mission with all of its responsibilities.

So it is for us who have said yes to God's choosing. The choosing is not so that we can gloat or feel we are home free. It is so that we may declare with our words and with our lives the praises of him who called us out of darkness into his wonderful light.

Our very life is to be a form of worship. We are to radiate the light that God has called us into, and that takes a disciplined approach. For example, we cannot wake up on Sunday morning and decide then whether or not we will go to worship. Being regularly in corporate worship is one part of belonging to God's chosen people, his royal priesthood and holy nation.

DAY TWO

Intentional Priorities

Come, let us bow down in worship, let us kneel before the LORD our Maker; for he is our God and we are the people of his pasture, the flock under his care.

PSALM 95:6-7

These verses are a call to corporate worship. When it comes to corporate worship, we are a flock, not individuals. Our individual lives and needs are absorbed into the corporate "we" of that time together.

Corporate worship is what informs our private devotions during the week, not vice versa. When we reverse that statement, we end up with people thinking it is okay to miss Sunday morning worship because they are going to the mountains or the beach or the lake, and they always feel close to God there.

Corporate worship needs to be seen as the high point of the week, the point from which the rest of our lives and activities flow. Therefore, Sunday worship should be viewed as the primary focus of our week, with everything else being made subservient to and informed by that worship time.

In making corporate worship the linchpin of our week, we make a stand against the darkness. It also helps us keep our priorities clear each day and raise a generation of children who understand what the lordship of Christ means in their lives.

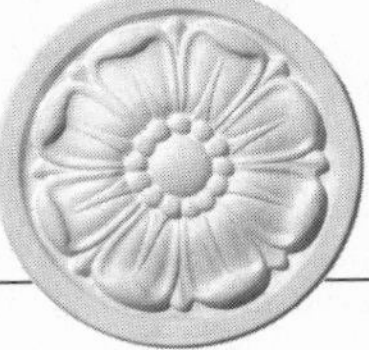

The Church Universal

Sing to him a new song; play skillfully, and shout for joy.

PSALM 33:3

This is a true story: At the end of the Palm Sunday worship service, a disgruntled parishioner came up to the organist and said, "This is the eighth year in a row we have had to sing that unfamiliar hymn."

When I finished laughing at this story, I reflected on how unwilling we can be to learn "a new song" to sing to the Lord. We can get so set in our ways as far as what is or is not "church music," if there should be formal liturgy or not, if there should be silence or singing during Communion, and if there is singing, does the choir or the congregation do it, etc. We can be so busy worshiping worship styles that we forget we are there to worship God.

We need to remember that Jesus is alive today and at work among his people, just as he has been since the Day of Pentecost (see Acts 2). Therefore the music we use in worship needs to reflect the church universal in all places and all times. We need to include old and new hymns, traditional and modern liturgies, chant and ethnic music.

In short, we need to open ourselves up to God at work everywhere and reflect that in our worship.

Small Changes

Also I gave them my Sabbaths as a sign between us, so they would know that I the LORD *made them holy.*

EZEKIEL 20:12

Many people dress more and more casually for Sunday morning worship. They come in jeans or shorts because they like the more relaxed atmosphere this creates. But on the other hand, I once heard someone say that by wearing a suit on Sunday morning, he was witnessing to his neighbors that he was going to church.

I've thought a lot about that comment over the years. When I get somewhat dressed up for church in the casual town I live in, I am aware of the silent witness I am making about where I am going and how I feel about it.

The negative side of this is when people judge others for what they wear to church. To paraphrase Saint Paul's words in 1 Corinthians 8:8, "We are not saved by what we wear or don't wear." However, clothes can often affect our feelings about an event. Maybe we are more open to God when we come casually to worship, like going to a friend's house. Or maybe we take God's Word in our lives more seriously if we dress up, as for an important business meeting.

The question really boils down to this: when we get dressed to go to church, how are we preparing ourselves to go? If God gave us the Sabbath as a sign of holiness, how are we responding to it? It is a question we should not take lightly, but it is also a question each person should answer for themselves.

DAY FIVE

Roots and Wings

You are worthy, our Lord and God, to receive glory and honor and power, for you created all things, and by your will they were created and have their being.

REVELATION 4:11

I like being an American. I value the freedom of religion that so many around the world do not have. However, as a Christian I am not free to worship God as I please. I am bound by the gospel.

It also behooves me to look at how the Holy Spirit has worked throughout the centuries in the church. The hymns, liturgies and prayers that have come down to us since New Testament times and even earlier enrich me with words and music used by Christians in many times and places.

It is important for us who are raising children in the Christian faith that we give them roots and wings. They need to hear the ancient words of the creeds regularly, and they need to hear intercessory prayers for immediate concerns in our individual faith communities. They need to sing liturgical words like those from the verse above to old and new tunes, and they need to sing songs that are newly written. Kids need to know the rhythms of the church year festivals and the unique traditions their own faith communities and families have created.

We as adults should try to wrap children in a rich array of ways to be in relationship with God so they will always have something to hang on to when the way gets rough.

DAY ONE

A Checklist

Let us not give up meeting together, as some are in the habit of doing, but let us encourage one another—and all the more as you see the Day approaching.

HEBREWS 10:25

Here are some questions to ask in order to assess a faith community:

- Is it biblically based and rooted in historical Christianity?
- Is corporate worship the centerpiece around which the rest of the church's life and mission rotate? What is the understanding of baptism and Holy Communion?
- Is the focus during worship on God or the worship leaders?
- Are children included in the whole worship service or dismissed part of the way through?
- Is the music taken from a variety of times and places in Christendom? Is it well led, making it easy for the congregation to sing? Do the people fully participate in worship?
- Is there a focus on outreach and the needs of the community?
- Is there intentional instruction in the faith and discipleship for all ages on Sundays or during the week?
- Is it close enough for you to easily participate in the life of the church during the week?
- Is there an expressed desire for godliness in the leadership and many of the members?
- Is there a place for you to volunteer in ministry?

There may be other questions that are important to you as well. Remember that although churches are not perfect, God uses them to do his work in the world. Therefore you need to enter a faith community prayerfully and carefully. It is also good to periodically assess the community we are in, especially if we have been there a long time.

DAY TWO

A Balance Beam

On the Lord's Day I was in the Spirit, and I heard behind me a loud voice. . . . And among the lampstands was someone "like a son of man." . . . When I saw him, I fell at his feet as though dead.

REVELATION 1:10, 13, 17

The opening chapter of the Revelation to Saint John sets the stage for a book full of wild images and precious promises. Christians have argued forever over what it all means. It is generally agreed, though, that one of the major themes of the book is worship, the main activity in heaven.

It is interesting to note that when John saw the risen Christ, he fell as though dead at his feet. John was one of Jesus' closest earthly friends (see John 13:23), yet he was overwhelmed by Jesus' glory.

In the New Testament, Jesus describes himself as a shepherd (see John 10:11), as a teacher (see John 13:13), as a waiting father (see Luke 15:11-32). These are not frightening images. In the Resurrection, Christ takes our breath away as Lord of the universe. Somehow our worship needs to reflect all of these truths.

If we focus too much on Jesus as our friend, we miss the glory and power that is his. If we focus too much on his glory and power, we miss the ability to see him as a friend. We must always keep a full picture in our mind as we worship, privately and corporately.

DAY THREE

Preparing to Worship

There are six days when you may work, but the seventh day is a Sabbath of rest, a day of sacred assembly. You are not to do any work; wherever you live, it is a Sabbath to the LORD.

LEVITICUS 23:3

The book of Leviticus has never been one of my favorites. For one thing, the endless list of laws seems to have little to do with my life. I mean, really—how many times do I have to worry about sacrificing a bull or a goat in the proper way?

But one day it was pointed out to me that this book is ultimately about worshiping God not only corporately but in the way we live our lives. This book is concerned that we keep a right view of who God is and that God is kept at the center of our worship. It is also concerned that we know who we are as the people of God.

Based on that knowing, there are certain ways God's people are called to act so that they might live well. A good rhythm of rest and activity is part of that living well.

For me, the idea of the Sabbath rest has become a question of *Am I living as well as God hopes I will?* more than a matter of doing no work one day a week. It is an attitude toward life that addresses my physical, spiritual, mental and emotional well-being. It is being grateful for each day, eating well, exercising, responding in love, and other practices that make for a good life. God wants us to live well because, among other things, it will help us worship well.

DAY FOUR

God Is God

Aaron's sons Nadab and Abihu took their censers, put fire in them and added incense; and they offered unauthorized fire before the LORD, contrary to his command. So fire came out from the presence of the LORD and consumed them, and they died before the LORD. Moses then said to Aaron, "This is what the LORD spoke of when he said: 'Among those who approach me I will show myself holy; in the sight of all the people I will be honored.'"

LEVITICUS 10:1-3

When I teach about worship, I often ask the question, if corporate worship were likened to a football game, who represents the players, who represents the cheerleaders and who represents the fans? Many people see God in the role of the players and the congregation in the role of the fans, but that is a false view that can affect the way we worship.

In reality, God is in the stands watching us, the players on the field, worship. We are being cheered on, so to speak, by the worship leaders. When we view ourselves as sitting in the stands watching, we may not be motivated to do our part. We may think we need to sit in the pew and watch while the pastor and the choir worship for us, or worse, entertain us. In truth, God is sitting in the pew watching as we worship. (This analogy is imperfect because God is also there in Word and Sacrament, hosting us in the Eucharist, inviting us closer to him in the Scripture readings; but for now we will focus on the other side of this worship reality.)

The root of the word *liturgy* means "the work of the people." Whether your church follows a historic liturgical form or has created its own worship structure, that liturgy is meant to be done *by* the people, not *for* the people. This concept destroys the notion that worship is to make me feel good. True worship of God may actually make us uncomfortable if we are honest.

DAY FIVE

Bodily Postures

Moses bowed to the ground at once and worshiped.

EXODUS 34:8

I will never forget my first visit to a midweek Lenten service in a Greek Orthodox church. At one point many of the people prostrated themselves on the floor in repentance. I remember one elderly lady in particular, stretched out flat with her face down and her arms out, praying fervently. As a Protestant, this was a new experience for me.

The faith tradition I was raised in incorporates sitting and standing in the worship service. Visiting a Roman Catholic church with friends in high school brought the experience of kneeling into my worship life. Later I experienced the charismatic style of raising hands in praise or prayer. Prostration was yet another posture to add to my worship repertoire.

We can use bodily positions to express inner feelings and to increase our understanding of worship. When we stand for the reading of the Gospel in church, it can symbolize our desire to stand for the Gospel in the world. When we fall on our faces in response to a movement of the Spirit, we are expressing with both body and soul the lordship of Christ.

Bodily movement in worship helps children connect to a worship service long before they can comprehend all of it. They can sit, stand, kneel, raise their hands and even prostrate themselves so that the worship service will touch them physically even if they may not understand much verbally. Worship that engages all of our senses will imprint our souls more deeply.

DAY ONE

Choosing Wisely

For where your treasure is, there your heart will be also.

MATTHEW 6:21

In Christian worship we are called together each week with brothers and sisters in Christ to spend time focusing on who God is, remembering who we are and being empowered to go out into a broken world with a word of grace. Worship is not to be an ivory-tower experience that has nothing to do with reality. True worship is meant to remind us of God's reality, which contradicts the messages the world around us is giving.

For many of us the collection of the offering during a corporate worship service is a time to relax, maybe to listen to the choir or a soloist. In reality the collection of the offering is a symbol of our giving to God our entire being—all that we are and all that we have. This isn't a time where we tip God for the good week we just had or where we help pay the minister's salary. While we may offer only a percentage of what we have been given, it is meant to be the down payment on the wholesale turning of everything, including our very lives, over to God.

We are then invited to go into the week with the attitude that God is Lord of everything, and that everything we do and every purchase we make is to be in line with his heart's desire. We cannot have the attitude that now that church is over, we can get back to our business. If we have truly worshiped, we will be seeking to be about God's business moment by moment in all of our tasks.

DAY TWO

Who Defines Worship?

You must not worship the LORD your God in [the pagans'] way. But you are to seek the place the LORD your God will choose from among all your tribes to put his Name there for his dwelling.

DEUTERONOMY 12:4-5

At a retreat, I went to a workshop called "Places Where We Worship." I like church architecture, so I was looking forward to seeing a variety of buildings and learning about their liturgical appointments and art. Instead the workshop showed a series of mountain vistas and desert sunsets. It was a nature slide show.

While I am in no way saying that God can't be worshipped in nature, I think we need to be a bit careful. Some people use this idea as an excuse to never join a church, to never (or rarely) gather with a local group of Christians for worship. They believe that by going out in nature and fishing or hiking or camping, they are encountering God (perhaps they are to some degree). But the question is, do they let God encounter them? A subtle danger here is that people will define where they will meet God, not letting God define where he would like to be met.

Today's verse seems odd to us New Testament Christians who worship anywhere and everywhere. The Israelites were commanded how and where to worship God. In fact, certain ritual practices, like animal sacrifices, could only be done at the temple in Jerusalem. The synagogues were places of meeting and studying the Torah (the Jewish Scriptures), but it was forbidden to do the sacrifices there that God commanded be done in the temple. This offers us a good reminder that God is God and that any definition of worship comes from him, not us.

This is why worship can be a discipline in ways more than just going to church regularly. It is also a discipline to seek worship practices, forms and rituals that are biblically true and that have been refined in the church by the Holy Spirit throughout the centuries.

It Is a Commandment

Remember the Sabbath day by keeping it holy.

EXODUS 20:8

Sometimes I think we forget that keeping the Sabbath is one of the Ten Commandments. Most of us who claim to follow Christ think we do pretty well with honoring God and not killing or stealing, but somehow we manage to rationalize that keeping the Sabbath was for ancient Israel and not for us New Testament Christians. Nowhere does Jesus say he came to abolish the law. In fact, he clearly states that he came to fulfill it (see Matthew 5:17). So why do we so often think that keeping the Sabbath holy is not relevant for us today?

The spiritual disciplines are not meant to be legalistic, nor are they meant to burden our lives. In fact, they are meant to yoke us more firmly to Christ, who says that our burdens will then be easier (see Matthew 11:30). So the point of this commandment is not to suddenly impose a rule in your family that everyone has to sit in the house and read the Bible all afternoon after church on Sunday. Besides worship, keeping the Sabbath involves doing acts of justice and mercy. It involves resting (or stopping) and remembering that God will take care of the universe even when you are not focused on your work. It means remembering that joy is to be the hallmark of a Christian (see John 15:11).

One way to start returning this commandment to a level of functionality in our lives is to do nothing that interferes with regular corporate worship. So don't do anything on Saturday that will exhaust you so much that on Sunday morning you need to sleep in or are too tired to focus on worshiping God. Plan the rest of your week so that you will have time to go to church instead of needing to catch up on everything you didn't get done Monday through Saturday. Even if you can't keep a whole day set aside for worship and rest, keep what you can of the day for a Sabbath.

Being Perfect

Be perfect, therefore, as your heavenly Father is perfect.

MATTHEW 5:48

Talk about laying a guilt trip on someone! I am supposed to be perfect as God is perfect? Who is Jesus kidding?

But perfect doesn't mean what we tend to think of as perfect in our culture: perfect hair, perfect dress, perfect car. The root word of *perfect* means "complete, finished." In the Sabbath commandment given in Exodus 20:8, the root word for *holy* means "whole," and the root word for *whole* means "healthy." So the ideas encompassed in being perfect and keeping the Sabbath holy mean to act in a way that is whole, complete, healthy. Of course, we know that we won't do any of that perfectly (completely), but that is the goal Jesus invites us to pursue.

All of us have goals, even if they are short-term ones like making it to the end of the workday so you can go home and watch TV. Jesus invites us to make our goals the same as God's goals: becoming people who are finished, complete, healthy. Corporate worship, which is a part of keeping the Sabbath holy, is only part of the picture. It also includes living 24-7 in a complete, healthy, finished way, a way that reflects how Jesus lived his life here on earth.

This is why worship is considered a spiritual discipline. We must worship in such a way that we let God transform us into people who are complete, healthy, finished. This transformation process will not be completed in this life, and yet this life is also not God's waiting room for heaven. This life is meant to make us the people God wants us to be now. We need to hear what that means on a regular basis.

DAY FIVE

Citizens of Two Worlds

At this, Job got up and tore his robe and shaved his head. Then he fell to the ground in worship and said: " . . . The LORD gave and the LORD has taken away; may the name of the LORD be praised."

JOB 1:20-21

Job lost everything, yet he was still able to worship God because he knew that "my Redeemer lives, and that in the end he will stand upon the earth" (19:25). Job grieved the loss of his children and all of his worldly possessions, and he struggled greatly with the question "Why me?" but he never lost sight of God's omnipotence. He asked God hard questions, but he refused to "curse God and die," as his wife suggested (2:9).

I know people who have left the church and even their faith commitment over losses not nearly as severe as Job's. I also know people who have drawn closer to God through suffering. We always have a choice in how we respond to circumstances we may otherwise have no choice over.

One of the hardest things to teach children in this culture is to separate who they are in the kingdom of God from what they have in terms of possessions or relationships. So many messages around us tell us we are not complete without this or that. We need to be intentional in teaching children that who they are and how they respond to life is not dependent on the external circumstances of the moment. All of us need to know the Redeemer who will someday stand upon the earth.

DAY ONE

Defining Worship

When Solomon finished praying [at the dedication of the temple], fire came down from heaven and consumed the burnt offering and the sacrifices, and the glory of the LORD filled the temple. The priests could not enter the temple of the LORD because the glory of the LORD filled it. When all the Israelites saw the fire coming down and the glory of the LORD above the temple, they knelt on the pavement with their faces to the ground, and they worshiped and gave thanks to the LORD, saying, "He is good; his love endures forever."

2 CHRONICLES 7:1-3

I enjoy the classic Judy Garland movie *The Wizard of Oz*. When Dorothy and her companions first encounter the great wizard in the Emerald City with his booming voice and mysterious head floating in the flames, they are in awe and kneel down—or in the case of the Cowardly Lion, shake in fear. They seek to honor the wizard in their language and attitude, letting him know they respect his power and authority even as they are asking for his help in getting Dorothy home again.

When I read the above verses, I am somewhat reminded of that old movie. Can you imagine what it would be like if God descended in the form of fire upon our gifts and offerings sitting on a table in the front of the church? I imagine I would do more than kneel with my face to the ground and recite part of a psalm!

When we come to worship, we are called to acknowledge through words, actions and bodily postures that God is indeed God of the universe, that there is no other god worthy of honor and glory. Worship reminds us that while we have infinite value, we are not the center of the universe.

This is why it is so important that we are regularly involved in corporate worship with a local body of Christians. We need to remind ourselves frequently that our lives, our problems, our accomplishments are to be kept in perspective according to God's desires and commands for his kingdom in the world—not the other way around.

DAY TWO

It's More Than Just Showing Up

Therefore, since we are receiving a kingdom that cannot be shaken, let us be thankful, and so worship God acceptably with reverence and awe, for our God is a consuming fire.

HEBREWS 12:28-29

Next to these two verses in my Bible I wrote, "We treat God like he is a flashlight." That is, instead of realizing that God is a consuming fire, I act as if he is a light to be turned on when I need help and turned off when I'm running fine on my own steam. Obviously, that is not an accurate view.

In light of this I must ask, have I really worshiped on Sunday if I taught Sunday school, skipped the worship service to set up for feeding the homeless afterward and then stayed to help with that lunch?

We must remember that service flows out of worship, not the other way around. Service in place of worship is a subtle form of idolatry. Worship is to be the center of our lives; it is to inform everything we do and say, and acts of service are certainly a part of that.

Does your congregation have people who perform acts of service but who rarely participate in the worship service? Mine does, and they are not a good witness to those who may be struggling to understand who God is. If as a faith community we are okay with people just hanging around the church building on Sunday mornings, helping out where needed or catching up with friends during the worship service, can we really offer a radical message of healing and forgiveness to the people who may have come looking for more than just a community-service group?

Going to church and *worshiping* may be two completely different things. It is important that the latter takes priority over the former.

DAY THREE

Soft Hearts

Therefore, I urge you, . . . in view of God's mercy, to offer your bodies as living sacrifices, holy and pleasing to God—this is your spiritual act of worship.

ROMANS 12:1

Because I work at a downtown church, I see all kinds of people come in to the office and ask for assistance. Some of them I just want to shake and tell them to get a job! Others are mentally ill and are on the streets because there is no place else for them to go. Sometimes it is hard to tell what is really going on.

When I am faithful in worshiping God regularly with others on Sunday morning and in my personal times with God during the week, I tend to be less judgmental toward others. When I remember who I am in relation to God, and that if it weren't for Jesus I would have no hope in this life or the life to come (see 1 Corinthians 15:19), then I am better able to be compassionate toward those who wander in looking for food or money or other kinds of assistance. It is easier for me to remember the adage "There but for the grace of God go I."

Worship is not just a nice little addition to a full life. Worship is meant to be our life. That doesn't mean we stand around singing hymns and praying all day; it does mean we live in a spirit of knowing who we are, who God is and what we are called to do with that knowledge. We are invited to be living sacrifices. We are invited to lay down our agendas and our preconceived notions of how things ought to be and respond with love, honesty and integrity to those people and situations God puts in front of us.

Burnt offerings have an odor. Is the sacrifice of my life to God a pleasing smell (see 2 Corinthians 2:16)?

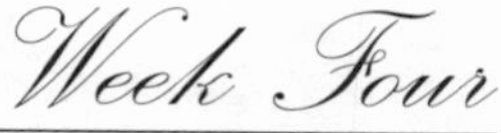

DAY FOUR

Eternal Worship

All the angels were standing around the throne and around the elders and the four living creatures. They fell down on their faces before the throne and worshiped God. . . . Therefore, "they are before the throne of God and serve him day and night in his temple."

REVELATION 7:11, 15

The standard comic-strip view of heaven depicts people standing around on clouds playing harps. The idea of heaven being one continuous church service does not appeal to a lot of people. Yet through the Revelation to Saint John we are given a glimpse of heaven, and worship is a critical part of what God's people will do in eternity, in the new Jerusalem, the city described in Revelation 21 and 22. It is interesting to note that throughout Revelation heaven is described as a city, not a garden. There is a big difference between a city and a garden. How does that description impact your understanding of the next life? How does it impact your understanding of this life?

An expanded view of worship is critical. If we define worship narrowly to mean an hour or so of singing hymns and listening to a sermon, then that would not be an appealing vision of eternity for most of us. But if we define worship as a way of thinking and living, then a lot more can be included in the vision.

Of course, we have very little idea of what heaven will really be like. If you could ask a child in the womb what they think the world outside will be like, I imagine that their idea would be fairly limited at best. And so it is with us. Our view of worship in eternity is limited, not in the least because we have such a limited view of what worship is meant to be here in this life.

All of us worship something and engage in that worship everyday. Whether it is worship of material possessions or health or knowledge or the God of the universe, something defines our use of time and possessions every minute of every day. The biggest choice we have to make in this life is who or what will ultimately get our worship?

DAY FIVE

Planning Ahead

There remains, then, a Sabbath-rest for the people of God; for anyone who enters God's rest also rests from his own work, just as God did from his.

HEBREWS 4:9-10

One of the greatest gifts we can give ourselves is a Sabbath. That may seem like an impossible task, but it is a worthy goal. Our culture is not one of rest. Even our leisure can be exhausting when it becomes competitive or complicated.

We need to be intentional about finding times of rest and rejuvenation. Nature abhors a vacuum, and calendars fit that category as well. We must plan in advance for regular and significant times of restorative play. It should be fun for everyone, and it doesn't need to cost anything, though occasionally spending money on a fun activity can be worthwhile.

When our children still lived at home, my husband and I would sit down with our calendars and plan to set aside certain days: days for family Christmas activities, spring-break activities, weekly "adventure days" in the summer, vacation and travel. Those family days were sacrosanct and were on the main family calendar so everyone knew about them. Even when our children came home from college during breaks, one of the first things we would do was plan out the important family and friend events. With those special times protected on the calendar, less important activities were scheduled as time was available.

My husband is a pastor, but we also made several hours available for family time at some point each weekend. My girls have a very close relationship to their father because he regularly spent time with them. And neither my husband nor I feel burnt out after years in ministry.

The Discipline of Guidance

THE DISCIPLINE OF GUIDANCE has a twofold focus: one is the guidance we seek as individuals and the other is the guidance we seek as a group of Christians in a meeting related to our faith community or other ministry. Both focuses work together.

As individuals, we seek to find what God's will is for our life in small as well as broad ways. As a church or a group within a church, together we seek to hear the voice of God in finding a solution to a problem or a direction to go for ministry, a voice that works through consensus, a voice that says everyone has a gift to contribute to the whole discussion.

There is no such thing as a Lone Ranger Christian. We must be in close association with a group of other Christians to verify that any call we think we are hearing is truly from God as we meditate on and study Scripture and as we seek to serve or live in a way that reflects Christ's values. If we try to do this all on our own, we could end up putting ourselves at risk. History is littered with the ruined lives of people who thought they heard a word from God, but with no accountability to a biblically sound faith community, they went off in a strange direction.

Honest accountability will also engage us fully in the discipline of submission, which teaches humility, because we may think we have a brilliant idea until we share it with other mature Christians who show us its fallacies. That can be very humbling.

Most of the other disciplines will also come into play as we seek God's will for a major decision in our life. Probably more than any other discipline, the discipline of guidance requires an honest engagement with many of the other disciplines, like fasting, confession, worship, prayer, meditation and solitude, to be sure that we hear correctly. And if we are walking in faith with someone else who is trying to make a decision, we too will need to use the other disciplines to be worthwhile partners in that person's discernment process.

As with all the disciplines, learn to practice this one through small, faithful steps. Begin by letting go of the idea that you are the only one who hears God's voice correctly. Submit yourself to an accountability group as you learn to go deeper in your walk with God. Then rejoice; God will guide you in the paths of righteousness for his name's sake (see Psalm 23:3).

Each week choose one or two suggested activities from the list below to help you practice this discipline:

For Anyone

- Think about a decision you are facing, such as a job change or the possibility of a surgery. What will be the impact of your decision on friends or members of your family? Process your decision within that smaller community.
- When praying for guidance in a situation, pray also for a willingness to follow and obey.
- When praying for discernment about an issue, pray for the ability to further the coming of God's kingdom here on earth in whatever direction you eventually choose.
- What can you do to make better small decisions each day? These may include better diet and exercise choices or more discipline in the area of your finances or use of time. Find an accountability partner to help you make those better choices.
- As you work on discerning between the best choices each day, ask yourself these questions as part of the decision process: Is the choice against God's commandments or against an accepted understanding of Scripture as taught historically by the church? Will the choice make life difficult for someone else, or will it cause someone else to turn against Christ? Should you still make that choice, trusting that God will deal with other person's struggles?
- How does a group that you are involved in (such as a book group, Bible study or church committee) come to consensus? Which of the spiritual

disciplines can you use in that process so feelings aren't hurt and everyone has an equal voice in the decision making?

- Think of a decision you are currently facing. Write down all that you can see of God's hand moving in your life up to this point. Does that past movement seem to point in one direction or another for the future?
- Get rid of any games or books you have that help you "tell the future." Even if they are meant for fun, they can lead you into the dangerous waters of idolatry, which is putting something other than God first in your life.
- Ask God for wisdom in a situation you will face today; then, believing God has given it to you, move confidently into that situation.

Especially with Children

- Teach children to listen to the "little voice" in the back of their minds but to process what it says with others. This can be a critical skill, such as when they visit a friend, and suddenly something doesn't feel right. If they know how to listen to that inner voice and share those concerns with an adult, a lot of grief could be avoided.
- In a group setting, such as at the dinner table, have everyone share some of the things they dreamed of doing as a child or still dream of doing someday. Ask any children what they think about doing when they get older; ask how you might help them achieve that goal.
- Let children plan a fun activity for the family or for a group of friends. Set parameters in terms of cost, length of time and distance from home. Talk about the plan, asking questions and discussing choices, to help them learn how decisions are made in community.
- Are you aware of inconsistencies in your Christian walk that your children might see? For example, do they have to go to Sunday school while you go to the grocery store or the golf course? Work to become consistent in your words and actions. Talk with them about being consistent in their own words and actions.

DAY ONE

We Belong to a Group

Then Moses and Aaron fell facedown in front of the whole Israelite assembly gathered there. Joshua son of Nun and Caleb son of Jephunneh, who were among those who had explored the land, tore their clothes and said to the entire Israelite assembly, "The land we passed through and explored is exceedingly good. If the LORD *is pleased with us, he will lead us into that land."*

NUMBERS 14:5-8

While God deals with us as individuals, he deals with us as individuals who live in community. Our actions are not isolated events done in a vacuum but rather are part of a bigger, interrelated picture. Therefore when there is a decision to be made, it's best done in some form of Christian community.

Caleb and Joshua, who had participated in spying out the Promised Land, wanted to move forward in faith, but the rest of the community held back in fear. God rewarded the trust of Caleb and Joshua by allowing them to eventually enter the land, the only two adults to do so out of that entire generation who had come out of Egypt.

It is interesting to note that Joshua and Caleb stayed with the community, suffering the consequences of forty years of wandering. They knew God was dealing with the Israelites as a nation as well as individuals. How many of us would have headed into the land on our own? Or found another group of people to associate with?

As Americans we love rugged individuality in movies and novels, but as Christians we are always called to community. We need to hear God's Word with others so it doesn't get skewed in our lives.

DAY TWO

Be Bold

In his heart a man plans his course, but the LORD determines his steps.

PROVERBS 16:9

We were all set to leave on vacation. The suitcases were packed and in the car. Arrangements were made for the cat, the mail and the plants to be cared for. Unexpectedly, however, the car would not start. Disappointed, we got out, unloaded it and watched as it was towed off to the mechanic. The problem was fairly minor, and we were assured that we would have the car back to leave by noon the next day.

The next morning in our mail was a returned envelope containing a missionary support check. Apparently there was a problem with the address. So I fixed it and remailed it right before we left for the trip.

I am convinced that our car had problems so that we would be home to get that check and send it back on its way. The missionary family must have needed it to come during the time period we were to be gone, not weeks later. Our trip was wonderful, and we did not have a bit of car trouble.

I take comfort from that story in knowing that I can proceed with plans, trusting God will change them as needed. If I am truly seeking God daily, I need never be afraid of moving forward in something. God will let me know, if I keep listening, what changes need to be made to my intended plan of action.

DAY THREE

Who Defines Whom?

Delight yourself in the LORD and he will give you the desires of your heart.

PSALM 37:4

Jesus also said something similar to this verse: "Seek first [God's] kingdom and his righteousness, and all these things will be given to you as well" (Matthew 6:33).

When I was in eighth grade I had a profound experience of wanting to follow God always and wholeheartedly. Over the last forty years, God has been showing me more of what that desire entails. For example, it did not involve being a part of the popular crowd in junior high and high school, but it did mean marrying a wonderful man I met in college. It has not involved having a lot of money or living a magazine-defined lifestyle, but it has meant wonderful children, good work, timely provisions and interesting travel. It has not meant the healing of all my struggles, but it has meant close friends, a good church and a good doctor. I am always amazed that when I give God a fraction of an inch of willingness to follow, God gives me miles of goodness and grace.

When we talk about guidance, we must remember that we are not the center of the universe. Ultimately our wants are not top priority. While God cares for us and provides for us, we are called to be a part of God's kingdom, fulfilling the role he created us to fill. God is not a part of our lives; we are a part of God's. But in being a part of God's life, we will be richly blessed and well cared for.

There Is a Due Date

Teach us to number our days aright, that we may gain a heart of wisdom.

PSALM 90:12

Within the last two years I have known three men in their forties who have dropped dead of heart attacks. Two of them were in very good physical condition. Part of the discipline of guidance is an awareness that we don't have tomorrow; all we have is today.

Too often we waste time agonizing over a job or school choice but spend no time thinking about how the myriads of little decisions we make every day regarding food and health issues, Bible study, prayer times and relationships are impacting us and others in significant ways. We forget that the smaller choices of each day are the critical ones when added up over a lifetime. One bad choice may not ruin us, but a lifetime of them will. Like payments on a loan, we will eventually have to ante up for all the small choices we assumed we could worry about later.

There are many ways Christians can remind themselves daily of death: an open grave in the monastery graveyard or viewing nighttime sleep as a mini death experience (see page 143). These ideas are not meant to be macabre (though some will find them creepy to think about and should not feel compelled to make them a point of meditation), but facing the issue of death regularly and realistically is meant to keep us grounded in the reality that none of us know when we will see Jesus face-to-face.

DAY FIVE

Intentional Behavior

If anyone causes one of these little ones who believe in me to sin, it would be better for him to be thrown into the sea with a large millstone tied around his neck.

MARK 9:42

When we talk about the discipline of guidance, we often think of making decisions for ourselves as adults. We also must keep guidance in mind as it relates to children. In the long run what we *do* as parents or teachers is more critical than what we *say.*

Children are great observers but poor interpreters. That is why we must guide them clearly when they are young while still giving them lots of room for exploration on their own. For example, if we forego intentional instruction in the Christian faith, letting them make their own decisions with no guidance from us and other mature Christians who are also modeling following Jesus intentionally, it is like sending them to sea in a boat with no oars.

Years ago I read an article about a mother who was careful not to let her children have sugary snacks. However, she kept a stash of them hidden for herself in the pantry. The article described the outcry of her children when one of them discovered her stash and ultimately her hypocrisy.

Adults must do everything in their power not to cause children to fall away because of a lack of integrity in their own behavior.

DAY ONE

Following the Call

In the past God spoke to our forefathers through the prophets at many times and in various ways, but in these last days he has spoken to us by his Son.

HEBREWS 1:1-2

When we helped our girls look at college choices, we took into account who they were as people. We also looked at how God had been leading them through their interests and talents. As we looked back over their growing-up years, we could see God opening doors in some areas and closing them in others. We used those signs to help them determine what seemed like the best next step.

God draws a continuous line through our lives, though at times we may not see that line. God seeks to bring out gifts and soften rough edges in many and various ways. God gives us desires and a personality that is unique, and he designs opportunities for those desires and that temperament to be useful to others for Christ's sake.

When we are trying to decide which way to go next, we can safely step forward on the continuous line of where we have been. It may be a giant next step or it may be a baby step, but it will be a step in the direction God has been leading us all along.

DAY TWO

A Willingness to Act

By day the LORD went ahead of them in a pillar of cloud to guide them on their way and by night in a pillar of fire to give them light, so that they could travel by day or night.

EXODUS 13:21

How wonderful that kind of guidance must have been! The Israelites didn't have to worry about a thing. Not only did they not move unless the pillar of cloud did (see Numbers 9:19-23), but the cloud—God himself—protected them from their enemies (see Exodus 14:19-20). What an easy time of it the Israelites had, never having to wonder what to do next. They camped when the Lord stopped, and they moved on when the Lord moved on.

But one major element was missing: thankful obedience. Even though the Israelites had this clear guidance and the promise of a new home, they were constantly carping and complaining. Numbers 21:4-9 tells of one particularly harsh time of griping and the Lord's response to it. The people had forgotten that if they wanted the Lord to be their shield and guide, they would have to trust and obey his guidance. Unfortunately, they couldn't get past fretting over their next meal.

Our call to obedience is no different from ancient Israel's call to obedience. If we are seeking God's guidance, then we must obey that guidance. We must ask for direction with a teachable heart and a willing spirit. We must, like Israel was called to do, be willing to follow where God shows us, even if it seems like a wilderness experience on the way.

Did I Get It Right?

For this God is our God for ever and ever; he will be our guide even to the end.

PSALM 48:14

We all know Christians who are forever questioning whether or not they are doing God's will. One way to look at it is this: if you are someplace doing something, then it is in some way God's will. Otherwise you would be somewhere else doing something different. We are called to thank God for where we are and what we are doing, trusting that he will move us to a different spot if necessary.

Another way to discern if you are doing God's will is to ask yourself two questions: Do you like what you are doing? Does the world benefit from what you are doing? If your answer to both of those questions is no, then you need to go through a process of discernment for change.* For example, if you love teaching but are currently in an inner-city school where you feel afraid, then the answer to question two is yes but the answer to question one is no. If you like your job as a designer but it involves creating provocative clothing for young women, then the answer to question two is no.

God's will involves our joyful service to others. If either component of joy or service is missing, then something needs to change. Otherwise, relax; you are where you are supposed to be for now.

*Adapted from Frederick Buechner, *Wishful Thinking: A Seeker's ABC* (San Francisco: HarperSanFrancisco, 1993), pp. 118-19.

DAY FOUR

Pray, Then Act

Therefore everyone who hears these words of mine and puts them into practice is like a wise man who built his house on the rock.

MATTHEW 7:24

A woman who was struggling with a situation came to me for advice. At first glance it seemed she was caught in a cross fire of opinions and options covering all sides of the issue. As we talked, though, it became apparent what the real problem was. She knew what God wanted her to do, but didn't really want to do it. She kept seeking advice from others, hoping she would be able to avoid doing what needed to be done by hiding behind "seeking God's will and guidance."

At that point I had to withdraw myself from the conversation. I could not in good conscience continue to help her avoid the necessary obedience by allowing her to hash out supposed choices with me. My calling was to tell her to do what she knew she was supposed to and stop avoiding her call.

Children often do this. They seek to have a discussion about the finer points of a homework assignment or chore. Sometimes I thought my girls really were trying to understand something deeper until I realized at some point in the discussion that they were simply seeking a way out of whatever needed to be done.

Jesus ends the Sermon on the Mount (Matthew 5–7) with a warning that wisdom means obeying his teachings. Many Christians try to argue the cultural or historical issues of why a certain teaching no longer applies. Jesus says in the verses following our verse for today that these avoidance attempts won't withstand the storms of life.

DAY FIVE

Nudges

Make plans by seeking advice.

PROVERBS 20:18

I don't mind driving in snow, so when snow is in the forecast, I generally stick to my planned schedule for the day.

One day in early spring the forecast called for a huge storm. Everyone was talking about it. At first I didn't think much of it. I had planned to do errands and grocery shopping the next day, but suddenly I had a strong urge to go that day. I talked it over with my husband, and we worked out sharing the car that morning so that I could follow my hunch.

That afternoon the rain started, and by the next day we had the beginnings of a snowstorm that was the worst in ninety years. The entire area was shut down for three days. I was glad that I had listened to the nudging voice and had discussed it with my husband. We snuggled in for three days, well stocked, able to enjoy the beauty of the storm.

The discipline of guidance must always be viewed from a corporate perspective. My intuition meant we had plenty of food to last through the storm, but it had also impacted my husband's plans because of my unexpected desire to use the car. Even so, my vague sense of things isn't always as accurate as it was that time.

DAY ONE

A Peaceful Heart

Where you have envy and selfish ambition, there you find disorder and every evil practice. But the wisdom that comes from heaven is first of all pure; then peace loving, considerate, submissive, full of mercy and good fruit, impartial and sincere.

JAMES 3:16-17

I was the leader of a small musical ensemble, but I often sought input from others. It was a benevolent dictatorship, I always joked. One Sunday morning we were warming up to play in church. One member, who had been trying to sow seeds of dissension in the group for several weeks, challenged the entire way the piece was being done and my ability to lead it. All the pent-up frustrations toward this person came out, and suddenly the group was in a fight, complete with screaming and yelling. The choir, who was assembling for a warm-up nearby, witnessed this ugly scene, a living example of the first part of today's passage. Needless to say, we did not play very well during the service.

I'm sure all of us have a story that exemplifies these verses. Fortunately, other spiritual disciplines can help overcome envy and selfish ambition in practicing the discipline of guidance within a group. The disciplines of meditation, prayer, fasting and study can help each member of a group listen for God's voice. The disciplines of submission, solitude and service can help each person let go of a driving need to have the situation go the way they think it needs to. The discipline of confession can be used when pride and egos rear their ugly heads. It is difficult, though, when members of the group are not willing to practice these disciplines.

The disgruntled member in the musical ensemble ended up leaving the group. While it left us short on covering the parts, the spirit in the ensemble changed dramatically. Rehearsals went back to being peace loving, considerate, full of mercy and good music.

DAY TWO

Looking Backward and Forward

When you have entered the land the LORD your God is giving you as an inheritance and have taken possession of it and settled in it, take some of the firstfruits. . . . Then go to the place the LORD your God will choose as a dwelling for his Name. . . . The priest shall take the basket from your hands and . . . you shall declare before the LORD . . . : "My father was a wandering Aramean, and he went down into Egypt with a few people and lived there and became a great nation, powerful and numerous."

DEUTERONOMY 26:1-2, 4-5

God was instructing the people coming to worship him in the temple of Jerusalem with the firstfruits of their harvests that they were to stand and recite the history of God's delivering their ancestors from Egypt. Through that recitation they were connecting themselves with that history, ending with these words: "and now I bring the firstfruits of the soil that you, O LORD, have given me" (Deuteronomy 26:10). The command here was to rejoice in the present while remembering the past works of God in the lives of their ancestors.

When we look at our lives and wonder how best to proceed in the future, we can begin our process of discernment by remembering the way God has worked in the past, not only with us but with his people throughout history.

As we seek guidance regarding a new job, school opportunity, marriage or anything else, we are invited to remember that we have a history of goodness from God's hand. In remembering that goodness, we can begin to look for the continuation of God's goodness in the next opportunity or decision.

This is a place where the discipline of worship and the discipline of guidance intersect. When we are reminded in weekly worship of God's work among humanity in all times and all places, we can be confident of God's guidance in the decisions of our daily lives, knowing that he is always calling us forward into a greater harvest of the fruits of the Spirit (see Galatians 5:22-23).

DAY THREE

Plugged Ears

Then you will call, and the LORD will answer; you will cry for help, and he will say: Here am I. If you do away . . . with the pointing finger and malicious talk, and if you spend yourselves in behalf of the hungry and satisfy the needs of the oppressed . . . the LORD will guide you always; he will satisfy your needs in a sun-scorched land.

ISAIAH 58:9-11

This passage is part of a section in which the Lord is pointing out that the spiritual disciplines are meant to be an internal reality and to have an outward manifestation. For example, a few verses earlier we read, "Your fasting ends in quarreling and strife, and in striking each other with wicked fists. You cannot fast as you do today and expect your voice to be heard on high" (Isaiah 58:4).

We must be very careful that we don't develop a theology of causality (something bad happens to you because you did something bad; see Jesus' words against this kind of thinking in Luke 13:1-5). But if we are not getting a sense of guidance from God in an issue, we can still ask ourselves if there is some obvious disobedience we need to clear up in our life.

For example, if we are seeking guidance about our future yet we are cheating on our income taxes, we must repent of the stealing before we can hope to hear God clearly about other issues. Or sometimes we get an answer but we don't like it or it isn't the answer we wanted, so we keep asking and then get frustrated that God is not responding to our plea for help.

God is full of grace and mercy and works in our lives in spite of ourselves. But if we are truly seeking God's face about an issue and feel we are not getting an answer, it behooves us to ask God if there is something else getting in the way of our hearing where God is calling us next.

DAY FOUR

Prayer and Action

Devote yourselves to prayer, being watchful and thankful.

COLOSSIANS 4:2

We parked at one of our favorite trailheads in Rocky Mountain National Park. There was a new sign telling about the flora and fauna we could expect to see, as well as giving precautionary hiking tips. In bold letters at the bottom of the sign were these words: *The mountains don't care!* Even though we are seasoned hikers, we caught our breath. What a stark warning for ill-prepared hikers, one to remember when a lightning storm comes up and you are above the tree line or a rain storm comes through as snow at the higher elevations and you are in shorts. We had read enough tragic stories of people injured and killed over the years to know how serious this warning was.

Today's verse tells us to devote ourselves to prayer. In addition, we are to pay attention (be watchful) and be thankful. We are invited to talk to God about our needs, our choices and the decisions that have to be made, but we are also to look around us, learn all we can about those choices and decisions, and prepare ourselves to recognize the answer God sends our way.

To go hiking in the Rocky Mountains in the summer with no water, no extra food or rain gear and no understanding of the terrain and weather patterns, and then expect prayer to protect you, is a serious misuse of faith in God. We are to trust our walk to God, have a backpack with survival materials and then be thankful for the glorious creation around us. Living our daily lives should be approached in the same way.

Different Plants

For you created my inmost being; you knit me together in my mother's womb.

PSALM 139:13

I heard a story about a man who planted some broccoli. One plant simply did not do well, so he fussed and fussed over it: he gave it lots of water and fertilizer, then tried less water and fertilizer. Still it was nothing but a stick with curled and wrinkled leaves, so finally he just ignored it. When it was time to harvest the broccoli, the man discovered that one plant was a stalk of Brussels sprouts! He had done all he could to take care of a broccoli plant when in reality he had a Brussels sprouts stalk mixed in with the flat of broccoli plants he had bought.

Sometimes we do this with children. In our concern to guide them well through life, we may inadvertently try to make a Brussels sprouts into a broccoli plant. We think they should look like we think they should look, and we fuss over them or yell at them or end up ignoring them because we are trying to grow broccoli. But in reality God created this child to be a Brussels sprouts plant. Both broccoli and Brussels sprouts are good, but they aren't interchangeable in most recipes, and they don't require the same type of care.

While the analogy only goes so far, the basic point is an important one: our job as adults is to guide children into the path God has created them to walk, even if it goes a direction we would not want it to.

At various stages of their development, I've encouraged one or the other of my daughters to be a bike racer, a firefighter, an Iditarod racer and a bush pilot. Along the way I've had to swallow hard more than once while trying to smile as a bright face looks up at me and says, "Mom, wouldn't it be cool to do that?" The good news is that God has gifted our children in ways he hasn't gifted us, and God is most definitely smiling.

DAY ONE

Modern Heresies

When Saul saw the Philistine army, he was afraid; terror filled his heart. He inquired of the LORD, but the LORD did not answer him by dreams or . . . prophets. Saul then said to his attendants, "Find me a woman who is a medium, so I may go and inquire of her."
"There is one in Endor," they said.

1 SAMUEL 28:5-7

God will not be mocked. Saul, who had lost favor with God because of direct disobedience, was unable to hear God's voice regarding his future in the upcoming battle. (See 1 Samuel 15, complete with a classic rationalization for Saul's disobedience.) But instead of waiting for God's timing, Saul went to a medium to see if he could force a word from God. Saul himself had expelled the mediums and spiritists from the land (see 1 Samuel 28:3) at God's command; therefore Saul again deliberately disobeyed God by seeking out someone God had told him to rid the land of. The answer Saul got from the spirit the woman conjured up caused him to faint with fear (verses 16-20); it did not bring him peace, as a word from the Lord would have done.

In today's culture there are plenty of ungodly ways of seeking answers to questions. Tarot cards, Ouija boards, horoscopes, palm readers and other seemingly harmless games can be toeholds into our souls for the forces of darkness. Many people think this is overreacting—"I just do this for fun," they say. But they don't realize that any time we seek guidance from someone not in the service of the God of the universe, we are playing with fire. Children are especially vulnerable because they are not always able to clearly discern what is pretend and what is real.

The discipline of guidance must be practiced within a strong faith community. When we need answers, we also need our brothers and sisters in Christ around us to make sure we are hearing God's voice, that we are waiting prayerfully for that voice and not trying to jump-start a word from God. God knows our motivations and our heart's desires, and he will not be fooled by our subtle attempts to seek direction from sources other than him.

DAY TWO

God Will Provide

"Ah, sovereign LORD," [Jeremiah] said, "I do not know how to speak; I am only a child." But the LORD said to me, ". . . You must go to everyone I send you to and say whatever I command you."

JEREMIAH 1:6-7

I have had enough experience with this to know it's true: if I ask God how to respond in a situation, I will be given the words when I need them, often without having any idea of what what I am going to say until I say it.

For example, I had a difficult situation I needed to confront. I had to tell someone that it was not working for him to be in a particular group. Yet it was due to a chronic physical condition that he was not able to do the work. I prayed about it and talked with another trusted Christian. I thought about the options I could offer and the phrases I could use (or should not use). Unexpectedly a window of opportunity opened up for me to talk to this person privately. So I plunged in. In the mercies of God, the conversation went well and a good resolution was found, one that left his dignity intact and also led to the possibility of the group moving forward well.

I realized later that while it was my voice, the words spoken were God's. I never could have scripted that conversation on my own. By plunging in and trusting the Holy Spirit to work, I simply became a conduit for God to speak and respond to this person. All I could do was give thanks when it was over.

Many times we are in situations where we need to speak a word that frightens us. Certainly that was the case for the prophet Jeremiah. Yet we have the Holy Spirit with us, giving us words from God that could bring truth and healing to situations that desperately need it.

DAY THREE

Solid Footing in the Storm

If any of you lacks wisdom, he should ask God, who gives generously to all without finding fault, and it will be given to him. But when he asks, he must believe and not doubt, because he who doubts is like a wave of the sea, blown and tossed by the wind.

JAMES 1:5-6

At some point we have to move out in faith. That sounds like an obvious statement, but I know I can get myself all wrapped up around the axle, wondering if I really heard God, if I really know what I should do and how it should be done, etc., etc., etc.

Peter discovered this when he asked Jesus to let him walk on the water (see Matthew 14:22-32). Peter wanted guidance to know if the "ghost" the disciples saw walking toward them over the water was really Jesus. The test—"Lord, if it's you . . ."—was whether Peter could also walk on the water. And he did until he realized what he was doing, freaked out and started to drown. Jesus had to reach out to him and pull him back into the boat.

How many times have I moved out in faith in something God was calling me to do only to look at the wind and waves of the situation, panic, start to drown and have to have God drag me, dripping wet and frightened, back into the safety of the boat? Today's verse reminds me that God will generously give me wisdom when I ask, but then my job is to take hold of that wisdom and walk with it in faith.

DAY FOUR

A Trial

Daniel resolved not to defile himself with the royal food and wine, and he asked the chief official for permission not to defile himself this way. . . . The official told Daniel, "I am afraid of my lord the king, who has assigned your food and drink. Why should he see you looking worse than the other young men your age? The king would then have my head because of you." Daniel then said to the guard whom the chief official had appointed over Daniel . . . , "Please test your servants for ten days: Give us nothing but vegetables to eat and water to drink. Then compare our appearance with that of the young men who eat the royal food, and treat your servants in accordance with what you see." . . . At the end of the ten days they looked healthier and better nourished than any of the young men who ate the royal food.

DANIEL 1:8, 10-13, 15

In this passage, Daniel, a captive from the land of Israel, was trying to maintain the integrity of his faith in a foreign culture. He and several other young men were handpicked to eat well, live well and become well educated (see verses 3-5). Daniel and those employed by the king to train these young men could have been killed if a deviation from the king's orders had resulted in failure. Daniel's request to not defile himself was risky and had to be made in consultation with those it would impact if it failed. Choosing death for yourself is one thing; choosing it for others is another.

The thing Daniel knew and that we are invited to know as well is that when we are sincerely seeking God's face and living according to his commands, we can trust God to take care of us. In being faithful, in offering a test that seemed to Daniel to be in keeping with God's commands, Daniel was letting God work out the end result. And God did. Daniel came through with flying colors. In fact, he did better than those who ate the royal food.

When we are seeking guidance in a situation where we are motivated to seek God's kingdom first in our lives, God will overcome the obstacles, which may include other people who will be affected by our choice.

DAY FIVE

Moving Forward

Paul and his companions traveled throughout the region of Phrygia and Galatia, having been kept by the Holy Spirit from preaching the word in the province of Asia. When they came to the border of Mysia, they tried to enter Bithynia, but the Spirit of Jesus would not allow them to. So they passed by Mysia and went down to Troas. During the night Paul had a vision of a man of Macedonia standing and begging him, "Come over to Macedonia and help us." After Paul had seen the vision, we got ready at once to leave for Macedonia, concluding that God had called us to preach the gospel to them.

ACTS 16:6-10

Thus began one of Paul's greatest missionary journeys. There are three points from these verses that can help us when it comes to seeking a new direction in our lives:

1. Paul kept moving in the direction he thought he should go, only stopping when the Spirit prevented him from going further. We need to learn confidence in moving forward in our lives, trusting that God will open and shut the right doors for us.

2. Paul functioned in community. He didn't get a vision and then run off on his own. Notice that it says, "We...[concluded] that God had called us." We need to learn that when we feel God is moving us, especially in an entirely new direction, we should seek godly, wise counsel so we don't end up out in left field somewhere.

3. After Paul and his companions concluded that God had called them to Macedonia, they went. We need to learn to act in a timely manner to obey the call of God in our lives.

It is important that children learn good decision-making skills from an early age so that they can be effective workers in God's kingdom, like Paul and his companions were. It is a good lesson for adults too.

The Discipline of Celebration

CALLING CELEBRATION A DISCIPLINE seems contradictory to many of us, especially if we are still struggling to overcome the negative associations the word *discipline* has picked up in our culture. Doesn't life have enough structure imposed upon it already without turning fun into a discipline?

If we view the spiritual disciplines as burdens or legalism, then the above concern is a valid one. However, if we understand that the words *discipline* and *disciple* have the same root, then we can view the discipline of celebration as a way of becoming a better disciple of Jesus Christ.

Simply put, this discipline teaches us to look at life from the perspective of the final chapters of the book of Revelation, where we get a foretaste of the end of civilization as we know it. Even when things seem hopeless, we can have within us a deep well of joy and say, "But I know how this all will end." This takes discipline to do on many days and in many circumstances.

This is not a Pollyannaish view of the world that is optimistic for the sake of optimism. This is not whistling in the dark, hoping the boogeyman won't be behind the next tree. This is walking in triumph because Jesus, the risen Christ, has walked this way before. This is having a deep confidence in God's goodness and the working out of that goodness in human history. This is knowing that while there are still battles to be fought, the war is over. This is being filled with joy and hope even while grieving the death of a loved one or the death of a dream.

But like all hand-dug wells, it will take time to access this deep aquifer of joy in our souls. We may have to chip through rocks of bitterness, resentment or anger to get down to the living waters that God promises are available to us. This is why the discipline of celebration needs to infuse our learning and practice of all the other disciplines. If the discipline of worship is the hub of the wheel and the other disciplines are the spokes, then the discipline of celebration is the round part of the wheel that surrounds everything, holding it all together.

Joy is to be the hallmark of a Christian. If that does not describe you, then this discipline can help you get down to those springs of joy that are meant to flow through us to refresh a tired and thirsty world.

Each week choose one or two suggested activities from the list below to help you practice this discipline.

For Anyone

- Choose happiness today. If that is not possible for you, find a spiritual mentor or counselor who can help you discover what is the little bit of yeast of malice or wickedness in your soul that is spoiling the whole batch of good dough (see 1 Corinthians 5:6-8).
- Organize a potluck for your small group or church to celebrate God's goodness in your lives as individuals and as a community.
- Do something to immerse yourself in creation, such as a long walk in nature. Try to imagine what it would have been like in the Garden of Eden. How does it still reflect some of God's creative goodness?
- Whenever you are processing a hard situation, acknowledge the difficulty of it, but also find a way to acknowledge the greatness of God over all.
- If you have a particularly unpleasant chore that must be done, find an uplifting piece of music that you can play and even sing along with while doing the task.
- Start planning now for next Christmas. Write down some notes to yourself on how you can make your family's celebration less connected to the commercial events that have come to surround this church holiday. Plan now how to introduce those changes.
- Reflect on Deuteronomy 28:47-48: "Because you did not serve the LORD your God joyfully and gladly in the time of prosperity, therefore in hunger and thirst, in nakedness and dire poverty, you will serve the enemies the LORD sends against you." Do the people you spend the most time

with help you serve God in joy and gladness? If not, can you find people who do?

- Write down all the complaints you make in one day. Then write down things that happened in the same day that you could give thanks for. Which list is longer? Take the complaints and look for different ways to think about them.
- Memorize the twenty-third Psalm if you don't already know it. Use it as a bold statement of victory whenever you become worried or discouraged today.
- Have you have ever wanted to dance spontaneously for joy before the Lord? What did you do with that feeling? Spend some time meditating on 2 Samuel 6:12-23.
- What would it be like to play a game such as tennis or bridge or basketball with no rules? It would eventually become unsettling; you wouldn't know what to do next. Think of an area in your life where you are trying to play with no rules, such as in overeating, excessive alcohol consumption or credit-card debt. Find one small step you can take to move yourself back to playing by the rules.
- Be intentional about encouraging everyone you can today. Even if someone is in a difficult place in their life and is not exactly fun to be around, find a way to say or do something that will encourage them to try to find their footing again.

Especially with Children

- Plan and prepare a small surprise for someone who needs a lift. Bake some cookies for an elderly neighbor, make an activity basket for a sick child, bring a homemade card to a person new to your community or church. While you are putting the surprise together, pray for that person.
- In a special notebook, write down the dreams your children have: what they would like to do and what kind of people they would like to be when they grow up. Look at it with them every year, maybe as part of their birthday celebration, adjusting the list as the years go by.
- Hold your children in your lap for as long as you can today. If they are too big to sit in your lap, sit next to them on the couch with your arm

around them. Tell them how much you love them and how proud you are of them. Imagine Jesus holding you while you are holding them.

- Buy some finger paints and a roll of newsprint. Spend some time doing finger paintings. Hang up the artwork to remind you of what it means to simply have fun.

DAY ONE

Celebration Is a Discipline?

O LORD, how many are my foes! How many rise up against me! Many are saying of me, "God will not deliver him." . . . I lie down and sleep; I wake again because the LORD sustains me.

PSALM 3:1-2, 5

The discipline of celebration cultivates the belief that no matter what happens in our lives, God has the final word, and it will be good. This discipline does not gloss over bad things or pretend that everything is fine. It looks evil square in the face and calls it what it is. But it goes one step further, as the psalmist does in the verses above: it allows us to rest in God's sustaining power.

There is a wonderful service called "Morning Office in a Celtic Tradition." It includes this canticle:

In the midst of dark powers
We magnify the greatness of heaven
In the midst of foul deeds
We magnify the greatness of heaven
In the midst of fearful thoughts
We magnify the greatness of heaven
In the midst of a blighted land
We magnify the greatness of heaven
In our time of need
We magnify the greatness of heaven
We praise you Lord of earth and heaven
We magnify you on earth as in heaven*

This takes a strong faith to say honestly. But by magnifying the greatness of heaven in the midst of the hard things recalled, we are affirming our belief in the end of the story. This is the discipline of celebration.

---

*St. Aidan Celtic Christian Trust—USA, *Resources for Ministry in the Celtic Tradition,* ©1994, P.O. Box 4241, Evergreen, CO 80437-4241. All rights reserved. Used by permission.

DAY TWO

The Plant Grows from the Root

One man dies in full vigor, completely secure and at ease, his body well nourished, his bones rich with marrow. Another man dies in bitterness of soul, never having enjoyed anything good.

JOB 21:23-25

Unfortunately, we all know people who used to be happy and fun to be around but over the years became bitter and complaining. Maybe it is because of a tragedy they could never quite overcome or a series of illnesses or other setbacks that caused them to lose perspective gradually. Sometimes people feel they are entitled to a "good" life simply because they are "good" people, and when things go wrong, bitterness and resentment creep in.

In the verses above, two kinds of people are contrasted; while both die, there is a sense that the second man missed out on so much because of his bitterness. We have a choice as to what kind of person we will be at the time of our own death, and we make that choice every day in the way we respond to the small things as well as the big events.

We must guard against a slowly building bitterness and resentment in our souls, attitudes that will flower fully in old age if we don't consciously choose joy and gratitude. One way to do that is through an accountability partner or group, where we can encourage each other to remember God's goodness in all things.

Starting Over

Yet this I call to mind and therefore I have hope: Because of the LORD's great love we are not consumed, for his compassions never fail. They are new every morning; great is your faithfulness.

LAMENTATIONS 3:21-23

The whole day started out wrong. My daughter was crabby the minute she woke up. We argued over what she should wear, clashed over what to eat for breakfast and disagreed over the pace of the morning. She was cantankerous and unpleasant, and I was beginning to match her attitude, ugly mood for ugly mood.

Finally she looked at me and said, "Mom, can we start this day over?" I burst out laughing. After a big hug, we climbed back into bed. Following a few minutes of quiet, I made a ringing sound and got up again. As I came into my daughter's bedroom with a cheery "Good morning!" she happily hopped out of bed, and we began again. The morning took a 180-degree turn for the better.

When things are not going well, we have to make a deliberate effort to stop the train and turn it around. We can continue to hurtle down the tracks of bickering and frustration, or we can pull the switch and get onto a different track. All it takes is making a concentrated attempt to change the way things are going. God offers us that chance daily.

DAY FOUR

Singing in the Storm

Then will I ever sing praise to your name and fulfill my vows day after day.

PSALM 61:8

Today we don't think much of vows except at weddings or special services where people are set apart for a life of service to God. But the psalmist's commitment to perform vows daily hit home for me one day.

It was a gloomy day outside, and my spirit wasn't much brighter. I was standing at the ironing board feeling pretty sorry for myself. Suddenly the most wonderful, lilting music came on the radio. I was mesmerized. It was as if God had hit the light switch in my soul. I actually began to feel better. Even the weather seemed more pleasant. I was able to go from grumping to gratitude.

All of us have daily vows, things that we have agreed to do at home or at work as part of our responsibilities and commitments. Some of those are pleasant tasks; others are not. We must be careful what we are teaching children about the drudgeries of life by our attitude toward unpleasant chores. We must not teach them to dread these tasks but to embrace them. One way is to find a way to praise God while performing them.

DAY FIVE

Rejoicing

Rejoice in the Lord always. I will say it again: Rejoice!

PHILIPPIANS 4:4

I love my job as coordinator of music ministries and organist for a wonderful church. One night, though, I found myself at home feeling restless and unsatisfied. I went down to the church, pulled out several of my favorite organ pieces and played. I didn't practice or think how the music might fit into a worship service; I just played. With my weekly focus on preparing to lead worship and music in a congregation, I was in danger of losing the joy of making music.

In our society there is such a heavy emphasis on productivity that to just enjoy doing something for its own sake can feel like a waste of time. If children like to do pottery or play the guitar, we fret over how they will earn a living. If they like a sport but aren't scholarship material, we wonder if they should waste their time with it.

To simply be able to do something for the joy of doing it can be foreign to many of us. What a relief to know that God invites us to rest through simple fun with no pressure to be highly gifted in the activity.

DAY ONE

It Takes a Group

Use the silver to buy whatever you like: cattle, sheep, wine or other fermented drink, or anything you wish. Then you and your household shall eat there in the presence of the LORD your God and rejoice.

DEUTERONOMY 14:26

A celebration implies more than one person. In fact, it usually implies lots of people. That is why many organizations offer free Thanksgiving or Christmas dinners to people who have nowhere else to go or no money to provide the fixings for a celebration of their own. Weddings, graduations, births, baptisms—all invite us to celebrate in joy with others.

And isn't it nice to know that the Lord commends, even commands, celebrations? In the verse above, God actually suggests a menu that is celebratory. And this is in the section of Deuteronomy where the command to tithe is laid out! How many of us approach the issues of tithing with the kind of joy the Lord commands in this verse? What would happen if our faith communities took 10 percent of all that was given to the annual budget and threw a big party for the community simply to celebrate the goodness of God once a year? I think that would require a different kind of stewardship campaign than many of us participate in year after year.

The discipline of celebration flies in the face of Lone Ranger Christianity—the idea that you don't need to go to church because you can encounter God on your own. But it is hard to celebrate on your own, and Sunday morning, if nothing else, should be a communal celebration of God's work among us as individuals and as a community.

What would our non-Christian neighbors think if they saw us excited about a weekly Sunday morning celebration held at our local faith community?

DAY TWO

Simple Celebrations

The Israelites who were present in Jerusalem celebrated the Feast of Unleavened Bread for seven days with great rejoicing, while the Levites and priests sang to the LORD every day, accompanied by the LORD's instruments of praise.

2 CHRONICLES 30:21

When was the last time you really celebrated Christmas? I'm not talking about the commercial event that starts before Halloween and ends December 26. I'm talking about the Feast of the Incarnation that the church of Jesus Christ celebrates for twelve days beginning December 25. I'm talking about a celebration that has been prepared for through Advent, those four weeks before December 25, and that begins when the world is putting its Christmas holiday away.

Imagine this scenario: during Advent, the family reads the daily Scripture readings of the Advent calendar together. The house is decorated gradually instead of the Christmas decorations appearing all in one day. There are no Christmas parties until after the December 25. Gifts and goodies are saved for the twelve days between Christmas Day and Epiphany (which is January 6 and celebrates the wise men coming to Bethlehem). During those twelve days, little work is done and much time is spent doing fun, restorative things both alone and with others.

Does this sound like a complete fantasy? We worship a God who commands feasting as well as fasting. We all need these kinds of rhythms in our lives. Isn't it nice to know that God blesses them?

DAY THREE

Music of the Universe

Happy are the people who know the festal shout, who walk, O LORD, in the light of your countenance.

PSALM 89:15 NRSV

What does the music of God's kingdom sound like? If you had to describe it or play it or sing it, would you be able to? I would say that joy is the music of God's kingdom; any time I encounter true joy, I am in the midst of the harmony the morning stars sang together at creation (see Job 38:7).

So the next question is: do you know that music, that festal shout that the psalmist talks about in the above verse? And what does that sound like in your life? Can other people hear it through your way of living?

A woman I know went through a difficult time, and in the midst of it she ended up surrounded by a lot of "downer" personality types for friends. These were people for whom the glass was always half empty, and it affected her mood, even the tone of her voice. Through a series of events that only God could have orchestrated, she began to seek out other friends, people who loved God and loved life. I began to notice the lift in her voice; her laughter came back, and life became easier despite the heavy demands of a full schedule.

So back to my question: if you don't know the sound of the festal shout of the people of God, maybe you need to consider finding a way to spend more time with people who do—people who hear that melody deep in their hearts even when they are facing difficulties; people who know that in Christ the glass is overflowing with fullness and goodness; people who live in that reality of joy and light.

DAY FOUR

Joy in Nature

And God said, "Let the water teem with living creatures, and let birds fly above the earth across the expanse of the sky." So God created the great creatures of the sea and every living and moving thing with which the water teems, according to their kinds, and every winged bird according to its kind. And God saw that is was good.

GENESIS 1:20-21

It was the end of Sunday dinner, and since we don't have a dishwasher, I was doing a lot of dishes by hand after the company had left. It was also a beautiful spring day. I stepped outside with a load of trash when all of a sudden I heard a high-pitched whistling noise, and something zoomed past my head. The hummingbirds were back after their long migration from Central America, a miracle that I never tire of witnessing!

The kitchen mess was forgotten as I rushed to find the hummingbird feeder. I filled it and hung it in the usual spot in the tree. I waited expectantly for one to come and drink and was again transfixed by the tiny bundle of beauty and remarkable endurance. I finished those dishes in a state of rejoicing. And I agreed with God: creation is good.

Treasure the things of creation. They bear witness to God's transcendent goodness and help us remember that celebration is an intentional way of seeing and thinking.

DAY FIVE

Models of Trust

I trust in your unfailing love; my heart rejoices in your salvation. I will sing to the LORD*, for he has been good to me.*

PSALM 13:5-6

We have a cat named Butterscotch, a flame point Siamese mix. Butterscotch lives a contented life of trust. He knows that he will be fed and petted. He knows where his litter box is and that it will be kept clean. He naps in total peace on the bed in the sunlight. On his occasional forays out into the backyard, he trusts that the door will eventually open to let him back in. And he trusts his spot in the closet to protect him from the vacuum cleaner, little kids who chase him and the howl of the coyotes outside.

He is also a lap cat. No matter what I am doing, Butterscotch jumps confidently into my lap and stands patiently as I adjust my book or my sewing to accommodate him. He then takes his time circling several times before finding the perfect spot to plop down. I love having him there. I pet him and rub his ears, and I'm often rewarded with steady purring.

Jesus wants me to come to him as Butterscotch comes to me. There is always room for me, and I can trust I will get his full attention and care. It doesn't matter what shape I am in or what I have done or how much time I take to settle down. Jesus is thrilled to have me come joyfully and confidently to him at any time. Now that is something to sing about!

DAY ONE

It Is a Choice

Therefore my heart is glad and my tongue rejoices; my body also will rest secure, because you will not abandon me to the grave, nor will you let your Holy One see decay. You have made known to me the path of life; you will fill me with joy in your presence, with eternal pleasures at your right hand.

PSALM 16:9-11

How many Christians do you know who are chronic complainers? Are you one? Do friends and neighbors sense a joy and peace in your life even without Jesus ever being mentioned? Do you often give thanks for things? Do you sleep secure at night, trusting God for all things? Are the children in your life going to want to stay in the Christian faith when they grow up because they have seen its joyful impact on your life?

These are hard questions that we must ask ourselves. If we don't like the answers to these questions, we need to find a way to manifest the joy of the Lord in our lives. This does not mean denying hard realities in a Pollyannaish sort of way. It does mean having a deep well of joy to draw from in all circumstances. And that well is dug by living a life of intentional gratitude.

DAY TWO

A Shout of Victory

You prepare a table before me in the presence of my enemies.

PSALM 23:5

Many of us know this psalm so well that we can recite it at a funeral without looking at the front cover of the service leaflet. Yet what a shout of victory these words are in the midst of seeming defeat! We are proclaiming to ourselves and those around us that though we may be sitting with death, we are eating a feast of victory with God.

The twenty-third Psalm has too often been domesticated into a "warm fuzzy," when in reality it is a statement of life and joy and resurrection in the midst of the shadow of death and enemies. This psalm is a battle call to rejoice in the bigger picture despite what the immediate circumstances may be. It is a victory cry of celebration against the overwhelming sense of gloom and doom currently surrounding us.

If we live the discipline of celebration, which is an acknowledgment of the victory of Christ over death in the face of everyday life, we will be powerful witnesses to a hurting, lost and unhappy world. If you can have a banquet in the midst of enemy territory, that is a strong statement that you believe there will be a different outcome than what may seem possible at the moment.

The discipline of celebration is not whistling in the dark to try to make ourselves feel better or faking a happy smile. It is a song of victory and a shout of resurrection power in the face of a bitter but ultimately defeated foe.

DAY THREE

Dancing for God

David, wearing a linen ephod, danced before the LORD with all his might, while he and the entire house of Israel brought up the ark of the LORD with shouts and the sound of trumpets.

2 SAMUEL 6:14-15

This verse flies in the face of the theologies of some of our churches, which would consider dancing spontaneously before the Lord to be shameful and heretical. In fact, Michal, David's wife, was watching David from the window and thought the same way; she despised David in her heart (v. 16). She was especially concerned that David was nearly naked and what will the slave girls think? (v. 20). David explains to her that he was celebrating before the Lord (vv. 21-23) because of all the blessings God had bestowed on him. In fact, this was such an act of pure worship that David tells Michal he would even be willing to become more undignified and humiliated if that would express more praise to the Lord. And to add insult to injury of our pious notions of what is proper in church, God sides with David and renders Michal barren for the rest of her life.

The discipline of celebration is a wild and risky discipline. It means that we are to rejoice in God and that rejoicing can be expressed in ways that can be seen by the others in our faith community.

Using an accountability group and the discipline of guidance, we must make sure that we really are focused on praising the Lord and not showing off. But on the other hand, we must be careful not to judge someone we think is too physically expressive in worship. We may end up "barren," like Michal.

Attitudes Are Up to Us

Don't you know that a little yeast works through the whole batch of dough? Get rid of the old yeast that you may be a new batch without yeast—as you really are. For Christ, our Passover lamb, has been sacrificed. Therefore let us keep the Festival, not with the old yeast, the yeast of malice and wickedness, but with bread without yeast, the bread of sincerity and truth.

1 CORINTHIANS 5:6-8

Frank Minirth and Paul Meier wrote a book called *Happiness Is a Choice,* which deals with the symptoms, causes and cures of depression. The basic premise of the book is expressed in a quote from Abraham Lincoln: "Most people are about as happy as they choose to be."*

We all know people who choose not to be happy. They are the ones at the family gatherings who, no matter how nice the event is, always find something wrong with it. Or they can never be fully happy or healthy despite the goodness surrounding them. Their little bit of complaining yeast can really work to dampen or even wreck an event for others.

In the discipline of celebration, we choose to be happy. Not in a naive, optimistic kind of frothiness, but in a deep place in our spirits. We know that we can keep the festival because Christ, the Passover lamb, has been sacrificed, and everything will ultimately come out as it should in the kingdom of God.

The analogy here is the anchor sunk into the bottom of the ocean, holding firmly despite the hurricane raging around the ship on the surface. This is where celebration becomes a discipline: we are making choices for life and goodness and wholeness in every situation of every day. And that is not always a natural choice to make. It takes practice and training, as do all of the other good things in life.

*Frank Minirth and Paul Meier, *Happiness Is a Choice* (Grand Rapids: Baker Books, 1994), p. 14.

DAY FIVE

A Larger View

Therefore, if anyone is in Christ, he is a new creation; the old has gone, the new has come!

2 CORINTHIANS 5:17

I have a card that I keep out on my desk. It shows a small kitten looking into a mirror. The reflection looking back at him is that of a full-grown male lion.* I find that card not only humorous but also hopeful. It reminds me of how we all want to see ourselves as something greater than who we are. And while there can be a dark side of megalomania to our thinking of ourselves as larger than we really are, there is also a side that is biblically based.

We can find a deep hope and joy in today's verse. A loose paraphrase of this verse would be my little card. When I am in Christ, I look in the mirror and see not the old me but a new creation, a creation that reflects Christ in me. That image can often be dim and hard to see clearly, but in the discipline of celebration, I am invited to act on what I know, not necessarily what I feel.

With God's help, I can remember the lion I am called to be when I feel like a small kitten.

*Alan Wnuk, "Roaring Reflection," published and distributed by Portal Publications Ltd., Novato, California <www.portalpub.co>.

DAY ONE

You Can't Have One Without the Other

This is love for God: to obey his commands. And his commands are not burdensome, for everyone born of God overcomes the world.

1 JOHN 5:3-4

All of us need solid boundaries in our lives so we can live life well. I think of the boundaries we had in the historic neighborhood where my children grew up. Because of the nature of the summer community and the physical boundaries of the neighborhood itself, my children ran free all summer long with groups of kids of all ages. They knew clearly where they could go without permission and where they had to ask permission to go.

One day I could not find my four-year-old. She was not at any of her little friends' houses, and she wasn't down at the swings (an area that was off-limits without permission). I could feel a rising panic and was about to go home to call the police when I saw her on the other side of a big grassy area with a little friend and the girl's nanny. This area was public and clearly out-of-bounds without express permission and adult supervision. While my daughter had the adult supervision, her purposeful refusal to seek my permission before she went that far needed to be addressed. She went through a time of discipline she never forgot because of her defiant disobedience of my commands, which were ultimately for her safety and not to ruin a good time.

When we obey God's commands, we are invited to play fully within very clear-cut boundaries. It's like a game of tennis where you can play the ball anywhere you want as long as you don't cross the line. Obedience leads to joy and fun; disobedience ultimately leads to misery and downfall.

DAY TWO

Odd Companions

This is what the LORD *Almighty says: "The fasts of the fourth, fifth, seventh and tenth months will become joyful and glad occasions and happy festivals for Judah."*

ZECHARIAH 8:19

We are reminded in the above verse that the spiritual disciplines all work in harmony together, and sometimes it is hard to separate out where one discipline ends and another begins. It is possible to have a blending of the discipline of fasting and the discipline of celebration, though most of us would not think these two disciplines could go together in the same sentence.

The best example for this is the traditional understanding of Advent. Advent begins four Sundays before Christmas in the church's calendar. Christmas is celebrated from December 25 through Epiphany on January 6. This is certainly not the way our culture celebrates the month of December, but if we allow ourselves to be molded by centuries of church teaching, we can have joy as we prepare for Christmas while using Advent as a time to fast from all those activities and foods that keep us from arriving at Christmas Day in a state of joy. (The season of Lent, those forty days before Easter, is another example of fasting so as to fully embrace the feast.)

What would happen if we used some of the days during the four weeks of Advent to fast so that we could intensify our joy? By fasting from some of the overabundance of food, shopping and other activities of our culture's December, maybe we could arrive at Christmas in the same state as the shepherd's arrived at the manager: full of awe and wonder.

DAY THREE

Softening Rock

Encourage one another daily, as long as it is called Today, so that none of you may be hardened by sin's deceitfulness.

HEBREWS 3:13

One of the most important things we can do for our family and friends is to help them find a deep well of joy within themselves. And one of the ways to do that is by encouraging them daily. This is not to say that you approve of everything they say or do, but it means you let them know they are loved and appreciated as people, even though they may be in a time of hard growing pains.

For example, there is much in our children's world that will not be encouraging or joy-filled, especially as they get older and eventually go on to college or the working world. No matter how hard we may try, we cannot protect our children from bad things. But if they have access to a deep well of joy in their hearts, they will weather those hard times better and be stronger for having gone through the experience.

When people don't feel good about themselves, they become hardened and go through life with a chip on their shoulder. They always have to be at the center of attention and don't get along well with others. One way to help children feel good about themselves is to give them clear boundaries, high but attainable goals and age-appropriate responsibilities. Catering to their every whim will leave them confused, irresponsible and ultimately with poor self-esteem.

The discipline of celebration includes fun times, but it is more than that. It is the ability to hear the distant triumph song of Christ's victory over sin and death while still in the midst of a great battle. And in that battle we are invited to be disciplined to the ways of the kingdom of God.

DAY FOUR

Looking Sideways

Therefore, since we are surrounded by such a great cloud of witnesses, let us throw off everything that hinders and the sin that so easily entangles, and let us run with perseverance the race marked out for us. Let us fix our eyes on Jesus, the author and perfecter of our faith, who for the joy set before him endured the cross, scorning its shame, and sat down at the right hand of the throne of God. Consider [meditate on] him who endured such opposition from sinful men, so that you will not grow weary and lose heart.

HEBREWS 12:1-3

This passage tells us that God redeemed suffering so that it could become a path to joy for us. Jesus kept his eyes on the joy set before him as he endured the cross. Joy is something you can't get by focusing on it. You have to focus on obedience to God's commands and gratitude *in* (not *for*) everything in life; joy will be the byproduct.

All of us have been in a situation where we had to "put on a happy face." I knew a mother who had a birthday a few days after she had miscarried a much-wanted baby. Her other children, not understanding the depth of her grief, tried to make her birthday a special day. For their sake she smiled and tried to be cheerful, but she told me later that the cake tasted like straw in her mouth.

In the discipline of celebration we can stand at a graveside with many tears yet know that death is not the end of the story. We can find a way to give thanks to God even in that circumstance.

This passage tells us that we are not alone. We have a cloud of witnesses who have finished the race themselves and now cheer us on. It's the idea that if they can do it, so can we. When I am aware of the cloud of witnesses, I tend to live better and more honestly, knowing I am being watched. It helps me be less sloppy in my tasks. Surprisingly, those are often the days that are most joyful because I feel strong and focused on the right priorities.

Unless we connect joy and suffering, we Christians have nothing new to say to a hurting world. The world knows how to grieve, but it doesn't know joy that can come at the end of a well-run race. What a wonderful message to share!

A Hug for All, from All

The Spirit of the Sovereign LORD is on me, because the LORD has anointed me to preach good news to the poor. He has sent me to bind up the brokenhearted, to proclaim freedom for the captives and release from darkness for the prisoners, . . . to comfort all who mourn, . . . to bestow on them a crown of beauty instead of ashes, the oil of gladness instead of mourning, and a garment of praise instead of a spirit of despair.

ISAIAH 61:1-3

Everyone, regardless of age, can personify this verse: little children, teenagers, adults, healthy or infirm, rich or poor—everyone. There are so many ideas that you can do to lift up and comfort someone else or brighten the day of another person. May baskets, carved pumpkins, plates of Christmas cookies, Easter baskets, festive napkins at dinner, picnics, homemade cards and handwritten notes, and on and on. There are books and Internet sites galore with ideas on how to make each day, each moment, holy and special, lived in gratitude to God.

The discipline of celebration isn't an occasional party. It is a daily attitude, a way of living and thinking that can include periodic planned celebrations but ultimately is a joyful life of gratitude. It is a strong statement of faith in the midst of a world that can be downright ugly at times. The discipline of celebration is knowing, deep down, every day, that Jesus Christ is risen! He is risen indeed! Alleluia!

Some Final Thoughts

THROUGHOUT THIS BOOK, the concept of accountability has been suggested. In many places, the idea of working with another person or a small group has been strongly encouraged. This is one of the best ways to know if we really are making progress in becoming a better disciple of Jesus Christ. When we have a person or a group who can regularly and honestly reflect back to us what we are saying or doing, then we can know where God is calling us to focus our attention.

Accountability also keeps us honest about engaging in the exercises suggested in this book. There have been many nights before my accountability group meetings when I am making the phone call or writing the letter I had committed to doing because I knew the next day I would need to share publicly whether I had kept my commitment or not.

Some of the exercises I suggested in each chapter are meant to be done over a period of several days or weeks. This makes them good choices to do with an accountability partner or small group that meets weekly, biweekly or even monthly.

Let me suggest a structure for how you might use this book with another person or in a small group:

1. If you don't already have an accountability partner or small group, look for someone who is willing to engage in mutual accountability, someone who understands confidentiality, someone who also desires to be a better disciple of Jesus Christ. This may not be the same person you would include in a group that is purely social. You aren't necessarily looking for a "bosom buddy" but rather someone who can help you mature in your faith, as you help them.

2. If you decide you want a group, limit the size to three to five people. Otherwise it will take too much time to share when you get together. You

want to be able to get through your accountability sharing in an hour and a half at the most.

3. Determine how often you are going to meet and where. Even if you meet biweekly or monthly, set a specific date and time in advance, and put it on your calendar. This time must be viewed as a priority or it won't work. So another thing to look for in a partner (or in group members) is someone who is able to keep commitments. If you try to do this over your lunch hour at work, find a private place where you will be undisturbed. This is not something to do in an open cubicle where anyone can listen in.

4. Commit to a specific time period, such as the summer or twelve weeks in the fall. That way if someone is not finding the experience helpful, there is a natural ending time to the commitment. At the end of the time period, people can better excuse themselves from the group or partnership without awkwardness or embarrassment. If everyone wants to continue, you can always commit to go on for another season. All groups, no matter how good or helpful, need periodic times of intentional evaluation of their usefulness and purpose.

5. Accountability can be done long-distance via phone or the Internet, though it shouldn't be your first choice. I have had experience in doing this, and it works as long as you can trust that the other person is being honest about how they are engaging in the exercises. It is better when possible to be able to share in person; it is easier to be honest if the person can see your face and hear your voice.

6. Plan where in the book you are going to start. As I said in the introduction, you don't have to start with chapter one, though you certainly can. However, to have a balanced understanding and practice of the spiritual disciplines, do go through all the chapters.

7. Decide how you will proceed through each chapter. One idea is to spend your time together reading the discipline's introduction to get an overall idea of what it is about. Then you can each pick an exercise (the same one for the group or a different one for each person) to focus on until your next meeting. If you only meet monthly, maybe you can choose one exercise for each week to work on together or as individuals. Write down what everyone commits to doing. That way you can pray for them as well as help hold them accountable.

8. Please note, the exercises are only suggestions to get you started. If you think of something to do that better suits your circumstances and needs within that discipline, have at it! But share the idea with your partner or group to make sure that you are honestly engaging with the principles in each discipline.

9. Another way to approach the book is to individually commit to reading the chapters ahead of your meeting time and pick an exercise (or two) to work on that will then be shared when you meet together. In your sharing, you can talk about what you learned, what you don't understand and how you tried to engage in an exercise.

10. A word of caution: in my years of using the spiritual disciplines with accountability groups, more than once we would discover that the exercise we chose to do was not the exercise God had in mind for us that week. That is fine; don't block the leading of the Holy Spirit. However, if someone is *always* coming up with something different from what they committed to doing, they either need better help in choosing what to focus on, or they need to be confronted about a lack of honesty in their engagement with these exercises.

11. Feel free to modify an exercise. For example, at one point in the discipline of celebration, I encourage taking a walk in nature. If you live in the downtown area of a big city or the weather is such that a walk in nature would not be pleasant or wise, modify it. Maybe you can go to an indoor botanical garden, greenhouse or florist and look at the plants there. Or you can save that exercise until you can get out of the city or until the weather allows you to get outside and enjoy God's good creation.

12. Encouragement should be the basis of your gatherings, never condemnation. That is God's job. If you feel that someone is not being honest with themselves or with you, find ways to gently point it out. If there is a nagging sense that you are not getting the kind of feedback you need from an accountability partner or the honesty of commitment from another person, find another accountability situation. Your job is to fix yourself, not someone else.

13. Remember, the main thing is to engage honestly with the ideas and exercises presented in this book. Use them to see where you are hindered from a deeper relationship with God and to encourage yourself where you

are moving in a good direction in your faith walk.

Here are some questions you can use to prime the pump when you gather with others:

a. Was this discipline already familiar to me?

b. What was easy?

c. What was hard or unfamiliar?

d. What did I learn about myself that I didn't realize before?

e. Where is God calling me to go with this new knowledge?

We are not saved by doing these disciplines; we are saved by grace. But in the grace that is offered in Christ Jesus, let us learn to fully embrace a life that reflects our gratitude for God's goodness and mercy, a life that looks more and more like the one Jesus lived.

Suggested Resources

BELOW IS A LIST OF BOOKS that have been helpful to me in learning the spiritual disciplines. This list is in no way exhaustive, as new books are coming out all the time, but these are in my library and have been very useful.

Baker, Howard. *Soul Keeping: Ancient Paths of Spiritual Direction.* Colorado Springs: NavPress, 1998.

Bonhoeffer, Dietrich. *Life Together.* New York: Harper & Row, 1954.

Calhoun, Adele Ahlberg. *Spiritual Disciplines Handbook: Practices That Transform Us*. Downers Grove, Ill.: InterVarsity Press, 2005.

Chittister, Joan. *Wisdom Distilled from the Daily: Living the Rule of St. Benedict Today.* San Francisco: HarperSanFrancisco, 1990.

Dahill, Lisa E. *Truly Present: Practicing Prayer in the Liturgy.* Minneapolis: Augsburg Fortress, 2005.

Foster, Richard J. *Celebration of Discipline: The Path to Spiritual Growth.* San Francisco: Harper & Row, 1988.

———. *Freedom of Simplicity.* San Francisco: Harper & Row, 1981.

———. *Money, Sex, and Power: The Challenge of the Disciplined Life* (now called *The Challenge of the Disciplined Life*). San Francisco: Harper & Row, 1985.

———. *Prayer: Finding the Heart's True Home.* San Francisco: HarperSanFrancisco, 1992.

———. *Prayers from the Heart.* San Francisco: HarperSanFrancisco, 1994.

———. *Seeking the Kingdom: Devotions for the Daily Journey of Faith.* San Francisco: HarperSanFrancisco, 1995.

———. Study guide for *Celebration of Discipline.* San Francisco: Harper & Row, 1983.

———. Study guide for *Money, Sex, and Power* (now called *The Challenge of the Disciplined Life*). London: Hodder and Stoughton, 1985.

———, ed. *The Renovaré Spiritual Formation Bible*. San Francisco: HarperSanFrancisco, 2005.

Foster, Richard J., and James Bryan Smith, ed. *Devotional Classics: Selected Readings for Individuals and Groups*. San Francisco: HarperSanFrancisco, 1993.

Graybeal, Lynda, and Julia L. Roller. *Connecting with God: A Spiritual Formation Guide*. San Francisco: HarperSanFrancisco, 2006.

Griffin, Emilie. *Wonderful and Dark Is This Road: Discovering the Mystic Path*. Brewster, Mass.: Paraclete Press, 2004.

Guenther, Margaret. *Holy Listening: The Art of Spiritual Direction*. Cambridge, Mass.: Cowley Publications, 1992.

Hansel, Tim. *You Gotta Keep Dancin': In the Midst of Life's Hurts, You Can Choose Joy!* Elgin, Ill.: David C. Cook Publishing, 1985.

Hess, Valerie E., and Marti Watson Garlett. *Habits of a Child's Heart: Raising Your Kids with the Spiritual Disciplines*. Colorado Springs: NavPress, 2004.

Lathrop, Gordon W. *Central Things: Worship in Word and Sacrament*. Minneapolis: Augsburg Fortress, 2005.

MacDonald, Gordon. *Ordering Your Private World*. Nashville: Oliver-Nelson, 1985.

Peterson, Eugene H. *Eat This Book: A Conversation in the Art of Spiritual Reading*. Grand Rapids: Eerdmans, 2006.

———. *Reversed Thunder: The Revelation of John and the Praying Imagination*. San Francisco: Harper & Row, 1988.

Rimbo, Robert A. *Why Worship Matters*. Minneapolis: Augsburg Fortress, 2004.

Smith, James Bryan. *A Spiritual Formation Workbook: Small Group Resources for Nurturing Christian Growth*. San Francisco: HarperSanFrancisco, 1999.

Sparks, Jack N. *Prayer in the Unseen Warfare*. Ben Lomond, Calif.: Conciliar Press, 1996.

———. *Victory in the Unseen Warfare*. Ben Lomond, Calif.: Conciliar Press, 1993.

———. *Virtue in the Unseen Warfare*. Ben Lomond, Calif.: Conciliar Press, 1995.

Thompson, Marjorie J. *Soul Feast: An Invitation to the Christian Spiritual Life.* Louisville, Ky.: Westminster John Knox Press, 1995.

Wallis, Arthur. *God's Chosen Fast: A Spiritual and Practical Guide to Fasting.* Fort Washington, Penn.: Christian Literature Crusade, 1968.

Whitney, Donald S. *Spiritual Disciplines for the Christian Life.* Colorado Springs: NavPress, 1991.

Willard, Dallas. *The Divine Conspiracy: Rediscovering Our Hidden Life in God.* San Francisco: HarperSanFrancisco, 1998.

———. *The Great Omission: Reclaiming Jesus's Essential Teachings on Discipleship.* San Francisco: HarperSanFrancisco, 2006.

———. *Renovation of the Heart: Putting on the Character of Christ.* Colorado Springs: NavPress, 2002.

———. *In Search of Guidance: Developing a Conversational Relationship with God.* San Francisco: HarperSanFrancisco, 1993.

———. *The Spirit of the Disciplines: Understanding How God Changes Lives.* San Francisco: HarperSanFrancisco, 1988.